'Tony Ellis is the latest addition to a new generation of ethnographer/theorists who seek to move beyond the obsolete and sometimes prejudicial constructivist positions that clutter the social scientific study of male violence. This book is a resounding success, the first to analyse data from groups of violent working-class males in a transcendental materialist framework to produce a crisp, clear and credible explanation of persistent male violence. Essential and paradigm-busting reading.'

Steve Hall, Professor of Criminology, Teesside University, UK

'*Men, Masculinities and Violence* is an outstanding ethnographic study that should be read by everyone with an interest in criminology and the sociology of violence. Ellis leaves the comfortable confines of the university behind and heads out onto the streets in the company of men committed to violence. He returns with detailed stories of gang violence, football hooliganism and other forms of criminality, and he develops a detailed theoretical framework to make sense of it all. This is precisely the sort of research criminology needs to jolt itself out of its present inertia.'

Simon Winlow, Professor and Co-Director, Teesside Centre for Realist Criminology, Teesside University, UK

'Grounded in exceptional ethnographic engagement and written in an accessible and considered manner Anthony Ellis has produced a fantastic book on the origins and reality of men's criminal violence. While the topic and focus is sometimes unsettling, the picture of normality fused with occasional stark brutality, which underpins the lived reality of the participants, both as perpetrators and victims, never falls into the trap of romanticism. This is a brilliant book, and one that every serious social scientist should read.'

James Treadwell, Lecturer in Criminology, University of Birmingham

Men, Masculinities and Violence

Why do some men use physical violence against others? How do some men come to value physical violence as a resource? Drawing on in-depth ethnographic research conducted with men involved in serious violence and crime over a period of two years in the North of England, Anthony Ellis addresses these questions and the complex relationship between these men and their use of physical violence against others.

Using detailed life-history interviews and extended periods of observation with these men, *Men, Masculinities and Violence* describes their 'inner' subjective lives and experiences, exploring how they came to value violence, why they are willing to use it against others and risk serious harm to themselves in the process. Over the course of the book a picture emerges of a group of men who have experienced and perpetrated serious violence throughout their lives. This book advances a critical psychosocial understanding of such violence by situating these masculine biographies within their immediate contexts of de-industrialisation, fracturing working-class community and culture, and broader shifts within the political economy of liberal capitalism.

With its synthesis of rich ethnographic material and new developments in criminological theory, this book is essential reading for students and academics interested in issues of gender and violence.

Anthony Ellis is a Lecturer in Sociology and Criminology at the University of Salford, Manchester, UK.

Routledge Studies in Crime and Society

Sex work

Men, Masculinities and Violence

An ethnographic study

Anthony Ellis

Routledge
Taylor & Francis Group

LONDON AND NEW YORK

First published in paperback 2017

First published 2016
by Routledge

2 Park Square, Milton Park, Abingdon, Oxon OX14 4RN
and by Routledge
711 Third Avenue, New York, NY 10017

Routledge is an imprint of the Taylor & Francis Group, an informa business

British Library Cataloguing-in-Publication Data
A catalogue record for this book is available from the British Library

Library of Congress Cataloging-in-Publication Data
A catalog record has been requested for this book

ISBN: 978-1-138-81909-2 (hbk)
ISBN: 978-1-138-04027-4 (pbk)
ISBN: 978-1-315-74482-7 (ebk)

Typeset in Times New Roman by
Florence Production Ltd, Stoodleigh, Devon, UK

*I dedicate this book to my family
and to the loving memory of my grandma,
Barbara Ellis, who passed away on
26 December 2010*

Contents

Acknowledgements

This book represents the culmination of over five years of work. It began life in 2010 as a Ph.D. study, which was undertaken at the University of Sheffield and was funded by the White Rose Network under its 'Crime and Insecurity' theme. Since then I have been fortunate enough to have gained the friendship and received the support of numerous individuals who I want to thank unreservedly for everything they have done for me over the years.

I want to begin by acknowledging the men who participated in the research that informs this book. It is a cliché, but none of this would have been possible without their participation. Despite scaring the life out of me on several occasions it has been an immense privilege to have learned about and documented their lives in such detail. They were kind enough to talk to me and let me 'hang around', they introduced me to their families and to their friends, all with genuinely very little to gain for themselves. I thank them for their generosity. I must also thank my various 'contacts' who helped me to gain access and gave such glowing references of my character to participants. For obvious reasons I cannot mention them here, but they know who they are.

I am indebted to various academic colleagues whose friendship, support, guidance and encouragement have helped me to reach this stage. I have to begin by thanking Maggie Wykes who supervised my Ph.D. and has continued to support me since. The friendship, guidance and advice that Maggie has provided me over the years have been invaluable and I cannot thank her enough. I must also extend my deepest thanks to Rowland Atkinson and Simon Winlow, who I was fortunate enough to have on my supervisory team and who have both supported, encouraged and inspired me immensely. I am grateful to Matthew Hall, who always had his office door open for me while I was a doctoral student at Sheffield. Matthew did a sterling job as the internal examiner for my Ph.D. and also offered some very helpful comments on the proposal for this book. I am indebted to Steve Hall who examined my Ph.D. and whose theoretical work has been inspirational. Steve was kind enough to give up his time to look over and offer his thoughts on a draft of Chapter 7 that appears in this book. Any errors are my own of course. My thanks must also go to numerous other academic colleagues who at various points over the past several years have given me good advice, support and friendship: Matt Bacon, Cormac Behan, Dan Briggs, Steve Farrall,

Sara Grace, Jamie Grace, Paul Knepper, Gwen Robinson, Maurice Roche, Joanna Shapland, Jennifer Sloan and James Treadwell.

I would also like to thank my colleagues in Sociology and Criminology at the University of Salford for providing such a friendly and supportive place in which to work. A huge thank you to Marian and Jon for welcoming me into their lovely home in Salford, usually after long working days, and saving me from making the trek back across the Pennines to my home. Thanks as well to Tom Sutton and Heidi Lee at Routledge for agreeing to publish this book and the support they have offered during its production.

Finally, I want to acknowledge my family and friends; they are the people who have always been there for me, while developing this book and long before I began working on it. My mum, dad and my 'big' sister Julie deserve a special mention, as does my partner Amanda, for putting up with me and my occasional grumpiness.

Glossary of terms

Belting – to be violently assaulted.

Blow – slang term for Cannabis/Marijuana.

Bottle – displaying courage and daring.

Bottled – term used to describe being hit/attacked with a glass bottle.

Chinned – to punch/hit someone on the chin.

Clobber – term for clothing, usually qualified with the adjective 'decent' or 'good' to signify designer, branded clothing.

Cock – term used to describe an individual male who is regarded to be the best fighter, or the 'hardest' individual within a particular geographical area or institution, such as a particular housing estate or a school.

Coke – Cocaine.

Cracked me/him – to be punched or to punch someone else.

Fatha – vernacular for father.

Fella – Most often used as a term of endearment between men.

Firm – in the context of this book, reference to a 'firm' or 'the firm' denotes a collective of men that identify with a particular professional football team's hooligan group. This group of men will engage in violence with rival 'firms' that identify with other professional football teams. Men who associate with football firms will also wear particular branded and 'casual' clothing that is associated with the football hooligan culture.

Flip out – term to describe becoming angry or losing your temper.

Front/Fronted – to give the impression to others of being volatile and willing to fight; this image is amplified in threatening circumstances. This is often done in an attempt to bring an end to the confrontation through the opponent's submission.

Fruit bowl – used generally to describe someone who behaves 'abnormally' or displays signs of having a mental health condition. In the context of this book, the expression is used to describe someone whose behaviour is unpredictable and volatile.

Game/Gameness – term used to describe someone who is willing to involve themselves in violence.

Gear – illicit drugs, but often used when referring to heroin.

Gypo – offensive term used to refer to an individual from the Gypsy Traveller community.

Handy – an individual who is adept at using violence.

Headcase – term for an individual who is considered dangerous and unpredictable.

Hiding – a slang term for violence.

Lay out/Laid him out – in this context to physically assault someone or defeat them in a fight.

Muppet – offensive term for someone who is considered naïve and devoid of dignity.

Nutter – term for an individual who is considered dangerous and unpredictable.

Our lass – term used to refer to girlfriend or wife.

Paki – offensive term used to refer to an individual of Pakistani heritage, but also often used indiscriminately to describe anyone with ethnic ties to the Indian sub-continent.

Phet – Amphetamines.

Pills – Ecstasy.

Playing the big 'un – to behave in an ostentatious manner that suggests you are a competent fighter. Equivalent colloquial expressions are '**acting hard**' or '**cocky**'.

Rattling – experiencing withdrawal symptoms.

Scrap/scrapping – term to describe physical violence.

Shooter – firearm.

Smackhead – derogatory term for a heroin user.

Sniff – Cocaine.

Tapped – term to describe someone who is unpredictable or volatile.

Tenner – ten British pound sterling.

1 Let's get ready to rumble

One morning, a few months into 2014, I was driving to the supermarket. The route I had chosen was a familiar one, taking me through a community that I know fairly well. The secondary school that I attended many years ago is located about half a mile away, and for a period of several years I had lived on a housing estate that is only physically separated from this community by a large and very busy dual carriageway. It is a community that has suffered considerably during the past several decades. At the end of the 1980s, two large coal mines located in nearby villages were closed – two mines that had historically provided generations of local people, men in particular, with abundant and stable employment. In the 1990s a nearby river flooded, forcing many local families out of their homes. Despite calls in the aftermath to improve flood defences, the river flooded for a second time several years later. Once again, many families were forced into temporary accommodation, in some cases for several months while their homes were made habitable again.

As I headed towards the supermarket I drove down the main high street where the few businesses still operating in the area are located, having to stop at the traffic lights as they turned from green to red. This street is the main road which runs through the heart of the community, connecting it to adjacent areas and the nearby motorway network. At the height of the flooding, most of the street had been under several feet of water and you can still see water marks almost four feet high on some of the walls of the buildings that line the street. The main street itself contains a pub, where on particularly warm days large groups of men and a few women will congregate on the pavement outside, drinking and smoking. A little further up the road from the pub is a fast-food takeaway, which never seems to have anyone in it but, I have been told, does an excellent curry. While a little further down the road from the pub a newsagent has recently opened in what had been, prior to its opening, a dour derelict building bearing all the classic physical features of community decline.

As I waited at the traffic lights, trying to remember what I needed to buy from the supermarket, I noticed in the periphery of my vision sudden frantic movement; the kind of movement that immediately draws your gaze because you sense potential threat in it. As I turned my head to look out of my window, I was confronted with two adult men fighting in a bus shelter located at the side of the road. As is most 'real' violence it was a desperate, painfully unskilled contest. One of the men was dressed in a t-shirt, jeans and boots, and had a shaven head; I estimated his age at around early 40s. His opponent was shorter in height, looked slightly younger and was probably aged early to mid-30s. He had short dark hair, and was dressed in jeans, a hoodie and trainers. The two were swinging punches wildly at each other, with most of their punches failing to properly connect. The older fighter then threw a punch which landed on his younger opponent's chin. The impact of the blow forced his opponent to stagger backwards into the shelter, leaving him momentarily slumped on the bench inside. The landing of the crucial blow brought the wild flailing of arms to an abrupt halt. The slumped male attempted to stand up, but his legs seemed to give way slightly as he fell back onto the bench. As the lights shifted to green and I began to move forward slowly, still transfixed on the two individuals, I faintly heard an exchange of words between them, with the older, victorious male shouting something to the effect of 'Shouldn't have fucking started should you?'

This book provides an account of an ethnographic research project that explored the lives of men who use interpersonal violence against others. This incident happened after I had completed my research, so some time had elapsed since my immersion in the lives of the men who had participated and I had finally been able to begin focusing my thoughts on things other than violence and masculinity. The ethnographic research that informs this book and supports the theoretical arguments it advances, was carried out over a prolonged period with a group of men who had grown up, and continued to reside, in what had been staunchly working-class communities in northern England. Like the place I found myself in that morning as I made my way to the supermarket, these are communities that have been devastated by the collapse of heavy industry and its allied socialist politics following de-industrialisation. As I unexpectedly bore witness to this incident, it was like the sudden abrupt and unannounced return of the repressed, which had slowly begun to drift from my thoughts. It was a stark reminder, not that I needed it, that there are still many individuals, particularly men, whose lives are affected by the use of interpersonal violence. This is a book about the lives of men like this, the violence they perpetrate against others, and why they do this. To begin, I feel it is necessary to provide a rationale for the importance and significance of a book that addresses these issues in the contemporary context.

First of all, it is in no way contentious to claim that men commit the majority of recorded and unrecorded interpersonal violent crime (DeKeseredy and Schwartz, 2005; Wykes and Welsh, 2009). And second to this, neither is it 'contentious to claim that the majority of these men come from working-class, marginalised or excluded social locations' (Winlow, 2012, p. 203). The validity of these two statements is borne out by a large amount of empirical evidence: men are far more likely than women to commit violence (Wykes and Welsh, 2009) with the evidence indicating strongly that young, economically marginalised men, are the most likely perpetrators (Hall, 2002; Ray, 2011; Zedner, 2002). Though paradoxically, these trends are mirrored when one looks at violent victimisation, as socio-economically marginalised men are more likely to be victims of violence, particularly in public settings (Wykes and Welsh, 2009).

Some recent data from the Crime Survey for England and Wales (CSEW; formerly British Crime Survey) supports these aforementioned trends. The risk of being a victim of violent crime[1] was highest for young men aged 16–24 and the same group were found to be most likely to commit violence (Office for National Statistics, 2013). These patterns of victimisation and offending are consistent with those uncovered in previous measurement periods (see Hall and Innes, 2010; Roe *et al.*, 2009), with the 2008/2009 sweep indicating that the risks of violent victimisation are highest for those experiencing a variety of indicators of deprivation: including living in social-rented housing, in communities with high levels of poverty, and not being in employment (Roe *et al.*, 2009).

There are of course methodological issues associated with the data sources cited here and their potential to accurately measure various violent crimes (see Ray, 2011; Walby and Myhill, 2001; Wykes and Welsh, 2009). Yet, the overwhelming involvement of men in violent crime has become something of a criminological truism and 'possibly the nearest that Criminology has come to producing an indisputable fact' (Hall, 2002, p. 36). These patterns of men's violence are neither specific to the contemporary period nor only to England and Wales. Men's use of interpersonal violence is a global issue (Hautzinger, 2003), transcending both cultural contexts and historical epochs (Emsley, 2005a, 2005b; Eisner, 2011; Nivette, 2011; Spierenburg, 1998, 2008; Wykes and Welsh, 2009). However, available historical evidence points strongly towards a gradual shift in the socio-economic composition of men using physical forms of violence. Regular physical confrontations and highly ritualised duels once common among groups of socially elite men became increasingly less prevalent from the seventeenth century onwards, as Spierenburg (2008, p. 66) explains:

> Dueling did not stay fashionable enough to prevent the gradual pacification of the upper and middle classes . . . Many lower-class men, on the other hand . . . stood ready to attack those who insulted or hindered them.

Despite a strong evidence base linking men to the use of interpersonal violence, criminology has been slow to explore the nature of these links. Masculinity, and its relationship to offending, has remained marginalised within criminological thinking, despite its obvious salience within patterns of offending and victimisation. This is not to deny the recent, though long overdue, advancements that have been made in the study of men, masculinities and crime since the early 1990s, which has generated a substantial body of literature and empirically-based research that will be examined in Chapter 2. However, even within sections of the more recent violence literature, the pressing necessity for a critical engagement with questions of masculine subjectivity in the perpetration of violence have often been sidelined and obfuscated at the expense of other variables/issues that were granted greater explanatory credence, such as youth, race, 'gangs', and troublingly, victim/women blaming (Howe, 2008; Wykes and Welsh, 2009). And so, questions of gender within criminology have often continued to be associated with what women do, rather than with what men do, think and feel (Collier, 1998).

Like gender though, social class is also a marginalised discourse within criminology, although this has not always been the case. Once a fulcrum of criminological and sociological theorising, academic interest in social class has slowly dissipated amid the growing hegemony of postmodernist theories across the social sciences. The transition in Western societies into a 'postmodern' epoch has contributed greatly to the effective marginalisation of discourses around social class within political and everyday rhetoric more generally (see Charlesworth, 2000; Hall, 2012a). Changing patterns of consumption, demographics, and alterations to traditional labour markets, have led some commentators and scholars to suggest that classificatory mechanisms and analytical frameworks based around social class are no longer useful or relevant. This has been extremely damaging for criminological theory and its ability to adequately grasp the subjective motivations that underpin criminality (Hall, 2012a), particularly crimes involving violence, given the aforementioned socio-economic backgrounds of most persistently violent offenders.

Despite some progression, then, in the study of men, masculinities and violence, there remains much more to be said and understood about this complex relationship. Making a contribution towards exploring these issues is a primary aim of this book. Before discussing the book's content, and the ethnographic research upon which it is based, in more detail, I will briefly outline the contemporary scholarly and socio-economic political contexts that frame what is discussed here, as these have been significant in determining the book's focus and theoretical orientation.

Violent times? Post-crash crime and criminology

The research for, and the writing of, this book took place at a time when overall recorded crime rates were reported to be falling in the UK and across the globe. Predictably, some politicians have spoken proudly of the success of their law and order mandates in reducing crime rates, while some criminologists have been quick to start considering the reasons behind the 'drop'; particularly as these trends have continued in the midst of one of the worst economic recessions of recent times, when it was anticipated that crime rates would actually increase. It is not my intention here to engage in a lengthy critical debate about the validity of the 'crime drop' discourse and the methodological rigour of the survey data that is being used to support it. However, a brief cursory discussion of some important issues in relation to this is worthwhile to help formulate the context for this book and the arguments I will make in it.

Significantly, rates of interpersonal violence were reported to have followed this broader trend of decline. Commenting on findings from the UK Peace Index showing declining rates of violent crime, the BBC's Home Affairs Editor Mark Easton has suggested recently that the findings might indicate the emergence of a growing peacefulness and potentially a new morality that is increasingly repugnant towards violence (BBC, 2013). This certainly is an interesting set of trends, but caution is required, as overall rates of violence and criminality when measured nationally/internationally mask concentrations of crime within particular localities and spaces. Research indicates that the majority of violent crime tends to occur in highly specific geographical spaces and communities (see Ray, 2011). The findings acknowledge the places in the UK with the highest concentrations of recorded violence, those being several highly deprived urban areas experiencing multiple disadvantages. Yet, quite contradictorily, the report then seemingly rejects evidence that inequality is a predictor of violence. Moreover, disappointingly, there was no further discussion of the conditions and issues impacting those deprived and marginalised communities that continue to experience frequent violence and criminality. One must ask, is regular exposure to violence not an inequality in itself? And is this not an issue worthy of consideration for its potential impact upon those who routinely experience violence and intimidation? The report also seemed to quite conveniently circumvent the weight of evidence that indicates violence often takes place within familial and social/communal networks of individuals known to each other (see Stanko, 1990; Wykes and Welsh, 2009). These relationships and contexts within which interpersonal violence most frequently take place, actually constrain attempts to uncover the extent of it, while at the same time providing victims with little incentive to come forward and report the violence they are experiencing.

Regardless of any reported statistical declines in criminality, the inescapable reality is that for the individuals who occupy communities where violence and crime are regular features, like the men involved in this study, evidence of a crime drop is distinctly absent. For men like those who you will meet in the following pages, they are unlikely to report instances of crime or violence. As data presented in the later chapters of this book will indicate, violence and the threat of it (however *real* or imagined), has remained an enduring feature of these men's biographies. Violence is not 'alien' to these men, but is more akin to a structuring force that is negotiated routinely (see Stanko, 1990). The genuine possibility of encountering violence is something that they attempt to face stoically, with their own personal resources. The men involved in this study, and those communities where crime and violence are visibly present, are the largely forgotten and neglected groups of much recent criminological theorising and research (Hall, 2012a). Unfortunately, the 'crime drop' discourse appears to be in danger of further glossing over the realities and disadvantages of everyday life for marginalised populations. Although we may be witnessing a genuine fall in overall crime rates, this should not be taken as an opportunity to celebrate victory in what has been a lengthy 'war on crime'. Early in 2014 police recorded crime figures, for many years deemed a fairly reliable indicator of crime rates when combined with national victim survey data, lost the approval of the UK Statistics Authority amid concerns of unreliability (Casciani, 2014). Despite the evident need to err on the side of caution when interpreting these figures, we have instead already seen subtle attempts by political elites to seize upon these trends in order to give further justification for certain agendas (primarily austerity measures) with the former

Home Office Minister Norman Baker suggesting recently that now 'there is less for police to do' (BBC, 2014).

Further to this, when one takes into account the West's current socio-economic and political context that constitutes the backdrop to these discussions, the whole notion of a 'crime drop' is perplexing. Quite unbelievably, few criminologists, with the exception of a small contingent of critical scholars (see Burdis and Tombs, 2012; Hall, 2012a), have had anything to say about the various harmful (criminal?) practices that actually plunged the economy into recession, and the various 'harms' that have resulted from this incredibly deep and complex global economic decline; unemployment and austerity are just two examples. Yet still, debate about a miraculous 'crime drop' has continued during the post-crash period when widespread and multifarious harms[2] and crimes continue to take place globally, and are being uncovered, reported on, and which have emerged from economic and political systems, and from the actions of individuals; for instance: the 'expenses' scandal within British Parliament; the transatlantic banking crisis and the uncompromising levels of corporate dishonesty and recklessness that contributed to this; the 'phone hacking' scandal involving several high-profile tabloid newspapers and journalists; the routine sexual abuse of children and young people, some involving high profile public figures, that have highlighted systemic failures on the part of police and social services to properly investigate, prosecute offenders and protect victims; ongoing political instabilities and the concomitant extreme violence affecting several nations in the Middle East; the UK summer riots of 2011; the violent rampages of Derrick Bird in Cumbria and former nightclub doorman Raoul Moat in the North East of England; the brutal and disturbing execution of a British soldier outside of Woolwich Barracks in London in May 2013; the recent terrorist attacks in Paris during early 2015 . . . and I could go on.

Of course, some of the examples referred to here of historic sexual abuses occurred many years ago and have only recently come to light. Yet, their emergence into the public eye should serve as a stark reminder of hidden abuses and harms that continue to go undetected. Furthermore, the nature of the harms that we face contemporarily, remain complex, multifarious and increasingly intertwined with the neo-liberal state and the global free market (Hall, 2012a; Hobbs, 2012). These harms often do not even fit neatly into the legalistic frameworks of particular nation states or the definitions/variables and recording instruments that many criminologists use to define and measure crime. Like their legitimate counterparts, criminal markets do not recognise sovereign borders, nor do they remain static in the face of technological innovations that might better conceal them (see Treadwell, 2012). They are often comprised of various flexible groups and loose networks of entrepreneurial individuals, some of whom are willing to resort to extreme violence and intimidation to secure their market position and share of it (Castells, 2000; Hobbs, 1995; Paoli, 2003; Varese, 2001; Wieviorka, 2009). Indeed, states' monopolies of violence are being increasingly challenged, contested and undermined from within the 'de-civilised' interstices of global governance that have been strategically severed and isolated from the economic benefits of global capitalism (Castells, 2000), for instance, politically de-stabilised areas in the developing world; ambiguous border regions; and the 'no-go' areas and inner city 'sink' estates of the West's de-industrialised urban wastelands (Spierenburg, 2008).

Given this highly complicated context of contemporary criminality and crime control, as well as various methodological problems and limitations, the reported decline in crime rates should be approached with extreme caution. As this introduction will hopefully have indicated, and as will the remainder of the book, the motivation to break laws and harm others is still very much present in contemporary UK society. And yet the core issue remains: how are we to make sense of and explain such behaviour? It has been rightly argued by several critically minded criminologists that the discipline has for long periods been locked in a state of aetiological inertia and crisis (Hall, 2012a; Hall and Winlow, 2012). This sense of inertia is starkly reflected in criminology's seeming inability to adequately address what is arguably its most pressing question: why do some people harm others? Gadd and Jefferson (2007) were, unfortunately, correct in their observation that if you want to know about why people commit crime, the last person you ask is a criminologist. And in the turbulent socio-economic times we are facing a need to provide better answers to this question has never been more pressing. Unfortunately though, as others have discussed at length (see Winlow and Hall, 2013), we appear to have reached a period of stasis following the famous proclamation that we have arrived at the 'end of history' having reached the pinnacle of our social and political evolution (Fukuyama, 1993). This sense of stasis has permeated the social, cultural, political, economic and intellectual spheres of our lives and has been accompanied by a fatalistic air of postmodern cynicism. Despite experiencing during the past several years arguably one of the most catastrophic and complex economic recessions of modern times we seem bereft of a way forward; barely able to muster any semblance of an alternative to our current economic and political arrangements as we remain gripped by a sense of impotence to intervene or change anything. Put simply, there is 'no alternative' to what Fisher (2009, p. 2) calls 'capitalist realism':

> the widespread sense that not only is capitalism the only viable political and economic system, but also that it is now impossible even to imagine a coherent alternative to it.

In a similar vein, the dominant right and left liberal wings of criminology appear content to continue working with theoretical frameworks and accompanying ontologies of the 'criminal subject' that promulgate those who harm others as rational, self-interested calculators, or, unfortunate impoverished individuals that are products of a draconian state, media-induced moral panics, aggressive labelling processes and powerful discourses. Slowly though it is becoming apparent that these cannot give sufficient critical consideration to contemporary market societies, their shadow criminal variants, as well as the lives, biographies and subjectivities of those who occupy them (Hall, 2012a; Hall and Winlow, 2012; Hobbs, 2012; Treadwell *et al.*, 2013).

Returning to the form of crime this book is concerned with, the current crime figures suggest that we might be physically harming each other a little less than several years ago and the broader long-term trend for interpersonal violence, which is discussed in more detail in the next chapter, is one of gradual decline over the last several centuries. However, despite talk of a 'crime drop', and the broader inferences drawn by some scholars from long-term violence trends as representing a 'civilising process' (Elias, 2000), there remain significant groups of men, however small in number, who are willing to use interpersonal violence against others. It is these men that this book is concerned with. I will now briefly discuss the ethnographic research undertaken to inform this book and discuss its design in relation to this, briefly overviewed, broader context.

A brief word on methods

As intimated earlier, this book provides an account of an ethnographic study that was carried out during 2011–2013. It was 'ethnographic' in the sense that I attempted, as much as was possible, to immerse myself in the lives of the men who participated, by conducting in-depth life history interviews and partaking in periods of observation with them. A study such as this immediately raises questions around securing access, gaining trust, ethics and personal safety. In respect of the first issue, access to the 'field' was not secured via the criminal justice system. I was very keen from the outset to avoid this method of gaining access to participants. As Polsky (1967) famously argued, there are potential epistemic limits to studying criminals from behind bars, but also related issues of establishing effective trust. Like several other ethnographers of crime (see Ancrum, 2013; Armstrong, 1993, 1998; Hall *et al.*, 2008; Hobbs, 1988; Treadwell, 2010; Wakeman, 2014; Winlow, 2001) I was fortunate that I possessed some of the cultural and social capital necessary to establish requisite trust and sufficient access to conduct this type of research. My biography had given me access to a range of trusted informal contacts to support my access to the field. I also possessed a certain form of cultural capital and knowledge useful for this project, which cannot be gained through 'formal' education or research training. Let me be clear here, I do not engage in violence myself nor have I been involved in the types of criminal activities engaged in by some of the participants. However, I do hail from a socio-cultural background that is similar to the men who participated and I have experienced some of the things that they have.

I am from a working-class family and grew up in a de-industrialised urban community in the north of England. Throughout my life I have been in regular contact with a number of men actively involved in acquisitive criminality and serious violence. I witnessed a fair amount of violence while growing up and have, on occasions, found myself in threatening situations. My own masculinity and personal biography were crucial in this respect, as I am familiar with the expression of the kinds of masculinities typical among the men who participated. This was a methodological resource and although it was difficult at times, I could play up aspects of my own masculinity in ways that these men would recognise and appreciate. If needed I could laugh at offensive jokes; take part in the objectification of women; tolerate racist language and views; drink large amounts of alcohol; listen to gratuitous descriptions and justifications of violence; while remaining calm in threatening circumstances or when witnessing criminal activities. My bodily capital could be emphasised to build rapport and fit in: my accent, local knowledge, tattoos, short hair, bodily demeanour and gait are all befitting of the 'types' of men I encountered during the research. In short, violence and criminality are not alien to me. And, more importantly, I understand the significance that violence can come to have in some men's lives and the cultural values that surround it, which are bound up with notions of shame, humiliation, personal reputation and status.

So from the outset I had the trust and respect of several participants and other contacts who could make required introductions and attest to my character. When recruiting participants for this research I set myself particular inclusion criteria: participants had to have experience of using physical violence against other men during their adult lives and on more than just one or two isolated occasions. In sum, they had to be men who possessed genuine reputations for violence and were known by others for their potential to use it. I understand this may be viewed as potentially vague inclusion criteria, but I expand upon and explain this later on. I did not restrict myself in terms of age either. I wanted to have a fairly diverse range of ages in my sample, which actually do range from early twenties to mid-forties. All of my participants were of white ethnic background, which generally reflected the ethnic composition of the areas where I conducted the research. These were northern, predominantly white populated areas and 'working class' in social composition. I, too, am a white male and my 'contacts' were also all white. During the ethnography I did encounter and interact with men from non-white backgrounds, but these were friends and acquaintances of some of the men who participated and did not have the violent reputations on which I was focusing.

Once in the field I could make use of my own cultural knowledge to think critically about what I was told, saw and heard. Entering the field inevitably meant encountering the vague hierarchies of 'hardness' that exist among men who occupy particular geographical areas: the hearsay, the rumours, and various 'reputations' that exist in these communities. Due to the significance that violence has in some men's lives there is genuine potential for individuals to exaggerate or distort their experiences in the name of 'saving face' and maintaining reputation. There is also potentially something to be gained from creating and maintaining a façade of 'hardness', which some men will actively pursue. It was important therefore that I had the ability to engage with these various complexities and recognise potential 'bull shitters' from those with genuine histories of, and potential for, violence and who would be able to properly assist my research endea-vours. I did this through several methods: my own specific cultural understandings and knowledge of violence from having spent time socialising with men willing to use it; my prior knowledge of certain participants (I knew who some of them were because of their reputations and I had also witnessed some of them behave violently before); and through the help and support of my research contacts.

The fieldwork took place in several urban areas across the north of England, many of which I was already familiar with prior to beginning the research. Interview and observational data was gathered from a variety of spaces and places that the participants occupied on a day-to-day basis, which included: their homes, bars, pubs, nightclubs, the streets, professional football matches, their workplaces, occasionally in their cars, and the visiting hall of a prison. Conducting research with these men, and among their wider familial and friendship networks, exposed me to a variety of ethical issues and potential dangers that had to be managed effectively. In the course of the research I witnessed violent and aggressive behaviour, drug use and drug supply and the distribution of stolen goods, and became privy to various ongoing criminal activities. Some participants described quite traumatic experiences and life events, as well as horrific personal experiences of violence. As I describe in the coming chapters of the book, particularly during Chapter 8, frequent exposure to this throughout the fieldwork was on occasions personally distressing and emotionally difficult. On these occasions the difficulty stemmed from both the traumatic character of what I was witnessing and hearing, which is a recurrent issue for researchers who study the lives of those affected by violence (Liebling and Stanko, 2001), but also because there were resonances with my own biographical experiences. As Wakeman has discussed recently (2014), the discipline of criminology has largely neglected the relationships qualitative researchers form with their participants and how these often intersect with the former's biography in ways that can have a significant emotional impact. Importantly though, Wakeman takes his observations of doing 'autoethnography' further and examines how they can be used to generate insightful analyses of field data. My emotional responses to gathering data are articulated intermittently throughout the book and these certainly provided some analytical insight. In Chapter 8, the final chapter, I return to some of these issues in more depth through examining my own emotions and biography in the research.

In an attempt to manage the various other ethical issues that arose from conducting this research, all of the names that appear in this book are pseudonyms to protect the identities of those who participated or were present during fieldwork, as well as anyone else discussed by the participants. The identity of locations has not been disclosed and, where necessary, I have also withheld certain information to maintain anonymity. The data were gathered through a combination of taped interviews and, where recording was not possible, field notes. I did not take notes during fieldwork and these were written up from memory as soon as possible after vacating the field. I accept the limitations of using one's memory as a tool for recording data and the possibility for inaccuracies. However, in an attempt to minimise this, subsequent checks were made with participants or relevant individuals to verify the data that had been written up from memory.

The fact that I knew some of these men before I began the research and was introduced to those who I did not know by individuals who are respected and well thought of, meant that I could get access to the lived everyday experiences of some of these men's lives. I could blend in quite seamlessly to such an extent that I am pretty certain that some participants would often forget the real reason I was present. The fact that some of these men engaged in criminal activities in front of me and made me aware of information that was particularly sensitive, is indicative of the trust I had gained. I spent sufficient time in these spaces with participants to 'ensure that we entered a mutual space that encouraged critical reflection and honesty' (Treadwell *et al.*, 2013, p. 4). I am willing to admit that I formed relationships with these men that could be described as friendships, as much as they were researcher–participant relationships. The nature of the research both necessitated and facilitated 'friendly' relations with the participants, which obviously brought benefits in terms of securing trust and access. I am aware, though, of the difficulties of this in terms of the questions it raises regarding neutrality and the potential for objectivity and critical distance.

To this end I cannot state unequivocally that I made no errors or mistakes during the course of this research. There were several occasions when I ruminated, often for days and weeks afterwards, on how I had phrased a question incorrectly; missed opportunities to probe and challenge things that were said to me during interviews and conversations; and had on occasions, unintentionally, perhaps colluded with some of these men or even unwittingly validated, in their own minds, some of the things they had done. Quite often I was immediately aware that I had made a mistake during the fieldwork, and I had to quickly put this acknowledgement to one side in my mind while I continued to gather data. I would then often return to it and consider it afterwards during reflective periods. Other mistakes became clear when I listened to the recording of interviews or during the process of writing up field notes.

In taking a critical realist ethnographic approach to the study of men, masculinities and violence, mistakes were unavoidably made while attempting to employ this approach in the settings that I entered. The varying pressures that accompany doing research among potentially dangerous and volatile groups of men makes having to temporarily suspend one's own beliefs, sentiments and values (see Calvey, 2008), and even sacrificing some of those sacred academic standards to 'objectivity', unavoidable pragmatic necessities (see also Ancrum, 2013; Hobbs, 1995). As Ferrell (1998, p. 25) argues, criminological ethnographic research

> unavoidably entangles those who practice it in complex and ambiguous relations to subjects and situations of study, to issues of personal and social responsibility, and to law and legality.

The process of forming research relationships under these conditions necessitates having to participate to some extent in the activities engaged in by participants, building rapport in order to generate sufficient trust, co-operation and access to gather data. This often required me to divulge information about myself and my biography, which a number of participants were interested in; particularly where I had grown up, where I went to school, who I knew, and my motivations for doing the research. It is unsurprising that participants would attempt to 'suss' me out given the potential dangers of sharing information with an 'outsider', and these appear to be common experiences for researchers who use qualitative methods to study crime and violence whether overtly or covertly (Maguire, 2008; Winlow *et al.*, 2001). I did not want to deflect nor dismiss this curiosity as I felt it was important, given that I was asking them to talk openly and honestly about themselves, to share something of myself in a reciprocal exchange (see Oakley, 1981; Polsky, 1967). Not doing so would have been pure hypocrisy on my part and potentially damaging, although on occasions such curiosity strayed into what I suspect were 'tests' that had to be managed in the situation (Calvey, 2008). One participant told his close friend, who is a known football hooligan, that I was an undercover police officer. This was clearly done as a joke, which the participant and his friend – once he realised I was not a police officer – both found highly amusing. However, I suspect that the ulterior motive was to test how I would react when suddenly placed in a highly pressurised situation. It was also a clear demonstration of this participant's power and the power he wielded over me while I was present in his world.

I do accept potential critiques of the biographical accounts that I received from the men who are discussed later in this book. I am referring here to the possibility that these were potentially partial and distorted. I am in little doubt that this probably was the case at times. In response to such suggestions I would argue that although there is a strong possibility of this, I did develop trusting relationships with these men, mainly because of my personal background and my contacts who made the introductions and vouched for my legitimacy and trustworthiness. Of course this does not automatically absolve me of any such criticism. Where possible I would check the reliability of what I was told, particularly certain information that I was suspicious about. I would often strategically ask participants at a later date to reiterate the event again, claiming I had forgotten what they told me, using this as an opportunity to check for inconsistencies. I also occasionally sought verification from gatekeepers, but used this sparingly, and with caution, as I did not wish to divulge what the participant had shared with me, which would contravene confidentiality. Occasionally during the ethnography, just through 'hanging around', I became privy to information that supplemented and verified things I had been told or suspected. This was often a way to access additional information on participants that they had not divulged themselves. In one or two instances this was the sort of information that I expected participants might not reveal to me; for example, instances when they had been badly beaten up or had been made to look foolish in a way that contradicted and undermined the images they occasionally sought to present of themselves to others, including me – although this technique was not without limits, as sometimes acquaintances simply did not know the answer or did not possess the information I sought. At other times I suspected they knew more than they were letting on and obviously did not wish certain information to be known by me. Media sources were also very occasionally helpful for verifying that particular criminal activities had taken place.

In his famous essay Howard Becker (1967) argued that undertaking research free from personal or political values was not possible and that instead

> the question is not whether we should take sides, since we inevitably will, but rather whose side are we on?

(p. 239)

Like Becker, I do not purport to occupy the position of a truly objective researcher who brings none of their own subjective background to the process. I do however, take seriously my role as a critical realist ethnographer: 'to unpack . . . experiences and events as much as possible' (Briggs, 2013, p. 21) and provide as accurate account of these as one can under sometimes difficult and stressful conditions. This also requires documenting what I am told and observe in a manner that is non-judgemental, but is ultimately not entirely devoid of an ethical position either. My research approached the issue of interpersonal violence through the eyes of men that perpetrate it against others. As discussed, I recognise that my participants behave in ways that are harmful to others, but that my participants are also 'harmed'. My methodological position, and approach to the research more broadly, is both ethical and political. And this is intertwined with my ontological and theoretical position.

A brief word on theory

This book is diligent to the complexities of these men's 'inner' lives that I have begun to allude to briefly already. However, the book also subjects their 'outer' lives to analysis and explores in particular the dialectical relation between the 'inner' and the 'outer' – or what has recently been referred to as the *psycho* and the *social* (Gadd and Jefferson, 2007). There are, as one might expect, individual differences within these men's biographies, which undoubtedly are partly reflective of the wider social and economic transformations characteristic of the late twentieth and early twenty-first centuries that have fractured what had previously been relatively stable and predictable life course trajectories and transitions for working-class men (see Charlesworth, 2000; Winlow, 2001; Winlow and Hall, 2006). Some of the men who participated were in employment and although none were employed in highly paid elite professions, there was some variability in the type of employment and sectors they worked in. Other participants were unemployed and some of these men had not been in employment for many years. Some of the men were fathers, they had wives/partners and others did not. Some had been, and still were, actively involved in serious acquisitive criminality; some had never been involved in any criminality other than violence. Despite this they all, nevertheless, have had some quite similar personal experiences, particularly with violence. These men share a broadly similar socio-historical lineage to such an extent that I argue that 'all hail from what was at the time of their birth unhesitatingly called "the working class"' (Winlow and Hall, 2009, p. 285). In addition to this point, and importantly given the focus of the study, like the samples of men involved in the small body of empirical work on masculinities and violence, among the men I worked with there were similarities in their personal experiences of violence and their feelings about it (see Winlow and Hall, 2009).

Although violence has been a feature of these men's lives (both as perpetrators and victims) and more so than it has for the majority of men, it is important to acknowledge that it is also not something that they engage in all of the time (see Collins, 2008; Gilligan, 2000). These men's occasionally violent and destructive behaviour is complex and as Jones (2008, p. 179) argues,

> must be understood as functioning within specific immediate circumstances, but also within their own histories and cultures . . . they are psychological events that are linked to wider social and cultural issues.

Crucially, these men possess, and have exercised, the capability to negotiate partic-ular confrontational situations and interactions with other men without making recourse to actual violence. This is discussed in much greater depth in the book. I recognise that these men, although capable of making decisions within particular symbolic socio-structural contexts, are also anxious, emotional human subjects who sometimes contradict themselves, exaggerate, distort, dissociate, lie, and do not always act and behave in ways that considered 'rational' or that 'make sense', even to themselves. Some participants actually found it incredibly diffi-cult to articulate the reasons behind their, at times, highly destructive behaviour. They genuinely lacked on occasions a clear understanding of 'why they do it'. Nevertheless, some of the violence perpetrated by these men and inflicted upon them by others, was truly disturbing and appalling. I have not sought to 'water down' any of the things that were described to me or that I observed, only enough to ensure full anonymity for those who took part. This book comes with a slight health warning, but I make no apologies for that. I took an empathetic and critical approach into this research and made it clear to the participants from the outset that my purpose was not to cast judgement, but to learn and understand. Although my observations and arguments are at times critical of these men and their occasionally violent behaviour, in no way does this represent an attempt to demonise or pathologise them. I want the reader, and so do the men who partici-pated, to acknowledge and better understand the occasional harsh brutalities that are perpetrated by, and inflicted upon, minorities of often severely marginalised groups of men who occupy the insecure, de-industrialised communities of advanced capitalism.

Furthermore, as well as developing a microanalysis of these men's subjective lives and the masculine identities they exhibit, the book situates this subjectivity within a broader context of social transformation and ubiquitous neo-liberal capitalist ideology. I acknowledge the role of humans in the creation of the social world, but as a critical realist my ontological view is that 'real' forces exist in that world, which have 'real' pragmatic material consequences for other humans that we can document and observe. The violence my participants commit against others and that they have been victims of are 'real' harms that have dire physical and psychological consequences. Such brutal violence is potentially transformative: it can shape individual perception, emotional experience and social engagement with others, and reverberates powerfully across an individual's life course, as we will see in forthcoming chapters. However, in a similar vein, the current structural arrangements of our socio-economic and political system are 'real'. I am in agreement with Winlow and Hall (2013) that advanced capitalism is an abstraction that possesses a profoundly transformative potential and dominates the lives of all social groups. The ubiquity of capital and neo-liberal ideology, which is the driving force behind its contemporary manifestation, is capable of engulfing humans, shaping subjectivity and producing potentially harmful effects, as this book will demonstrate.

Further to this, I adopted a broad approach to understanding these men, their masculinities and the violence they commit against others. As I discuss in more detail in the next chapter, the existing literature on masculinities and violence tends to begin with a focus upon a particular type of violence that occurs in a specific contextual setting (e.g., football violence/hooliganism; domestic violence; night-time economy violence etc.) and then focuses upon the men, and their masculinities, that perpetrate violence in that setting. My research was not focused on a particular type of male violence that occurs in a specific socio-spatial context, but was more concerned with exploring the life courses and subjectivities of men who perpetrate criminal violence against other men – whatever the specific context in which they are using it. The emphasis then, is upon men who use violence, why they use it, and how they came to value it.

This book incorporates and utilises some 'new theoretical directions' (see Hall and Winlow, 2012) to interpret the rich and highly complex data that I gathered from the ethnographic fieldwork. The book is aligned to an emergent body of perspectives that integrate sociological and psychological approaches to understanding gender, subjectivity and violence (see Gadd and Jefferson, 2007; Jones, 2008, 2012; Ray, 2011; Treadwell and Garland, 2011; Winlow, 2012; Winlow and Hall, 2009). The sheer volume of data and the complexity of it meant that utilising new theoretical approaches capable of dissecting criminal motivations and subjectivities was the only viable means of adequately making sense of these men and their lives.

Structure of the book

The book is comprised of eight individual chapters. The next chapter, Chapter 2, discusses and critically reviews empirical and theoretical literature on masculinities and violence to provide a broad context for my own research and theoretical arguments. Chapters 3 to 6 present various data gathered from the ethnographic fieldwork and outline the analytical themes that emerged from the analysis. Chapter 3 acts as a forerunner and signpost to these various analytical themes by documenting in detail the life history of one of the participants, who I refer to as 'Darren'. Darren's life history and experiences of violence, as both a perpetrator and a victim, provide a foundational context for the rest of the book. Chapter 4 explores some of the other participants' childhoods and the significance of violence within this phase of their lives. In Chapter 5, I look in more detail at perpetrating and experiencing violence from the perspectives of the men who participated and draw on interview and fieldwork data to explore the motivations for violence and its relationship to subjectivities that have been cultivated in marginalised, occasionally brutalising circumstances. Chapter 6 addresses the moral justifications for violence given by these men as well as exploring their reflections upon their identities as men, and how, for some of them, their experiences inform relationships with others, particularly significant male children. Chapter 7 provides an in-depth theoretical discussion of the micro-world of violent masculine subjectivity drawing on the qualitative data presented during Chapter 3 to Chapter 6. The broader socio-economic context to the 'inner' aspects of these men's lives is addressed in this chapter, particularly advanced neo-liberal capitalism and the general atmosphere of increased interpersonal competitiveness it has generated. The final chapter, Chapter 8, provides a brief afterword, which includes some personal reflections on doing the research.

This book is based upon a localised ethnographic study in de-industrialised urban communities. Readers will probably have detected from the discussion so far that I do not feel the traditional theoretical perspectives that have dominated and that continue to dominate criminology, important, though they are and have been to the discipline, suffice here. I have attempted to be ambitious in the way that I have tried to make sense, theoretically, of these men's 'inner' lives and the socio-economic context that envelops them. Importantly, I am in agreement with a growing minority of critical scholars who believe it is time to revitalise a critical criminology that is dynamic, theoretically innovative, with a strong ethical position and that is focused on revealing and making sense of crime and harms throughout the social order. I only hope that this book will make a suitable contribution to this much larger endeavour.

Notes

1   The definition of violent crime used in these surveys includes all types of physical assault, from pushing and shoving resulting in no physical harm, to wounding and murder.
2   I use the term 'harms' as despite the clearly harmful character of some of these examples, they were not always clearly labelled or defined as 'criminal'.

2 Theorising masculinities and violence

A review

This chapter critically reviews existing criminological literature on masculinities and violence providing a context in which to situate this book and its theoretical arguments. The review sketches out the theoretical developments that were made over the twentieth and into the twenty-first centuries within this literature. These advancements within criminological thinking were part of a much broader transition within the area of gender studies as a whole. This transition was characterised by a shift away from theories anchored in biological approaches to understanding gender towards more sociological, social constructionist and more recently, psychosocial approaches. These successive paradigmatic shifts (Hood-Williams, 2001) within the masculinities and crime literature drew attention to the plurality of gender expression, specifically the socially, culturally and historically contingent nature of masculinities. More recently, they have entailed an exploration of the psychological dimensions of male subjectivity at the nexus of these broader social conditions.

Gender 'blindness': biological and sex role perspectives

It was not until very late in the twentieth century that masculinity and its relationship with offending began to be considered or subjected to any requisite level of scrutiny. Prior to this, criminologists had acknowledged that men commit the vast majority of crimes, but this acknowledgement was implicit within their work rather than explicit. And this was the case within most social science research, which tended to use men as an all-inclusive term and failed to acknowledge gender as a variable (Hearn and Morgan, 1990; Beynon, 2002). So in criminology, the discipline had failed to engage with the masculinity of those being studied and had afforded men's evidently greater propensity to offend a degree of normality (Messerschmidt, 1997). Studies of violence did describe and analyse the actions of men, but this had been done in an indirect way, which did not address men as gendered beings. Criminologists had also systematically ignored women's place in crime and criminal justice until the 1970s when feminist criminologists began to engender the discipline, drawing attention to the endemic use of gender stereotypes and assumptions to explain men's and women's involvement in criminality as both offenders and victims (Smart 1976; Heidensohn, 1985).

For Walklate (2004), this legacy of gender blindness can be traced back to criminology's disciplinary inception. With its origins firmly rooted in two associated projects – the Governmental and the Positivist-inspired Lombrosian (Garland, 2002) – the discipline was founded on a scientific tradition with a specific ontology and epistemology concerned with identifying the causes of crime through rigorous scientific investigation and method. Heavily influenced by theories of evolution, the criminal anthropologists headed up by Cesare Lombroso, claimed that criminality was a product of atavism. Criminals were considered to be under-developed in evolutionary terms, their uncivilised behaviours and dispositions were manifestations of their inferior biological constitution. Criminals were therefore understood to be biologically different from non-criminals and could be identified through the presence of particular physical 'abnormalities'.

This early association between offending and biology is still perceived to be a strong one, particularly men's biology. The hegemony of biological positivism created a framework for thinking about men and women that is firmly rooted in biological difference (Walklate, 2004). In contrast to the meekness of femininity, it is often assumed that men are *naturally* violent and aggressive, with uncontrol-lable voracious sexual drives (Brittan, 1989; Smart, 1976). This is a powerful discourse that is still often evoked every day, within the media, and in some scientific explanations for acts of violence that are committed by men (Hearn, 1998; Whitehead, 2002). There have been numerous studies that have sought to locate the propensity to commit violence and crime at the level of the male (criminal) body, which is said to have dangerously high levels of testosterone surging through its veins, problematic chromosomal patterns, or to be at the mercy of instincts that have evolved in the human species as a means of gaining and then defending the resources (food, territory and sexual partners) necessary for survival (Edwards, 2006; Hearn, 1998; Jones, 2008). The presence of particular substances in the body, such as alcohol or drugs, are also often implicated in explanations for violence that are utilised both by scholars, practitioners and perpetrators themselves who can draw on such discourses to explain violence (Hearn, 1998). The media coverage of Raoul Moat's campaign of violence in 2010 made much of his reported use of steroids as a potential explanation for his aggressive, paranoid behaviour (Ellis *et al.*, 2013). It is understandable however, given men's evidently greater propensity for violence, that some scholars might assume a biological basis to that violence. Yet, strictly biological approaches encounter difficulty when explaining why only some men commit violence, and even then not all of the time or at every opportunity. Violence has strong cultural dimensions (Jones, 2008) both in how it is perceived, as well as its prevalence, which are influenced by temporal, spatial and contextual factors (Wieviorka, 2009). And much evidence suggests that social and psychological factors are far more important as causes of violence (Gilligan, 2000).

In spite of the discipline's gradual shift during the twentieth century, from explanations rooted in biological causation to theoretical approaches concerned with psychological, sub-cultural and social explanations for crime, the legacies of Lombroso and the Positivist tradition still linger on. For some time the discipline of criminology continued to cling to the implicit assumption that biological differences between men and women determine behavioural patterns that are natural to each sex; in some areas this assumption has yet to be fully dispensed with (Walklate, 2004).

Early theoretical approaches of the twentieth century, which drew on offenders' immediate social contexts and wider socio-structural conditions to explain their involvement in crime, were aware of the evident greater propensity among males to become involved in crime and violence. In light of this, attention was directed towards the differential processes of socialisation for males and females, in particular how these might create differing criminal opportunities. These approaches highlighted the significance of male and female 'sex roles' in creating patterns of crime by sex (Messerschmidt, 1993). Sutherland and Cressey (1966) captured nicely the recognition of these patterns during their discussion of the variation in sex ratios of offending populations:

> [V]ariations in the sex ratio in crime are so great that it can be considered that maleness is not significant in the causation of crime in itself but only as it indicates social position, supervision, and other social relations.
>
> (1966, p. 142)

For these theorists the 'maleness' of crime and violence was evident and acknowledged. However, a requisite interrogation of this masculine quality that seemed to lie at the heart of crime was disregarded in favour of an engagement with sex roles. Drawing on Sutherland's theory of 'differential association', in which crime is learned through exposure to criminal values and cultures, Sutherland and Cressey (1966) argued that boys were more likely to experience greater exposure to criminal cultures. Girls on the other hand, subjected to increased supervision and encouraged to adopt maternal roles in preparation for inevitable motherhood, had fewer opportunities to become exposed to these cultures. Boys were allowed greater freedom and encouraged to value 'toughness', which meant that involvement in crime and violence had greater symmetry with the male sex role. In a similar vein, Talcott Parsons attributed young males' greater involvement in crime and delinquency to a form of compensatory masculinity, stimulated by their sense of alienation within the feminising space of the family. Young girls identify with the familial context through their recognition of a future role within that space as a primary carer of children. Boys however, recognise that their role is external to the family unit. Seeking escapism from this context they are liable to become involved in delinquent activities to demonstrate toughness and bravado (Messerschmidt, 1993).

Cohen's (1955) study of delinquent youth gangs drew on the previous works of Sutherland and Parsons. Being 'characteristically *masculine*' (Cohen, 1955, p. 139), the activities of the delinquent gang did not compromise the qualities associated with the male sex role. The gang represented a solution for young men experiencing alienation from US society's respectable values embodied specifically in the middle-class institution of the education system. For Cohen, the female sex role was reducible to the need to find a suitable male partner for marriage, which would secure a future livelihood and respectable status. A role that was not compatible with the masculinity of the delinquent gang.

As Messerschmidt (1993) rightly noted, these early theoretical approaches displayed a solid awareness of how offending behaviour was heavily gendered and drew attention to the masculine quality of much violent crime. Yet, their theoretical approach remained partially anchored in biological differences between men and women and was deterministic in terms of gender identities and potential behavioural outcomes. This inherent biological orientation to sexed categories imposed a rigid dual dichotomy, each with its own associated role expectations which were assumed to be 'natural'. The female role was equated with passivity, nurturance, motherhood and the domestic sphere. While the masculine role with aggression, toughness, control and the public realm. What was missing and could not be explained through recourse to socio-biological approaches alone was an explanation for the evident differences that existed between men; specifically a further dichotomy between criminal and non-criminal men. If being violent and criminal represented the masculine role *par excellence*, then why do only some men behave violently and become involved in crime? Emulating and investing in such a tough, aggressive, rigid masculine role is not so well suited to contemporary means of gaining status as a man in Western societies (Archer, 1994). These extremely rigid models of masculinity and femininity, particularly the absence of any account of women's experiences of offending and victimisation, inspired a major shift in criminological thinking that was spearheaded by the growing influence of feminism.

Pro-feminist and structural perspectives: hegemony, power and performance

[T]he raw and unfinished business of 'becoming a man' sometimes comes at great cost . . . serving the ideals of masculinity can severely tax the resources of many individuals.

(Hatty, 2000, p. 110)

The development of critical approaches to the study of men, masculinities and crime is very much indebted to the work of feminist scholars on issues of gender and its relationship with offending. The problem of the evident 'maleness' of crime, particularly violent crime, long ignored by criminologists and obfuscated among other variables that were granted greater explanatory credence, was an issue that interested feminist criminologists from the outset (Gelsthorpe, 2002). It was feminist scholars who first drew sustained attention towards the pervasive levels of abuse perpetrated by men within the domestic context, an issue that had long been ignored by criminologists and criminal justice practitioners alike. Shifting the criminological gaze away from a concern with controlling public forms of violence and disorder committed by dangerous individual men (Stanko, 1994), feminist research drew attention towards physical, sexual and psychological forms of violence within the familial home and the threats posed to women by men closest to them (Kelly, 1987, 1988; Stanko, 1990; Dobash and Dobash, 1992). This rendered problematic, in a number of ways, the powerful masculinities that lie at the heart of the normalised heterosexual order of the familial and domestic sphere (Collier, 1998; Hatty, 2000; Wykes and Welsh, 2009). The much critiqued works of early radical feminist criminologists, perhaps epitomised by Brownmiller's (1975) approach to rape as an act of ideological power rather than a rare individualised pathological crime, significantly challenged traditional thinking, implicating all men in the oppression of women – although this model did suggest a rather limited and one-dimensional model of male dominance. Nevertheless, it generated more sustained interest in the area of masculinities (Gelsthorpe, 2002) among theorists who desired to more accurately theorise relations of power and dominance based on gender as not bound by biological sex, but acquired and variable over time and place.

Andrew Tolson was among the first to openly acknowledge and discuss masculinity as socially constructed. Tolson (1977) describes the nature of class-based masculinities and how these intersect with social institutions, patriarchy and the means of production. He argued that experiences within the family, school, peer group and the workplace, socialise men (of both working and middle-class backgrounds) into particular masculine roles, which emphasise their independence, privilege and dominance. Despite his analysis being still partially rooted in the inheritance of specific sex roles, Tolson's work represented a real theoretical advancement in the area of gender studies through his use of feminist theory, acknowledgement of power relations, and awareness of the potential variability of men's experiences by social class.

By the late 1980s the essentialist and inherently biological connotations present in early sex role theories were coming under sustained attack from the critical interrogation of the concepts of sex and gender, as well as the growing recognition of the potential social, cultural and historical variability of gender-based identities. Within the social scientific literature that has emerged since this period, masculinity has increasingly been referred to as 'masculinities'. The plurality of men's experiences and behaviour, even within the same cultural context, were recognised as evidently varied, multiple and fluid (Whitehead, 2002). The intersection with a multitude of other variables and social divisions produced a varied range of masculinities that are socially, culturally and historically contingent (Beynon, 2002; Morgan, 2005). Such accounts undermined the lingering, but still influential, assumption that particular manifest male behaviours are inevitable products of male biological constitution, rooted in a pre-social, pre-discursive realm (Butler, 1990; Beynon, 2002; Whitehead, 2002).

Identification as male was no longer theorised as a given based purely on the possession of particular physiological and anatomical features. Contrary to such thinking, in which masculinity was an assumed naturalistic biological quality possessed to varying degrees by all men (Brittan, 1989, 2001), phenomenological and post-structuralist-inspired theorists drew attention to gendered 'performances' which constitute and confirm gender. Accurate categorisation relies on an effective interactional performance in which social actors 'do' their gender in accordance with institutionalised expectations (West and Zimmerman, 1987). Men cannot simply 'be' masculine they must 'do' their masculinity and be seen to 'do' it. It is a context-bound performance that is subject to circumstances, involving active negotiation and agency (Morgan, 1992). For Judith Butler (1990), there 'is no gender identity behind the expressions of gender; that identity is performatively constituted by the very 'expressions' that are said to be its results' (p. 25). Butler's post-structuralist analysis locates gender identity within powerful medical and legal discourses, which promulgate and reproduce coherent sexed binaries and gendered comportment as 'naturalised'. Outside of these powerful discursive frameworks there exists no biologically determined essence to gender (Butler, 1990). When applied to men's violence, such a model of gender foregrounds the fleeting dramaturgy of the violent performance, which constitutes an expression of the gender outfit worn by criminal men. For Butler then, violence would be considered nothing more than performance – the materiality is inconsequential. Yet, for the next group of theorists to be discussed, such performances uphold dominant, oppressive gendered ideologies, which have very material and ontological consequences for men and women.

This group of theorists comprise what Edwards (2006) calls the second wave of men's critical studies and were among some of the first to critically examine the culturally and historically contingent nature of masculinities. Adopting a pro-feminist stance, this group of theorists were concerned with deconstructing the relations of power that exist between men, and between men and women (Hearn and Morgan, 1990). One of the seminal contributions was Connell's (1987, 2005a) conceptual approach to gender relations and masculinities, which theorises gender in relation to social structure and power. This work represented a backlash against biological and sex role theories of gender.

Connell, in the most updated edition of this work (2005a), argues that there is not a unitary masculinity, rather there are numerous masculinities, which must be located in relation to the 'gender order'. This order is constituted via relations of power, production and sexuality. Borrowing Gramsci's concept of hegemony – the term used to describe the elite's ideological control and domination of the proletariat via culture – Connell argues that a plethora of masculinities are constituted via their interaction with other social structures (namely class and race). At any given time there is one that occupies an ideologically dominant position. Hegemonic masculinity 'embodies the currently accepted answer to the problem of the legitimacy of patriarchy, which guarantees the dominant position of men and the subordination of women' (Connell, 2005a, p. 77). The form of masculinity designated hegemonic is neither fixed nor static, it represents a historically contingent mode of ideological dominance which can be challenged, contested and consequently transformed into a new hegemony. Although the gender practices and qualities of hegemonic masculinity are liable to change, Connell (2005a) argued that it is women and, in general, non-white, homosexual, and lower-class males that are subordinated. In the West, as Kimmel states, the

[H]egemonic definition of manhood is a man *in* power, a man *with* power, and a man *of* power. We equate manhood with being strong, successful, capable, reliable, in control.

(1994, p. 125)

The maintenance of this hegemonic ideology is not achieved exclusively through naked force, but physical coercion is not incompatible with the establishment and exercise of hegemony (Connell, 1987). Violence represents an instrument of power that is available to men, as Hearn (1998) explains:

[V]iolence is dominance, is the result of dominance, and creates the conditions for the reproduction of dominance. Violence is a means of *enforcing* power and control, but it is also power and control in itself.

(pp. 35–36)

Although the proportions of men who enforce hegemonic masculinity through violence may be small, the majority of men benefit and enjoy the privileges of a 'patriarchal dividend' that is then reaped from these practices (Connell, 2005a). All men are therefore complicit, sometimes indirectly and unconsciously, in the maintenance of the hegemonic form of masculinity; orientating themselves strategically to it in different situational contexts (Connell, 2005a). This secures the dominant masculinist ideology that *naturalises* the underlying inequality of gender relations (Brittan, 2001).

Connell's sophisticated theorisation shows how men's dominance and access to material and cultural benefits is secured from the structuring of the gender order. Yet, simultaneously, Connell drew attention to the ways in which men's experiences of power are not uniform and can be experienced as disempowering. As Kimmel (1994) has argued, hegemonic models of manhood place expectations upon men who are encouraged to compete with and out-do one another, which has generated feelings of fear and homophobia within men. Men pay a heavy price through having to suffer the pains of suppressing emotions that threaten or contradict the exercise of power. Patriarchy creates a contradictory experience for men who have exclusive access to restricted privileges and advantages, while experiencing pain at suppressing weakness, vulnerability and their emotions (Kaufman, 1994).

The need for men to achieve, and appear to be in possession of, a particular form of masculinity has relevance for understanding violent criminality, which can represent a means to exert dominance and power over others. Describing criminology as an 'inept' discipline on account of its gender blindness and failure to adequately explain men's dominance of recorded crime figures, Messerschmidt (1993) was the first criminologist to produce a theoretical framework that attempted to explain men's criminality. Heavily influenced by feminist criminology and Connell's work, Messerschmidt wove linkages between gender and crime through his theory of structured action. Messerschmidt's conceptual approach to understanding gender is based on the dialectical relationship between social structures and human agency. It takes account of both the constraining influence of social structures and individual men's capacity for agency based on their positioning relative to these. Drawing on West and Zimmerman's (1987) approach to gender as an interactional performance, Messerschmidt argues that men 'do' their gender and accomplish their masculine identity with the resources that are available to them. Men's 'crime may serve as a suitable resource for 'doing gender' – for separating them from all that is feminine' (Messerschmidt, 1993, p. 84), when other more legitimate avenues for gender expression are restricted or unavailable. Since then, Messerschmidt's work has integrated race, class and the role of male bodies in the process of 'doing' masculinity through crime (Messerschmidt, 1997, 1999, 2005).

Pro-feminist work on masculinities made huge strides towards explaining the bases of male dominance and challenging the assumed biological foundations of male aggression. This work exposed interpersonal violence as not a pure biological inevitability, but one possible strategy for the reproduction of dominance and gender inequalities that is potentially eradicable through social change and a commitment to transformation by men. These perspectives have not gone uncriticised however.

Since the late 1990s a wave of critical writings has emerged in response. Opposition was vocalised most strongly by British criminologist Tony Jefferson (2002), who spearheaded a paradigmatic shift within the masculinities and crime literature from structures towards psyches (Hood-Williams, 2001), which is discussed in more detail later. The general thrust of Jefferson's critique was that pro-feminist and structural perspectives had generated an over-socialised view of men, who simply internalise and orientate themselves in a predictable fashion to the masculinity which is rendered ideologically dominant and desirable. Jefferson made an important point here as theories of socially constructed masculinities, whether hegemonic or subordinated, had become imbued with the taint of causality despite some evident disagreement and confusion regarding their definitional and conceptual precision (see MacInnes, 1998). As MacInnes (1998) pointed out, social theorists have long theorised masculinity in isolation from the sexed bodies of men, which raises questions around how accurately the use of masculinity reflects what men, as a group, actually do and think in practice. Similarly, Collier (1998) suggests hegemonic masculinity is associated with a set of predominantly negative behavioural traits which reflect popular ideologies of 'being a man', equating these with men's criminality. Without doubt, aggression, competitiveness, egotism and dominance are qualities one might expect to find in violent, criminal men. But for Collier, the psychological complexities of men's subjectivities cannot be captured within an approach which theorises criminal masculinities as being confined to a range of ideologically popular behavioural traits.

More recently Steve Hall (2002, 2012a) has argued that those theorists using hegemonic models of masculinity are rather naïve in their assertions that interpersonal violence acts as a consolidator of power, which benefits men from all socio-economic groups by reaffirming a 'patriarchal dividend'. Hall argues that the concept lacks sufficient engagement with the changing historical usage of violence, which has gradually been divested of its function as a source of genuine power. Rather it is utilised predominantly by 'powerless' men occupying economically and socially excluded communities. A general point made by Arendt (1970) when she suggested that violence is present when power is absent.

Men's sense of agency within structural perspectives is therefore imbued with a rather rigid inevitability. Hood-Williams (2001, p. 44) captured nicely the thrust of these critical points:

> Why do only a minority of men summon crime when their masculinity is threatened? . . . what is the theoretical mechanism that enables us to discriminate between men who choose crime when their masculinity is threatened and that large majority of men who do not?

Without doubt, there exists 'plenty of support for the view that masculinity and gender relations are socially structured and varied' (Treadwell and Garland, 2011, p. 624). But whether these theoretical approaches can explain men's violence remains highly questionable. In spite of these criticisms, this theoretical work made some important and timely contributions to the criminological literature, and resonances of these theoretical approaches can still be detected in several contributions to the literature that have followed since. The important contribution from these theorists, particularly in terms of the impact made on subsequent literature, was the observation that men will often act in destructive and violent ways in contexts that they perceive to be threatening, an important theme which has permeated the literature since and that will now be explored in more detail with the suggestion made by some scholars that masculinity is experiencing a 'crisis'.

Masculinity in crisis

Alongside assertions that men are the most privileged and dominant social group there has emerged a contradictory theoretical current, which suggests that during the past several decades a series of global transformations have begun to threaten and de-stabilise the traditional historic dominance of men (Jefferson, 2002). This debate has emerged at the nexus of a variety of issues that Edwards (2006) describes as being confined to either 'without' or 'within' men. The former refers to broader socio-structural and economic shifts; the latter, to men's subjective experiences of these changes and their perceptions of themselves as men. The two, Edwards argues, are interconnected.

Generally, some of the following trends have been cited as challenging contemporary masculinities and have formed the evidential basis for the 'crisis': a widespread recognition of academic and educational failure among boys; growing concerns about the state of men's physical and mental health; the absence of men from some family units and the decline of the traditional nuclear family; greater gender equality, including the growing influence of feminism and increased educational and employment opportunities for women; de-industrialisation and the concomitant decline in opportunities for employment in semi-skilled and unskilled manual labour – traditionally the preserve of working-class men; global economic transformations which have altered day-to-day working practices, institutional bureaucracies and proliferated the use of information technology within the workplace; and, importantly, concerns about persistent male offending, particularly the destructive and violent behaviours exhibited by groups of excluded men occupying economically deprived communities (Beynon, 2002; Bly, 2001; Collier, 1998; Connell, 2005a, 2005b; Edwards, 2006).

While very few scholars would disagree that Western societies have altered in fundamental ways during the past several decades, claims that these changes have catalysed a crisis for all men have been rightly received with a high degree of scepticism (see Beynon, 2002; Collier, 1998; Edwards, 2006; Whitehead, 2002). Historical research reveals that masculinities of previous historical epochs have endured 'crises' in the face of challenges to their legitimacy (Hatty, 2000). Beynon (2002) suggests that masculinities are inherently disposed towards crisis tendencies during times of change. This does not constitute a refutation of claims being made contemporarily that some men are struggling to cope with material changes to their everyday lives and are experiencing subjective feelings of powerlessness and inadequacy as a result. However, as Whitehead (2002) has rightly noted, we should be wary of attempts that are made to grant legitimacy for the 'crisis'. Positioning oneself as being in a state of crisis may be potentially attractive to some men who may desire to identify themselves as victims to justify certain behaviours, particularly violence against others (see Gadd, 2004). This has added pertinence, given claims made by some writers that the evidential basis for the 'crisis' is, in many respects, rather weak (Beynon, 2002; Edwards, 2006). Beynon (2002) is perhaps much closer to an accurate description of what is being referred to as the 'crisis of masculinity'. He argues that the 'crisis' reflects a coalescence of various socio-economic and political changes that are unlikely to impact on men in a straightforward, uniform manner. In short, the impact will be experienced differentially by different groups of men.

Masculinity, marginality and violence

Literature that emerged in the late 1990s and post-Millennium began to consider in more depth this context of profound socio-economic and political transformation during the late twentieth century and its impact upon those men who have been disadvantaged most by these changes: those men who occupy working-class communities and marginalised social locations. The recent fracture and demise of working-class culture that had been established throughout modernity represents a momentous transformation within British society (Charlesworth, 2000). The harshness and the physical toils of day-to-day working life under industrial capitalism were uncompromising. The vexatious proximity of poverty and destitution made accepting the enforced dangerous working conditions and concomitant labour relations of this era an unavoidable economic necessity (Charlesworth,

2000; Engels, 1953). And this threat of economic insignificance became a potent symbol to all those unable to participate in the activities capitalism demands (Hobbs, 1988). Yet, by the middle of the twentieth century, amid this harsh socio-economic context, a nascent politico-symbolic structure based around collectivised social conflict between the working class and the owners of the means of production was fostered (Hall, 2012a; Wieviorka, 2009). In spite of the harsh inequalities that were inherent to the industrial phase of capitalism, this nascent symbolic order provided generations of working-class men and women with a sense of collective unity that allowed them to more effectively deal with the pressures generated by this socio-economic structure (Hall *et al.*, 2008). In particular, the difficult living and working conditions characteristic of the industrial phase of capitalism's history (see Engels, 1953) engendered highly durable and unreflexive embodied forms of resilience and hardened emotional dispositions among the working class. These were occupational cultures characterised by distinct forms of masculine chauvinism, toughness, stoicism, physical strength and tradecraft skills. It was not, and still is not, uncommon for working-class men in particular to revel in their capacity for physical and mental fortitude in the face of arduous external conditions and backbreaking manual work (Hall, 1997). Working milieus containing anti-authority attitudes and sentiments were common, as were the activities of 'pilfering' and 'fiddling' as manifestations of workers' informal attempts at regaining a semblance of mastery and control over the work process (Tolson, 1977; Willis, 1977). Hall (1997) describes these as 'visceral cultures', actively cultivated as adaptive and pragmatic responses to the enforced circumstances of this historical context, which valued

> physical 'hardness', mental sclerosis and egocentrism . . . producing subjects whose fierce devotion to these practices was held in place by the enforced development of a suite of brutalizing sensibilities.
>
> (p. 465)

These qualities became rigidly embodied in what Hall (1997) terms the durable visceral habitus. Hall drew on Bourdieu's (1984) work, which defined class habitus as 'the internalized form of class condition and of the conditionings it entails' (p. 101), representing an unconscious internalised guide for approaching the everyday social world that is inter-generationally reproduced. This equips the individual with embodied forms of habitual comportment, practices, speech and bodily gestural sets that are deployed without recourse to premeditated or calculative rational thought.

It was during the immediate post-war period that some advances in levels of equality were made under what has been termed the 'solidarity project' (Hall, 2007). At this time rates of crime and disorder remained relatively – in comparison with the contemporary period – low (Reiner, 2012). Rates of lethal and serious interpersonal violence were equally low. They reached 'some of the lowest points in history, and the claim that this was indeed the golden age of the pseudo-pacification process can be made with some confidence' (Hall, 2007, p. 92), as working communities were sufficiently stable, integrated and politicised to exert informal forms of social control upon their members (Lea, 1997).

These gains that were made by a working class that had successfully organised itself into a politically conscious population were, however, swiftly and uncompromisingly obliterated during turbulent economic change and the election of neo-conservative administrations in the US and the UK at the end of the 1970s, headed up by Ronald Regan and Margaret Thatcher respectively. Traditional forms of working-class employment began to rapidly disappear, much of which through de-industrialisation and the opening up of this sector to foreign competition and investment was relocated to areas of the so-called developing world with cheaper sources of labour (Harvey, 2005; Lash and Urry, 1987; Lea, 1997, 2002). The resultant declining demand for semi and unskilled manual labour was replaced by employment opportunities that place a high premium on formal education and qualifications, requiring employees to display dynamism, flexibility, and a set of skills designed to meet the requirements of a rapidly changing and highly competitive economic environment (Harvey, 1989). The job opportunities that now exist within growing consumer and service industries, which have largely replaced unskilled manual work, are very often, in contrast to their industrial predecessors, expendable, low-paid, menial, with a determinate contract length, de-unionised and vulnerable to the whims of a mutative post-industrial economy that may suddenly render them obsolete in the name of 'efficiency' or 'cost-effectiveness' (Lloyd, 2012; Sennett, 1998; Taylor, 1999; Winlow and Hall, 2006, 2013).

During this tumultuous period of British history recorded crime rates began to rise rapidly, reaching unprecedented levels in the 1980s and 1990s (Hall, 2007, 2012a; Reiner, 2012). It was during this period that a dramatic increase in rates of lethal interpersonal violence occurred, which was 'concentrated almost exclusively in men of working age living in the poorest parts of the country' (Dorling, 2004, p. 186). These increases occurred in spite of an overall longer-term decline in rates of interpersonal violence across Europe since the Middle Ages, that some scholars argued was a product of a 'civilisation process' (Elias, 2000; Fletcher, 1997) and an attendant transformation in masculine cultures that began to embrace passivity (Spierenburg, 2008). The last few decades have also experienced almost cyclical outbreaks of large-scale urban rioting in the UK, most recently in the summer of 2011, involving predominantly large groups of young men. Being in stable paid employment is a central prop of masculinity and male culture in Western societies (Morgan, 2005). Men 'are brought up to value work, as an end in itself, and to fix their personal identities around particular occupations' (Tolson, 1977, p. 13). These disturbances, particularly those in the early 1980s and 1990s occurred in rapidly de-industrialising communities experiencing high levels of unemployment and deprivation. Many of these, and similar working-class communities, have remained in states of permanent recession ever since, dogged by long-term intergenerational unemployment (Hall *et al.*, 2008; Willott and Griffin, 1996).

The once economically functional visceral cultures that emerged to service the economic imperatives of the heavy industrial phase of capitalism were then, quite suddenly and abruptly, divested of their economic utility in the wake of de-industrialisation (Hall, 1997; Hall and Winlow, 2004). Despite being discarded as a set of archaic dispositions that are (largely) no longer functional in an economic sense to the advanced capitalist project, the durability of the visceral habitus has left it tragically unreflexive and unable to comprehend and recognise its economic obsolescence (Hall, 1997). Yet, its valorised qualities continue to be repro-duced among generations of working-class men, for some of whom, a potential for violence lies at the core of their self-identities (Ayres and Treadwell, 2012; Winlow and Hall, 2006, 2009). Of course, the majority of men from lower-class backgrounds are not violent. However, there tends to exist within working-class male culture a general appreciation and recognition that violence does exist and that it happens. Tolson (1977) argued that working-class masculinity largely revolves around the local neighbourhood, embracing territoriality and a firm commitment to a tough, aggressive style. Violence is, and has always been, part of working-class life (see Hobbs, 1988) and continues to offer men from such backgrounds a potential means of earning the respect of male peers (Armstrong, 1998; Winlow, 2001). This is particularly the case when taking part in fights that are construed as 'honourable' and which affirm an idealised masculine identity (Whitehead, 2005). Historical analyses of England have found some working-class families endorsing and actively encouraging their children to behave aggressively, revelling in their children's potential for violence, particularly in the presence of a local audience (Emsley, 2005b). Davies (1998) discusses violence as a pervasive feature of both domestic and public life in the working-class communities of late nineteenth-century Salford and Manchester. It was likely in these neighbourhoods that young males would witness violence in the home and on the street regularly. The father–son relationship was often punctuated with regular bouts of corporal punishment and the gradual inheritance of appropriate codes of masculine behaviour, which had at their core aggression and toughness (Davies, 1998).

Men who are socialised in this socio-historical climate become acutely aware of their close proximity to other men who are willing to use violence, and the cultural benefits and respect often afforded to these individuals (Winlow, 2012). Experiencing violence is a distinct possibility particularly for young working-class men – a possibility that requires regular negotiation (Willis, 1990). Within socio-cultural climates that are characterised by proximal threats to physical safety, a demonstrable willingness to defend oneself is elevated in significance and often considered to be an unavoidable necessity (Anderson, 1999; Winlow, 2012; Winlow and Hall, 2009). It is still not uncommon for working-class men to be bombarded by those close to them with exhortations to 'not take any shit' and 'stand up for yourself'; sentiments which are largely defensive in nature and designed to encourage self-preservation and the maintenance of self-dignity (Winlow and Hall, 2009; Winlow, 2012). The desire to adequately prepare the young boy to defend himself and to 'be a man' may become abusive and be justified as necessary to toughen him up (Winlow, 2012). Some qualitative research with men who have committed violent crimes has found evidence of physical and emotional abuse within their biographies, in most cases at the hands of family members and carers (Athens, 1992; Hobbs, 1994, 1995; Jones, 2012; Messer-schmidt, 1999, 2005; Stein, 2007; Winlow, 2012, 2014).

There is strong evidence to revoke suggestions that sudden and dramatic increases in crime, and violent crime in particular, towards the end of the twentieth century were solely due to changes in policy and police recording practices (Hall, 2012a). Rather, as Hall (2007) has argued, the evidence points, potentially, towards the return of violence as a routine part of daily life, particularly within the most economically marginalised communities of the West as the gains that were made under the solidarity project rapidly unravelled. And it is the unequal redistribution of capital on a global scale that has coincided with these explosions in rates of violent crime within highly specific urban spaces and communities (Ray, 2011).

After conducting an analysis of the urban riots of 1991 in Newcastle, Cardiff and Oxford, Campbell (1993) situated the disturbances within a wider context of growing unemployment and a New Right governmental agenda indifferent to the plight of an increasingly excluded sub-section of the industrial working class. Crippled by deprivation, chronic unemployment and a lack of state support, these communities had reached crisis point. For Campbell, these violent disturbances were a culmination of the actions of both powerful (the uncaring, indifferent politicians and aggressive police officers) and powerless men (the violent and aggressive young men who took to the streets wielding bats, stones and petrol bombs). Economically obsolete, and without a sense of purpose, they destroyed their communities in anger at the sudden and swift transformations to what had been an established way of life and masculine identity.

Indeed, such public violence, destruction and nihilism, has been theorised by other scholars in relation to a sense of loss felt by groups of men who are finding themselves increasingly excluded from traditional forms of employment, institutions and the resources that once affirmed working-class masculinity. Instead, some of these men seek alternative meaning frames and sources of status in football 'firms', leisure, consumption of clothing, alcohol and drugs, and through involvement in occasional violence (see Armstrong, 1998; Ayres and Treadwell, 2012; Bairner, 1999; Canaan, 1996; Collison, 1996; Slaughter, 2003; Treadwell, 2010).

Given the long-standing historical relationship between working-class masculinities and the qualities that connote 'hardness' as discussed, several scholars have noted how some marginalised men's personal reputations remain contingent 'in part upon the maintenance of a credible threat of violence' (Daly and Wilson, 1988, p. 128). Such men are often willing to resort to occasionally extreme violence, sometimes with minimal provocation (Anderson, 1999; Polk, 1994). Focusing upon the foreground and emotive aspects of violence, Katz (1988) noted the importance of humiliation and its close relationship to rage. Such traumatic emotions, that are likely to motivate violence, arise when the individual's masculinity, reputation and sense of 'honour' are threatened or challenged (Polk, 1994; Spierenburg, 2008). Very often these are considered 'trivial' matters by outsiders, but for some groups of men they represent a challenge or threat to the value systems that prop up their sense of self-worth and identity, requiring an aggressive confrontational response in order to prevent their loss (Archer, 1994). And violence is particularly likely in such circumstances when men lack other non-violent means of coping with shame (Gilligan, 2000). Gregory (2012) analysed cases of homicide–suicide where men kill an intimate partner, their children, and then themselves. She suggests that when faced with the imminent loss of proprietary over intimates masculinity is threatened, so much so that they feel this can only be resolved through lethal violence towards others and then upon themselves. Ray *et al.* (2004) in their study of hate crime noted the presence of unacknowledged shame in the accounts of offenders, which was transformed into rage against South Asians. Importantly, Ray *et al.* noted that this shame–rage cycle was rooted in the broader socio-economic context of the offenders' lives, which was characterised by multiple disadvantages.

Other scholars have found that extreme violence is increasingly being used for more instrumental, economic purposes. In the absence of traditional routes into stable employment that existed under industrial capitalism, brute strength, physicality and violent potential represent forms of cultural capital and, when fused with entrepreneurial acumen, creates masculinities suited to a highly competitive globalised marketplace (Winlow, 2001). As Hobbs (1995, p. 108) explains:

> The residue of traditional masculine working-class culture, the potential for violence and instrumental physicality that remains from industrial domestic and employment cultures, once it is divested of the potential for communal action via collective responsibility, is ideally suited for engagement with serious crime.

Within a rapidly mutating society, where the market for legitimate manual occupations is shrinking, the criminal milieu and those legitimate markets that place a hefty premium on physicality, represent contexts where the visceral habitus and violent potential still retain their commercial utility (Hall, 1997; Hobbs, 1994, 1995; Hobbs *et al.*, 2003; Treadwell, 2010; Winlow, 2001).

Criminological literature from the US and Australia has also contributed to these debates around marginalised masculinities in a changing and turbulent economic environment. Mindful of ethnicity and the impact of migration on gender relations, Bourgois (1996, 2003) explored the adaptive responses of second and third generation Puerto Rican immigrant males to acute poverty and structural disadvantage. In the absence of the traditional indigenous familial and gender structures of native Puerto Rico, in which men were domestically and economically privileged, the young males in Bourgois' study found themselves increasingly marginalised in a rapidly restructuring global economy. These men rejected employment opportunities in the US economy's low-level service sector, which they perceived as feminine and emasculating. Instead, they turned to localised drug markets, and interpersonal and sexual violence in a desperate search for masculine affirmation. Similar conclusions were reached by DeKeseredy and Schwartz (2005), who theorised violence against women in intimate relationships within

Messerschmidt's (1993, 1997) masculinity as structured action framework discussed previously. The cumulative effect of economic and demographic alterations has, within many familial households, inverted traditional patriarchal relations between men and women. Violence against women within a domestic context equips men with a means to reassert these relations (DeKeseredy and Schwartz, 2005).

In line with these broadening conceptual approaches to masculinities and violence, Australian criminologists Carrington and colleagues (2008, 2010) have explored the varying impact of socio-spatial dynamics and geographic locations on masculinities. Responding to high rates of violence in rural locations of Australia, they explore the ways in which the rural and the masculine coalesce to produce culturally valorised rural masculinities. Rural masculinities, like the masculinities of industrial visceral cultures in the UK (Hall, 1997), are aligned with rugged manual work, brute physical strength and bodily resilience. This is a form of masculine identity deemed authentic and genuine, and one which has been valorised by some new men's movements. Yet social, economic and cultural changes are threatening traditional working practices and gender relations in rural locations. Rural men with limited access to more varied expressions of masculinity are likely to resort to exaggerated physicality and violence as a response to this growing fragility (Carrington and Scott, 2008).

As an extension to this conceptual approach, Carrington *et al.* (2010) discuss the recent growth in mining and resource extraction industries in remote locations of Australia. The multi-national companies that control these industries employ and rely heavily on a large non-resident population of men from lower/working-class backgrounds who are skilled in manual trades and live, temporarily, in these resource rich communities. These are men whose sense of identity has been cultivated within 'a culture that valorises hard physical labour, big machines and conspicuous consumption and normalises excessive alcohol consumption and displays of aggression' (Carrington *et al.*, 2010, p. 404). Frequent violence and disorder involving the men working and residing within these communities are manifestations of the subterranean convergences of frontier masculinities that characterise these rural communities, and the aggressive corporate masculinities of the multi-national companies that mobilise and organise them for effective resource extraction (Carrington *et al.*, 2010).

In contrast to pro-feminist, structural perspectives on men's violence explored earlier, this section has focused upon literature that addresses more directly the impact of a changing socio-economic environment upon men and how these transformations might be linked to violent criminality. This literature is characterised by a clearer acknowledgement of the sub-groups of men identified by Hood-Williams (2001) who use physical violence against others: socio-economically marginalised men. These various studies have taken a more nuanced approach to the expression of masculinity through being more attentive to issues of subjectivity and emotion, some of which have explored subjective feelings of worthlessness, shame, anger, and the embodiment of particular corporeal and mental qualities collectively referred to as 'hardness' among men within marginalised communities. These developments are certainly promising, particularly these early discussions around the role of emotions in relation to masculinity and violence. Yet, a more fully developed subjective reading of violent men informed by psychology is absent from these contributions to the literature. The remainder of the review will focus upon more recent perspectives that have explored men's 'inner worlds'. The focus here has been upon the subjective and psychological dimensions of masculinity, in particular how men interact, psychically, with broader socio-structural forces, and what relationship this might have with violence.

The turn to 'psyches': psychosocial perspectives

As previously discussed, the critical backlash against hegemonic masculinity and socio-structural approaches to men's offending heavily influenced by this concept, paved the way for a paradigmatic shift from structures to psyches (Hood-Williams, 2001). Suggestions that men accept and seek to emulate, without question or difficulty, idealised hegemonic masculine identities, were subjected to extensive criticism. Jefferson (1994) instead highlighted the complex ways in which individual men orientate themselves psychically towards dominant discourses of masculinity, sometimes in a spectacularly unsuccessful fashion. Jefferson began to assemble his theoretical foundations through a psychoanalytic case study of the former world heavy-weight boxing champion Mike Tyson (Jefferson, 1996, 1998). A reportedly withdrawn, passive child from a difficult family background in a poverty-stricken community of Brooklyn, New York, Tyson was a prime target for local bullies. This childhood image of acute vulnerability and victimisation serves as a drastic contrast to Tyson's awesome physical prowess and uncompromising brutality demonstrated during some of his professional boxing bouts. But as Jefferson argues, this transformation in Tyson's biography was not straightforward. The history of a 'painful psychic legacy of emotional neglect and the resulting pattern of anxiety' (Jefferson, 1998, p. 94) have punctuated Tyson's adult life, inducing feelings of powerlessness and a consequent return to his former withdrawn state of passivity (Jefferson, 1996).

Through this case study Jefferson offered a highly detailed and nuanced account of the complexities involved in the construction of male identity and how recourse to physical violence may be implicated in this process. His discussion of Tyson's changing subjectivity is informed by a theoretical framework that is premised upon the individual's attempts to ward off and defend against overwhelming anxieties. With Hollway (Hollway and Jefferson, 2000) this theoretical approach to understanding subjectivity was developed further through the positing of the individual as a 'defended subject', who is constantly attempting to manage and defend against anxiety-inducing emotions and memories that are deemed threatening to the self. Much of the theorising here around the defended subject relies heavily on Kleinian-inspired approaches to psychoanalysis, which focus on the infant's early and then subsequent experiences of persecutory anxiety and how these are defended against through the use of splitting and projection (Jefferson, 2002). Difficult biographical experiences can leave individuals heavily reliant on this form of primitive defence used to alleviate feelings of anxiety, and it is this which formulates the theoretical bedrock of much of Jefferson and colleagues' writings on crime and violence.

This broad theoretical framework was utilised by Gadd (2000) in his study of men who regularly abused their female partners. Critical of approaches to men's violence based solely on social structure and discourse, Gadd exposed the ambivalences and anxieties ridden in one man's account of the violence he had inflicted upon his female partner. Rather than acting as a context for the performance and affirmation of a masculine identity based upon power, control and dominance, physically abusing his partner acted as a means to defend against persecutory anxieties and vulnerabilities stemming from a difficult childhood. This induced an array of ambivalent emotions in regards to his violence, which complicate and render problematic the straightforward assumption that violence, particularly against women, equates a masculine affirming experience.

Jefferson and colleagues' early works were heavily psychoanalytical and have been subjected to numerous criticisms on that basis. Howe (2008) is critical of psychoanalytically-inspired theoretical approaches to understanding men's use of interpersonal violence, particularly Jefferson's work for writing in, what Howe describes as, a sympathetic manner about the motives and behaviours of men who commit acts of violence. Approaches solely rooted in psychoanalysis fail to sufficiently engage on a critical level with problematic forms of masculine sexuality, culture, and a powerful discourse 'that render men's violences as "normal" and, thus, inevitable' (Whitehead, 2002, p. 38). It is, therefore, largely devoid of the potential to be mobilised into a political project that might facilitate positive social changes (Collier, 2004).

The more recent *Psychosocial Criminology* (Gadd and Jefferson, 2007) attempts to better theorise the human subject by taking account of the social world, the discursive realm and the psychic inner world of 'unconscious as well as conscious processes' (Gadd and Jefferson, 2007, p. 4). The defended subject at the heart of this text is positioned as a purveyor of complex, contradictory and often inconsistent narratives on their lived experiences. Rather than theorising masculinity as rooted solely in structural conditions or discourse and being understood as a manifestation of power, their more psychoanalytic readings of gender suggest men will seek to occupy particular subject positions that avoid subjective feelings of insecurity and powerlessness in order to conceal feelings of weakness. Gadd and Jefferson's psychosocial approach, rightly focuses upon the under-theorised realm of men's subjectivities, which had for long periods been marginalised at the expense of a theoretical engagement with socio-structural conditions. This move towards a greater recognition of the complex interaction between individual biography, psychology and the social world is a positive one. As discussed, early literature had tended to portray men as rather static, ready-made fighting machines, willing and capable of 'doing' violence when masculinity was threatened. Gadd and Jefferson make a compelling case for a more nuanced approach to the study of masculinities and interpersonal violence, one that is capable of capturing the subtleties and nuances of this relationship.

Some criticisms still remain along similar lines to those already discussed. Wykes and Welsh (2009) suggest that psychosocial criminology still represents a rather reductive return to the psychoanalysis of individuals through case studies. They argue this is to the detriment of what is a much-needed critical engagement with problematic aspects of culture around masculinity and violence. Indeed, an analysis of interpersonal violence that is rooted too deeply within the individual biographies and psyches of men, runs the risk of pathologising those individuals (Treadwell and Garland, 2011). I would argue that it is imperative, if we are to understand why men commit acts of violence, to not discount significant moments within men's biographical histories and their potential for analytical value, so individual psychology must enter our analysis of men's violence to some extent. This is a point that has been made by several other scholars (see Hall, 2012a; Jones, 2008). However, in a similar vein to the critiques that have been outlined here, I too would argue that Gadd and Jefferson do fall short of a significant engagement with aspects of what they call the 'social', privileging instead a greater focus upon individual psychology and experience. Crucially, Gadd and Jefferson's (2007) *Psychosocial Criminology* does not clearly acknowledge the group of men who were discussed in the previous section and are most likely to commit interpersonal violence and be its victims, particularly in public settings, that is, socially and economically excluded men. Neither do their analyses of masculinities and violence subject the changing historical, material and social conditions of this group of men's existence to requisite critical scrutiny. Being firmly anchored within these approaches severely limits the potential for theoretical speculation beyond individuals to the more troubling and problematic aspects of our social world.

This incipient psychosocial literature has recently drawn contributions from more critical branches of criminology that have retained a strong focus on issues of the political economy of advanced capitalism. Building on the previous theoretical foundations of their earlier works, which have been described earlier in this chapter (see Hall, 1997, 2002; Hall and Winlow, 2004; Winlow, 2001), Winlow and Hall draw on critical psychoanalytic and continental philosophical approaches to subjectivity. They conceptualise violent/criminal masculinities as products of a fusion between individual psychology/subjectivity and historic socio-economic transformations in the fabric of capitalism's political economy.

Winlow and Hall's (2006) qualitative study of young people and interpersonal violence within the night-time economy addressed, in some detail, the unprecedented transformations that took place during the second half of the twentieth century and the psychosocial consequences of this for young people growing up within what has become an increasingly atomised, competitive and consumer driven culture. The hedonistic consumer milieu of the night-time economy is designed specifically for the narcissistic display of one's conspicuous and competent ability to consume, which can inspire fear within individuals and an atmosphere of intense competition. Young working-class males socialised in a durable habitus that clings to largely redundant notions of idealised, tough masculinity, make recourse to inter-personal violence in this milieu to temporarily avert incessant feelings of humiliation, insecurity and anxiety. This restores a temporary semblance of balance and triumph over their individual victim(s), who represents one of the threatening atomised 'others' that audaciously attempts a spectacular affront of ostentatious individualism (Winlow and Hall, 2006).

These evidently emotive aspects of men's interpersonal violence have been explored in further works through examining humiliation and shame within violent men's biographies (Winlow, 2012; Winlow and Hall, 2009), emotions that have been alluded to already in this chapter, but which Winlow and Hall connect to the political economy of advanced capitalism. Winlow and Hall claim that within contemporary postmodern culture, the anxious, insecure subject, who has been released from the fetters of collectivised identities that are capable of better insulating against insecurity and feelings of personal isolation (Hall, 2012a), experiences a strong compulsion towards instant gratification and *jouissance*, which is now achieved predominantly through various forms of consumption (Hall *et al.*, 2008). In contemporary market culture individuals become embroiled in a process of constant reappraisal of their individual identities. They ruminate on missed opportunities and individual mistakes, all the while tormented by a reorientated superego injunction that mocks them for their personal failings and commands them to enjoy. The durable habitus works in tandem with this reorientated subconscious ethical agency, forcing violent men's psyches to recall violent encounters in idealised terms. In reality, this subverts and represses the actuality of the violent incident – the actual reality of which may be too painful to remember completely. The experience of being physically dominated, and of failing to act in socially and culturally expected ways, is likely to be powerfully humiliating for men who have emerged from marginal social locations that continue to cling obsessively to an image of powerful, invulnerable masculinity. Difficult memories, and the emotions they evoke, are harnessed and utilised when perpetrating violence against others (Winlow, 2012; Winlow and Hall, 2009).

Jones (2012) suggests feelings of personal shame and inadequacy in relation to others have become more acute in late modernity with the increased potential of experiencing social isolation within what are now more individualistic cultures. Yet, physical violence as a means to deal with feelings of shame only serves to lock these men further into spirals of ultimately pointless altercations that bring no discernible rewards (Hall, 2002). Treadwell and Garland's (2011) research on racist violence among English Defence League (EDL) members approaches physical violence as 'a psychological process of individual identity making' (p. 632) in circumstances of structural marginality. These men target their anger and frustration at the 'Islamic other', who is blamed for their disadvantage. Yet, such violence harbours no genuine potential to create any lasting solutions to these men's experiences of structural marginality and exclusion – only a brief interlude to expel their anger and rage, which inevitably returns.

Discussion

This chapter has examined important contributions to criminological literature addressing the relationship between men, masculinities and violence. From early, and somewhat unsophisticated, perspectives based on crude biologically assumed differences between men and women, the literature since then has grown in both size and theoretical sophistication. The early 1990s saw the first significant contributions to this literature, which has undergone several significant paradigmatic shifts since then. There is overwhelming evidence, despite the very positive and important contribution made by this early literature, to suggest that purely structural or social constructionist accounts of masculinity cannot sufficiently theorise the complexities of men's subjectivities and how these are related to the use of interpersonal violence. In this respect, the subsequent shift within the literature towards better understanding men's psyches and how these interact with gender structures has evidently been a positive one. However, this shift certainly did, initially at least, push theory in this area too far towards the individual male. More recent contributions that attempt to fuse psychoanalytical, philosophical and sociological approaches into an understanding of masculine subjectivities and violence, provide a potentially more useful and promising theoretical framework for exploring this relationship, in particular, those perspectives that emanate from the critical tradition and that integrate ideology, culture, history and political economy into their analyses (see Hall, 2012a; Jones, 2012; Treadwell and Garland, 2011; Winlow, 2012; Winlow and Hall, 2006, 2009).

The existing masculinities and violence literature reviewed here is very often focused upon particular contexts and therefore a specific type of violence which takes place within those contexts (football violence/hooliganism; domestic violence; violence within drug and other criminal markets etc.). What constitutes the existing literature are a collection of theoretical and empirical studies of different types of violence that are committed by men, which have produced important ideas about the relationship between men, their masculinities and violence. However, the nature of the current literature mirrors, as Winlow (2012) has argued, the tendency within criminological and sociological studies to approach the issue of interpersonal violence as tangential to another discussion (urban deprivation, drug markets etc.) without necessarily focusing critically upon the violence itself and the subjectivities of those perpetrating it, a point echoed by Ray (2011), who has also commented upon the fragmentary nature of perspectives on violence within sociology and related disciplines that have lost 'sight of the intimate connection between violence and the human condition' (p. 2). Given this current situation both theorists argue for more integrated approaches to researching and theorising violence that grant it a more centralised position within criminology and associated social science disciplines. This review of literature, and the points made by Winlow and Ray, lead unavoidably then to questions of ontology and the nature of (violent) masculine subjectivity, which this book will now attempt to develop in the forthcoming chapters.

The next four chapters present detailed qualitative data gathered from the ethnographic fieldwork that was described in Chapter 1. The purpose is to sensitise the reader to the experiences, lives and subjectivities of the men who participated. In Chapter 7, I return to theory and posit a critically informed psychosocial theoretical framework that is anchored in this data.

3 Top lad

A violent biography

You might want to watch this

Come on Tony, get yourself outside, you might want to watch this.

After imploring me to join him Darren walks to the exit of The Fox, a pub famous for being one of the 'roughest' in town and a regular haunt for the large group of men who identify with the local professional football team's 'firm'. I immediately follow, still carrying a pint of lager in my hand. Previously Darren, having recently become a father for the first time, had told me that he was trying to avoid the 'bother' that occasionally occurs on match days. Now, standing on the pavement outside The Fox with around ten other young men clad in Stone Island jackets, bouncing up and down in nervous anticipation of potential violence with men from the pub next door, all under the watchful gaze of a CCTV camera perched on the opposite side of the street, Darren is showing little evidence of hesitancy. This is his story . . .

Darren is aged in his early 30s and stands around six feet in height. His physique is stocky and heavy-set. One of his arms is intricately tattooed from the wrist up to the shoulder and his wife's name is tattooed onto his chest. Darren possesses the physique of a man who looks more than capable of handling himself during physical confrontation. This physical appearance certainly does not lie. Since his late teens he has cultivated a fearsome reputation for violence in the large town where he grew up and currently lives. For well over a decade he has been a committed member of a football hooligan firm. His violent exploits at home, and abroad, as well as his presence in localised drug supply networks, have secured him a respected place and an almost celebrity-like status among some of his friends and a wider group of male peers. In the parlance of the football hooligan sub-culture Darren is known for his 'gameness' during confrontations with rivals. Despite a reduction in his involvement in football violence during recent years, he is still recognised and respected, by many of the other men involved, as one of the 'top lads' (Treadwell, 2010).

Young rogue

Darren was born and spent the early years of his life with his parents in a mining village that lies in a large, de-industrialised conurbation where he now lives with his wife and their young child. When one of Darren's younger brothers was born, the family moved to a new housing development nearby where Darren lived until his late teens. Darren described himself as 'a bit of a rogue' during his childhood and youth. He was first arrested during his mid-teens for vandalism. He began using drugs and was able to acquire enough quantities of amphetamine and ecstasy to begin supplying to his close friends on a regular basis, providing him with sufficient funds to cover his own personal use. Darren developed a reputation for violence early in his life course. A reputation that emulates that of his late father's, who was also known and respected by a number of local men for his violent credentials. School provided Darren with a context in which to flex and cultivate this incipient reputation:

> I was always known as a rogue, always in trouble at school, just got into fights, just enjoyed the buzz of a fight really . . . a lot of my family have got younger kids and they all say 'Oh such and such is a right bastard, he's just got expelled from school' and they still use me to this day as an example, saying 'Oh god he's not as bad as Darren though' . . . But I just saw everything as a bit of a challenge . . . babysitters were a challenge, know what I mean? I had the best of the best babysitters coming to look after me, and I saw it as a challenge to get rid of them. I remember this one lass, she was the daughter of my mum and dad's long friends, known them years, and apparently she were some sort of ice maiden they called her, and my mum goes 'Oh you've had it now, she's coming to babysit you' and all I did was up my game. Think she lasted two visits and she ended up having some sort of breakdown or something, and I felt brilliant do you know at the time.

Several babysitters later Darren finally met his match in a woman from the housing estate where he lived:

> . . . there was only one that stuck with it like . . . And I used to just push her and push her, I remember like it was yesterday . . . I once called her fat. And obviously you don't call women fat do you? . . . and she absolutely hammered me, like really hammered me . . . proper punched me, like the lot, booted me. I can remember being really, I mean that were the first hammering I'd ever had, and I can remember crying, I was 14 something like that, crying to my mum and dad, and they were just like 'no' kind of thing. And I was going 'no she really beat me up', and they just said 'well serves you right'.

At 16 years of age Darren left school and spent several years completing a paid work-based apprenticeship at a local college. He currently works in the skilled manufacturing sector and has done so since completing his apprenticeship. Several years ago he was promoted to a supervisory position. During some of the more formalised interviews I conducted with Darren he was keen to point out to me his commitment to work and evidently takes a huge amount of pride in his occupation, particularly the talent and skill he possesses within this particular trade. He spoke proudly about how he had always been in employment since leaving school and emphasised quite strongly what he believed was the normality of his familial background and upbringing, contrasting this with some of the highly negative media depictions of men who are violent:

> . . . no broken home really, no crappy school story, no stereotypical kind of bloke you know . . . I'm not that at all. Always been in work, never claimed a penny off the state ever . . . I do smile to myself how the papers usually say 'these drunken thuggish', I mean sometimes, a lot of times I've never even been drunk at a match, do you know what I mean? It's never been about that, broken home all this lot, my mum and dad were married, do you know what I mean? Just like a normal other family . . . never judge a book by its cover, cos I've got an ONC from college, and it's pretty hard to get, well certainly difficult for someone who messed about all the time at school.

Although Darren had been regularly involved in fights during his teens, particularly in school, he remembers quite vividly an early encounter with serious violence in the local night-time economy, during which he was seriously assaulted outside a fast food outlet. A group of men from a notorious local housing estate assaulted Darren in what he described was an unprovoked attack that began when he was accused of talking to a woman who was in a relationship with one of the assailants. Darren described his stoic, but ultimately futile attempts to fight back, as he was punched to the floor and repeatedly kicked in the stomach and ribs by his numerically advantaged enemy.

> It makes me laugh cos a couple of the lads who were with them at the time, I know them now and they are proper right up my ass, I mean these lads didn't actually hit me like but they were there part of that group. And I always wonder if they know that I know they were there, cos at that time I was a nobody.

Darren was unfortunate enough to experience the random violence that so often characterises contemporary urban night-time economies and which can often erupt with minimal provocation and forewarning (see Hobbs *et al.*, 2003; Tomsen, 1997; Winlow and Hall, 2006). Darren ruminated on this event for considerable time; a painfully humiliating encounter that cast a haunting shadow over his developing identity and self-image as a young male capable of 'looking after himself'. As his narrative recollections suggest he attached great significance to this event, particularly his firm conviction that it was the beginning of a transformation within him. As Darren explained himself, he was 'a nobody', but in the aftermath of this event he emerged from its shadow determined to become 'somebody'.

I don't fear dying

When Darren reached his late teens his father became seriously ill. Darren had left the family home by this point and had bought a house with his then girlfriend. Despite some initial improvements in his father's condition following treatment, he then suddenly and unexpectedly worsened. Despite being readmitted to hospital he passed away:

> **Darren**: . . . it were just horrible, I still think about him every day . . . we always do stuff and kind of remember him, all my birthdays and every Christmas we go up to the cemetery where he is buried. But yeah just horrible.

> **AE**: What sort of a relationship did you have with your dad before he passed away?

> **Darren**: We were very close, I didn't, I don't think I took the illness, I mean I'd got a huge chip on my shoulder about it at the time. I were going out with a lass from down south at the time, and I was travelling to and from hers every weekend or she'd be coming up here. Wrapped up in my own little world really . . . I didn't take it seriously enough I don't think, well no I didn't take it seriously enough cos if I did, if I knew he wouldn't be here I would have spent every single fucking day with him . . . that's a huge regret that I've got, is not spending more time with him . . . it's alright in hindsight isn't it looking back, but yeah that's about it just a normal relationship, more like matey than anything. Cos at that age, 18, 19, your dad starts being cool again doesn't he? And it's like he's your hero like until you're 13, then you don't want nothing to do with him until you're ready for an ale, and then it's kind of stuff like that. So then he starts being more of your mate kind of thing.

Darren had begun attending football matches with his father. His father, during his youth, was a member of a gang of skinheads that hailed from a deprived council estate and was himself regularly involved in football violence as a young man. He was well known and respected within the club's hooligan outfit, which was the early forerunner to the 'firm' that Darren is now involved with:

> . . . he used to go to the football matches and get involved in the bother when it was boot boys kind of thing, skin heads, he were one of the first skin heads round here and that . . . He were from a rough background, school and that, but he made himself . . . he were intelligent, he got a good job, did well for the family, we weren't wealthy but we didn't go without much. But he were the same, I used to listen to stories, they were my bedtime stories as I got older . . . like I remember being mesmerised by stories, he didn't used to glorify them, but he told me about when they went to Tottenham and they had this fight, do you know what I mean? So I used to get hooked on it, I used to love all that . . . And he's well known among other fans in fact I have beers with blokes who were his mates, who knocked about with him . . . brilliant

like, brilliant bloke, one in a million. Even now everybody who says it, they can kind of see me in him kind of thing, just stuff like that.

The trauma of losing his father had a significant impact on Darren's life and as his narrative suggests, he was struggling with intense feelings of grief, regret and loss. His memory of this period was blurred and Darren often found it difficult to recall specific details concerning this particular phase of his life course. It was in the wake of his father's death and following the severe beating he had taken outside the fast food outlet that Darren strongly sensed that there had been a significant shift and transformation within himself – from the young 'rogue' and its connotations of a youthful, rebellious flirtation with deviance, into something far more 'sinister':

> I were always a rogue at school . . . had trouble with the police more than a 13, 14-year-old kid should have . . . I think at that time when I was, when that happened with my dad it took a more sinister kind of path . . . the way I deal with things, the way I started dealing with things like . . . just them capabilities that everybody's got kind of thing of going that step further, but actually carrying it out . . . sort of like no fear . . . so maybe it was just laying beneath the surface, that sinister no fear kind of thing, and then that brought it on . . . . way I can only describe it is, I didn't have any fear of dying, cos I thought, in my opinion I'll get to meet my dad again, know what I mean?

Darren's relationship with his then girlfriend ended and she moved out of the home they had bought together. Darren sold the house and moved into a council flat with a friend. He began using illicit drugs more regularly and heavily, and following a series of tense arguments with his mother, became estranged from her and his brothers, having limited contact with them over a period of several years. Although Darren possesses a naturally large physique, he put considerably more effort into building this physicality, bulking up through weight training and steroids. He was also becoming more regularly involved in serious violence; particularly with the football firm. Prior to becoming involved in football violence, Darren already had a penchant for the casual clothing fashions that dominate the contemporary hooligan 'scene' (see Treadwell, 2008, 2010). Earning a regular wage from the age of 16, he had sufficient disposable income to adorn himself in expensive, designer clothing, which had begun to get him noticed at the matches:

> I know a lot of people now wear Stone Island just cos of the Football Factory film, but I used to be into the clothes anyway. I started working straight from school, so I got into my clothes straightaway, used to go to other cities shopping for my Stone Island gear. And at that time it was only ever football lads that wore it, and I wore it cos I liked it, it was good clobber. And obviously I used to stand out and I'd get kids, local lads who I recognised going 'you from around here?' And it just developed from there, you know on first name terms and all that lot.

Darren travelled to an away match with some members of the firm and became involved in a violent altercation which caught the eye of some of the more established and older men involved:

> . . . after the match I remember a big fight happening with a load of fans who had travelled to fight us lot and it went off in the train station. I were actually out on the station platform on my own and I ended up fighting with these rival lads, other lads from our firm were watching from the window, I laid one out and I were scrapping with the other one before the police arrived and chucked me on the train. I come onto the train just like a hero . . . I were obviously young, always been a biggish lad, and they just loved it, I were getting drinks bought and that were it then it just progressed from there, they wanted me. They wanted me to come with them and that, and I did.

Knock out

The socio-economic transformations that characterised the latter end of the twentieth century had a profound impact on criminal opportunities and cultures, which men with sufficient entrepreneurial acumen and reputations for violence were able to exploit (Hobbs, 1995; Winlow, 2001). Treadwell's (2010) ethnographic research with men involved in football violence and criminality, found that some men who have forged their reputations on the terraces are increasingly able to utilise and orientate this towards the more instrumental requirements of criminal markets; particularly drug supply (see also Treadwell and Ayres, 2014). Having supplied small quantities of drugs to his close friends for some time, Darren found there was a growing demand in the night-time economy for his services, where his reputation was getting him noticed:

> **Darren**: I started dealing quite a bit.
>
> **AE**: So were you actually starting to make money out of it at that point?
>
> **Darren**: Yeah, but it was still mainly to my mates, like mainly with pills. And I remember I was going downtown and all my nights were kind of took up by going to the toilets, and eventually it was mates of mates, then mates of those mates, and before I knew it, it was too easy money. And it were alright . . . I was always fighting, always, I started mingling a lot more with the football firm, and just fighting, every single week, every time I went out. And obviously it coincided with me making enemies, they obviously knew what I was doing.

In a local nightclub where Darren and several of his friends had been regularly supplying drugs, tensions had been mounting with a number of the bouncers who looked after the doors. One busy evening a fight ensued and several of the door staff were hospitalised:

It had been building up for a while, we had our little corner and there were a few of us doing little bits of dealing . . . we were always scrapping, never got chucked out cos the bouncers were wary of us. And this particular night they felt pretty confident, and we were out with the women, my missus was there . . . they actually started it that night for something very little. And it just went into a massive big riot, lights come on, club were full . . . we gave them a right hiding . . . as we came out some of the bouncers were begging us to stop.

Darren had been on bail at the time for a separate violent offence, but avoided arrest as he left the scene. His continued involvement in violence and his growing reputation within the town began to attract attention and he was arrested one evening on suspicion of possessing Class A drugs with intent to supply. Fortunately, for Darren, he had decided not to take any drugs out with him on this particular night having just started seeing his girlfriend, now his wife, who had asked him not to bring any with him.

We were going out, trying to get to know each other, and she never saw me cos I was always in the toilets knocking things out. And she'd said 'just this once don't go out with anything on you.' So I thought fuck it, yeah, I like her, like her a lot, I'll do it I'll prove to her . . . my girlfriend saying that to me at the time, it's like she's probably saved me, well she has. Cos usually I would go out with 20 or 30 [Ecstasy pills] easily . . . they strip-searched me and everything and I didn't have anything on me . . . and because they didn't find anything on me they couldn't search my house. So that obviously would have been a big jail sentence for that.

Darren suspected that it was one of his newly acquired 'enemies' who had informed the police that he was dealing. Feeling increasingly paranoid and not wishing to push his luck, Darren sold the remaining several hundred pills he had stashed at his house and ended his stint as a regular drug dealer:

I just thought no this is too much of a risk. So once I'd done that lot that was it. And from that just dabbled a bit, I learnt a big lesson from that, I mean I never really trusted anyone then, but never tell anybody anything as regards to stuff like that. And also I were just sorting my mates out again . . . It weren't hard to stop doing it, it were hard missing out on the money. I were never loaded with it, it just got me out kind of thing and that was it really . . . I was making enough money to go out and I never wanted to pack in work or anything like that because I always knew that would be my downfall.

The firm lad

Despite possessing many of the crucial ingredients that would be necessary for a successful career in criminality – violent potential and repute, respect, contacts and knowledge of local criminality – Darren retracted his own involvement and resumed his small-scale supply operation to a small circle of his trusted friends and acquaintances. The highly coveted cultural and material benefits that one can accrue from a successful career in serious criminality (Hall *et al.*, 2008; Hobbs, 1995) did not seem to hold much allure for Darren, who is committed to his employment and is evidently far more attracted to the excitement, thrills and the seductive aspects (see Katz, 1988) of the football hooligan sub-culture and identity:

> I was obsessed with being a hooligan, I were absolutely obsessed with it . . . if they could bottle that up, what you get, the buzz you get at a football match, actually fighting with the other lads, if you could bottle that up it would be worth ten times more than coke, there's no feeling like it ever.

Apart from these surface-level pleasures and attractions to committing violence, Darren described the pleasure and enjoyment he derived from being part of a fraternity of other men who fought together. Particularly the strong sense of camaraderie and the recognition he received from the older men involved:

> I don't actually fucking fight for nothing in my eyes, even though most people say 'Oh football is a load of bollocks, there's nothing to fight over football for', but it's not about that it's about like the whole mentality, the whole fucking bravado, the whole fucking, that little town mentality thing, come to football, come to here and try and take the piss if you want but you're going to fucking get it. And the same when you go away, little old us in your big city . . . and we're fucking tearing the place up, do you know what I mean? . . . I'm no psychologist but maybe, like I was obviously a young lad and most of the lads part of the hooligan element at that time were older lads, and maybe there is something in it somewhere that I was looking for that father figure kind of thing, do you know what I mean? Or not looking for a father figure, but I liked being around older blokes.

Football firms serve as contexts for the formation of collective and individual masculine identities through mutual involvement in violence and particular forms of conspicuous consumption (Ayres and Treadwell, 2012). By virtue of their established reputations and extensive experience of violence, older members can become approximations of iconic role models for younger members (Ayres and Treadwell, 2012). When pressed further on the subject of seeking an approximation of a father figure or male role model, Darren was ambivalent, initially suggesting that this was not the case. Later when relaying a series of anecdotes about a close friend of his, the issue of a father figure resurfaced, unprompted, in Darren's narrative:

> **Darren**: . . . my best mate at the time [says name] don't know if you've heard of him? Absolute fucking psychopath.

AE: I've heard that name before. So you and him were pretty good mates like?

Darren: Yeah . . . he's done it all mate . . . there's not many whose done more than him to be honest, he was just a fucking fruit bowl like. And we bounced off each other and that were funny like cos we were always trying to outdo each other all time. And at that period in time, I would say, just before I met my wife, I would say it was the best time of my life. Cos if anything, going back to that father figure, that's probably the one I did cling to. He's only 7 or 8 years older than me, but when I was younger I'd heard loads of stories about him. He wasn't like, it's hard to say, if you think of somebody, to say that they're a top lad, football lad, normal people would just think the hardest lad, but I know hard lads, really hard lads, who have lost their bottle before. And I've known lads who can't really fight, fucking never go anywhere like, know what I mean? Might be 9 stone wet through, but never go anywhere and will stand and fight all day long. So to me, a top lad is a mixture of both, and he were game as fuck, he never ever gave up anywhere.

Darren himself was rapidly gaining respect and becoming popular within the firm for his 'bottle' – the willingness to get involved in violence even in the face of strong opposition, which is highly valued within the football hooligan sub-culture (Armstrong, 1998). But more than this, it was his evident fighting skill, physical prowess, and his uncompromising ferocity and unrestrained rage during violent encounters that fuelled the general aura of menace that surrounded him:

Darren: I get to a point where you can't return kind of thing where I get all that nervous energy and start like laughing to myself and then that's it you're gone . . . in a fight I don't ever think to myself . . . oh best give over [stop] now or anything, it's just fucking go and do as much damage until you get pulled off or whatever . . . That's my style of fighting, I just keep going. Even though I'm a big lad and I am powerful with my fists . . . I don't just think to myself just punch them . . . I just go for it, I've bitten people before and all sorts . . . I've hit people with stools, chairs . . . ash trays.

AE: Do you ever feel any kind of sympathy for them [victims]?

Darren: No, I never have actually . . . that's probably where I'm wrong with it, cos a lot of people who I know . . . they do feel sorry for some things, but I don't . . . I've never started a fight with anybody who hasn't deserved, who I don't think has deserved it.

It was immediately after an away match that Darren's enthusiasm and his appetite for violence led him into dangerous territory:

We were walking up and there were loads of their lads coming over the road at us, and there were only two policemen with us. Police were trying to beat them back with batons. Meanwhile I'm walking down towards them [rival lads] saying 'Come on come on' like, and they were piling out of this boozer which I didn't see. My mates are further up and shouting 'get up here, stick together', I were away from our lot, still hell bent on getting these to come over and then next minute police cordoned them lot off, cordoned our lot off . . . and within a split second I was on my own, trapped down this street at the side of a bridge, and I got done over . . . I had some right bother down that side . . . From what I can remember they were coming at me, I was just fighting like fuck, I put one on the floor, and then another one I were having a good fight with him . . . then one just come flying in with a kick in the side, and then that were it, that's what did it. And I were just powerless to, I can't really remember, I didn't black out or anything but I can't really remember what happened then, it just seemed like it were going forever. I still remember what they were saying now, what were they calling me now, err, woolly back? Were it woolly back? Or sheep shagger or something [laughs] something like that.

Prior to this incident, Darren had enjoyed some 'good results' during confrontations with rival lads. Through a combination of his own evident skill as a fighter and the protection of large numbers of older and more experienced men, he had managed to avoid being seriously assaulted. Darren's narrative reveals the psychological and emotional traumas that can haunt the memories of men who have experienced, directly, the utter powerlessness and passivity experienced during physical domination. His inability to remember in much detail what happened to him is symptomatic of the traumatic nature of the event and his own psyche's inability to accept and memorise fully an event that threatens to shatter his ideal ego (Zizek, 2002, 2006) – the internalised ideal image that he aspires to be:

> I felt that down afterwards that I'd, not so much got a hiding, but my pride took a hammering. Cos, well I was always in bother anyway, but, put it this way I don't lose many [fights], especially at that time. So my pride took more of a hammering than anything else. Bruises heal after a few days, it were a pride thing.

Like the night he was assaulted outside the takeaway during his late teens, Darren found himself, once again, powerless in the face of a numerically advantaged enemy and tried doggedly to salvage a sense of dignity from the incident by fighting back. The aim here was to retrieve what little one can from a highly traumatising and humiliating situation through a display of stoic resistance and fortitude in the face of what are unassailable opponents (see Winlow and Hall, 2006):

> **Darren**: . . . that changed me as regards to my actual doings on a football day.
>
> **AE**: In what way did it change you?

Darren: Just mainly making sure that I was, I used my brain more kind of thing. Knowing when not to kick off . . . knowing that I'm not invincible for a start. But I sound a bit of a hypocrite because after that, I feel, there's times when I feel that confident and that, I feel like I can take on anyone. But it took something to make me feel invincible, not invincible sorry, you know what I mean? It's a weird kind of feeling, I'm not sure I understand what I'm trying to say, but its, yeah it took that to knock me down a peg or two, but in other ways it's probably made me as better hooligan as I'd ever be, do you know what I mean? If that had happened I might have just been one of these that went and did little bits and bobs when numbers were in the favour, rather than actually doing stuff, and not being the main man in the firm kind of thing, but being certainly one of them up there that makes decisions. I know it sounds a bit petty in a way, but there is decisions to be made.

Rather than serving as deterrents that may have induced passivity within him and a reluctance to experience those traumatic emotions again, his memories of experiencing powerlessness in such acutely undignified circumstances made Darren more determined than ever to be a competent fighter and football hooligan. For Darren, the humiliation of being badly beaten represented a learning process on the journey towards becoming the man that he became, and is, today:

. . . there's been times since then [since being violently assaulted] where I've had a confrontation and I've just fronted them and it's worked. Like I've had lads start shit with me, and I've said 'right get outside away from the cameras, cos what I'm going to do to you I don't want no fucking cameras watching it' and they've gone, 'Oh fuck you then' and they've backed off. But that's how you've got to be with people. At a match once I dove head first into opposition lads and I got escorted out of the ground by the stewards and about 12 or 15 of their lads come out after me. Gates got locked behind me and I'd got a load of their lads waiting, now I had nowhere to run, and if you run you'll only get done over worse down some fuckin back alley, so I just bounced up to them going 'come on then, lets fucking have it then' and they didn't do anything at first cos they must have been thinking, he's on his own, why is he so confident? There must be other lads with him, and there weren't, and a riot van pulls up couple of seconds later, police get out and grab me to put me in the van, and I were laughing at them all [their lads] and coppers were laughing at them too cos just me, one lad had fronted them all.

Darren's exploits, both home and away, continued to fuel his budding reputation, and not just locally. He began attending England international matches, meeting other men involved in football violence and acquiring contacts in other firms from across the country, which enabled him to play an increasing role in organising prearranged 'meet ups' and 'offs' with his club's rivals.

Went to England matches . . . Meeting other lads from other firms, meeting for drinks, going down meeting for fights and all that lot, and there were a time when . . . most football firms had heard of me. I've got a mate who goes to watch [local team], he knows some lads from their firm . . . Well he was trying to get me to go with them, cos he'd heard stuff, cos you do hear stuff on the grapevine. And obviously internet were a big thing, and it gives you that buzz, that buzz of going somewhere else and knowing [you are known among rivals].

Darren embraced wholeheartedly the football casuals' identity and culture, revelling in the notoriety and reputation that he was gaining. Living in a large conurbation with several rival firms in close proximity, the threat of violence remained a constant, and something that Darren had to manage strategically even when he wasn't 'looking for it':

Darren: It's all the lifestyle kind of thing, it alters all your way of thinking and everything.

AE: Have you ever had trouble when you've been out with your missus and that? Maybe off lads who recognise your face?

Darren: Yeah I've had quite a bit . . . We [Darren, his wife, and another couple] went up [nearby city] . . . and I said to my mate 'don't wear Stone Island or anything . . .' I know it's not important what we are wearing like but we had to think about it, cos we are going with the girlfriends . . . So we dressed down a bit, gets to the bar and it's just absolutely full wall to wall with [local firm] lads. Looked at my mate and I thought fuckin hell.

Darren was acquainted with several members of this firm who approached him while he was in the bar and engaged in friendly conversation with him. However, one individual took exception to Darren and his friend, and attempted to escalate the situation into violence. After Darren, his wife, and their friends had left the bar, at the behest of the door staff who had intervened in the developing confrontation, several men from the bar pursued them and a fight broke out in the middle of the street:

Gets round the corner from the bar, and about 20 of them come down, and it just kicked off in the middle of the street, we were fighting like fuck . . . I couldn't concentrate on fighting cos I were worried about our lass . . . my mate got hit over the head with a, they put pool balls in a sock, and thing with me is I don't mind [football team the men represented], I mean I don't like them, I'm glad when they lose. But their lads-wise, I just thought leave them to it like. And they've always had a grudging respect for us cos we hate their main rivals probably more than they do in a way . . . Tried to get hold of this kid's name, I did get hold of his name [lad who started the fight], but couldn't get hold of him. I put word out to his mates saying like I want to fucking meet you like one on one ... And I'm not saying he refused to, but it never materialised. So after that I just took it upon myself that any lads down here who were [members of that firm] we just turned them over, week after week ... every single week we were hammering lads just for revenge ... Just to show like, cos they were coming down here [before] and they got left alone.

Darren's persistent involvement in violence eventually resulted in him receiving a custodial sentence after he was involved in a fight between two large groups of men outside a city centre pub:

... it [prison] didn't do anything, went back to my old job [upon release], it just upset our lass. It wouldn't have upset our lass if I'd just got hours on a Sunday, give up my Sunday football I would have fucking hated it, but it wouldn't have interfered with anything she did, know what I mean? ... at that time she were only part time [working] cos she were studying at college. And you don't get benefits when your bloke's in jail, well you shouldn't anyway.

Despite the limited impact that prison had on reforming his views of violence, Darren's prison term was the catalyst for helping to rebuild relationships with his brothers and his mother, who he had not seen regularly for some time. It was not until I had got to know Darren a little better that he opened up more about some of the difficulties he and his family faced after his father had passed away:

... me and her [Darren's mother] are very alike, we clash. I wouldn't say I'm quick tempered but we can be if it's the slightest little thing, it could be a little thing that winds us both up and that was it really. And obviously my mood swings were, I was really caning the drugs at the time, unbeknown to me, only looking back now at it that it could have been that, but at the time you don't really realise that you've got bad moods or whatever ... every time I went down to the house, my mum's house, we'd be arguing, so then obviously with my brothers, she'd be saying 'I don't want you coming round to the house again' and all this lot. And I'd be like 'alright I'm not fucking bothered anyway' but obviously my brothers were down there ... so, yeah I didn't see much of them.

Darren was unable to say exactly for how long he did not see his family, but over a period of roughly four years it seems there had only been minimal contact.

Darren: ... see my brother always says to me that, I wrote him a letter when I was in jail, I can remember writing a letter ... And it was just saying like, I love you and all this lot ... Sorry we've not been, but I can't, I can't actually remember not getting on, so like it being that long, cos my dad died ... and

I remember it been about a year after that is when me and my mum fell out and I didn't see my brothers properly, erm, for about, I don't know, I can't remember to be honest . . . but it was a while, I mean I'd certainly not been to the house for a good 18 months anyway . . . And then, my brother seems to remember, he says he read this letter and he was crying when he read this letter and that's what made him, and since then we're like best mates, we're inseparable. And obviously I am like that father figure to my youngest brother. But yeah everyone says we're proper close, we are really close we do most things together. But I'm . . . surprised it was that long kind of thing. Whether he thought that I weren't really bothered about him, do you know what I mean? In them few years after. It just seems if you look back at it from like when I fell out [with his mum] . . . them four years, I wouldn't say I fell out with them or didn't have much to do with them for that four years, but it sounds like I have . . . Cos he says it was that letter that changed things like.

AE: So did he write to you first?

Darren: No, I wrote to him first. My mum came to see me in prison and my brother came, but I didn't want my youngest brother to come, how old was he? He'd have been 12, 13, but I didn't want him to come . . . didn't want him to go through that like, know what I mean? Ideally I wouldn't want anyone to have to go through, getting searched and all that bollocks. But obviously I wouldn't want our lass having to do it, but I obviously wanted to see her. So it's not right nice, especially for a woman to be searched and that. So no I just didn't want him bothered, he was still at school and that.

AE: So you actually did have some contact during that time but it just didn't feel like you'd seen each other?

Darren: Yeah that's what it must have been, must have been just little or nothing kind of thing. Cos I can't like, I just remember it being about 18 months when I like really didn't have much to do with them like cos of my mum, but they must have seen it as a bit longer period of time. Because when I got with my wife, she changed my opinions, well not changed my opinions . . . she encouraged me to go and sort things out with my mum, I mean we still fall out now me and my mum, but not like we did.

During the past several years Darren has been less involved in football violence for a variety of reasons: marriage, work commitments, and the recent birth of his first child, have reduced his time and opportunities. Serving a custodial sentence and the financial and emotional strains this placed upon his wife have also shackled Darren with a sense of guilt and regret. Being well known to local police Darren has genuine reason to be cautious. Match days for Darren tend to consist of putting on some 'decent clobber', having a few beers, and a few lines of 'sniff' with the other men involved. However, if he happens to find himself in a potentially violent situation he certainly won't hesitate, as the opening to this chapter indicated.

A new generation of enthusiastic, youthful hooligans have begun to step in, adopting and violently asserting the collective identity of the firm, many of whom clearly idolise Darren, as one of his close friends joked with me and some of the other lads while we travelled to an away match on a train:

Alright lads, form an orderly queue to shake Darren's hand.

Darren is rarely without an entourage on match days. Later that evening while we stood congregated in a nightclub, Darren, clad in a brightly coloured Stone Island coat with a bottle of beer in his hand, was constantly surrounded by groups of young men eager to talk to and to be seen with him. In the contemporary context, where many of the historical sources of working-class masculinity – heavy industry, manual work and unionised politics – have become increasingly less relevant for young men, personal reputation remains a 'surviving facet of masculine credibility . . . that can attain male respect' (Armstrong, 1998, p. 156). Despite his more intermittent involvement in the football hooligan 'scene', Darren still values violence immensely and maintains a strong attachment to the celebrity-like status that his violent reputation has bestowed upon him:

> . . . a lot of people know who I am in town, and not wanting to sound big headed or anything, they tend to stay away from me . . . I've always been quite loud, but as I've got older I've got not quieter, but I like to assess situations you know what I mean? And I just go into my own little world . . . Cos that's what my mates say, they say when I'm about to start fighting I start smiling at people, smiling at them and I'll just be sat there with my drink . . . And I know for a fact that they know my name, do you know what I mean? But they don't know that it's me, that's what's fuckin funny . . . that's why I laugh about stuff, I'm quite smug about stuff, I mean they're all 9, 10 stone wet through and I just think fucking hell, I don't even want to do it [use violence] cos it would be embarrassing like. Whereas they'll just see this biggish lad, who's a bit quiet . . . but if I said 'I'm Darren', which I wouldn't say . . . In fact I probably have said it before, or dropped it in conversation. Like if someone comes in and they're acting a bit clever, saying 'What's up with you like?' 'Where you from?' I'll tell them like, they'll say 'Do you know such and such?' I'll go 'yeah yeah'. They'll ask 'What's your name?' I'll tell them my name and they'll go 'Oh hey up mate, you alright? I've heard loads about you'. Or they'll know my brothers . . . But that does make me laugh.

Darren has recently reacquainted himself with boxing, having trained regularly during his youth. I saw him about a week after a fight: one of his eyes was still bruised and heavily bloodshot, and an old injury had resurfaced in one of his hands:

Darren: I'll definitely do it again, it were brilliant . . . he come out and all he wanted to do was knock my head off . . . My trainer said I was trying to box him now and again, but it's hard to box someone when they're fucking windmilling [throwing punches wildly and without skill] you, so I just windmilled back. And the first two rounds are just like a street brawl outside a fucking night club in town.

AE: [start laughing] Yeah?

Darren: [laughs] . . . yeah but it were fucking brilliant though cos that's what I do, know what I mean? . . . my trainer rung me few days later obviously when it had all calmed down, he says 'are you happy?'. And I said I was a bit pissed off I didn't like box as well as I could have. But he just said he thought I was brilliant like, he said he'd been doing it for 30 years and he's never known anyone have bigger balls than me, to come back like I did, that second round I took some big shots . . . Everyone said it was the fight of the night and it was, but yeah it were really good, right enjoyed it. All my family came, family travelled from other parts of the country to see it like, my granddad was there, he were right proud like. Like I say I loved it, I'll definitely do it again . . . I love the buzz out of it and I think you've got to get that aggression out. I have to get aggression out somehow . . . I do enjoy boxing. Love watching it, enjoy doing it and at end of the day I might be able to get a lot of aggression out in that way as well.

Stand and trade

Torrential rain falls steadily against the car windscreen. I wipe away some of the condensation that has begun to form on the windows with the back of my hand and stare out into the gloom, which is penetrated only by the sombre yellow and red lights from the other cars on the motorway. The conversation veers between the day's football results, one of the lad's recent trips to Ibiza, and Darren's fight that is taking place later in the evening. A large bottle of Peroni lager gets passed around; I take a swig and pass it on. We exit the motorway, following the Sat Nav to the working men's club. We park the car down the street from the club, jump out, and walk briskly through the rain; dodging the various puddles that are scattered along the street. Turning down an alleyway towards the entrance we are met by large groups of smokers huddled together either side of the entrance underneath the little shelter that is available from the downpour. Three middle-aged women stand just inside the main entrance exchanging tickets for wristbands; I handover my ticket to one of the women who promptly slaps a luminous green band around my wrist. I step past the imposing figures of the three muscular and heavily tattooed bouncers that guard the door to the main hall. Several hundred people are stood around the ring, which is situated towards the back of the hall. The aptly chosen Rocky 4 soundtrack plays in the background. I head to the bar and buy a round of drinks, which are handed to me in plastic cups; the management clearly aren't taking any chances with tonight's clientele. We stand towards the rear of the hall with our drinks and survey the room, some of which is populated by football hooligans, drug dealers, and other men with violent reputations. Occasionally I see lads I recognise from the football matches, who come over to us, shaking hands and exchanging brief pleasantries.

The compere announces that Darren's fight is imminent, which is followed by a chorus of cheers from the audience. We jostle for a good spot near the ring to watch the action. His opponent comes to the ring first with his trainer and is given a frosty reception with a few boos and jeers. Darren emerges from the back of the hall where we came in earlier, draped in the replica shirt of the football team he, and most of the other lads, support. The noise level in the hall cranks up a decibel, as his following of almost a hundred people make themselves heard. He struts towards his corner of the ring, weaving through the crowds flanked by his trainer and assistant. He steps into the ring and salutes his large following by raising his fist in the air. He and his opponent come to the centre of the ring for the referee to give his instructions; their gloves meet and they return to their respective corners in anticipation of the bell. It rings and both fighters meet in the middle, guards raised, and begin to trade punches. Darren starts cautiously, maintaining his high guard, trying to catch his opponent with his jab. The early stages of the round are fairly even, but it isn't long before Darren starts to encounter difficulty. His opponent has a longer reach and he begins to land punches to Darren's head. Darren tries to get in close to his opponent, keeping his guard up and trying to land punches of his own, but he is kept at bay. The punches become more intense, and following an exchange of blows between the two at close quarters, Darren drops to the canvas on one knee after being hit several times. Groans rise up from the crowd and Darren's disappointment and frustration is evident: he swears to himself while shaking his head in anger. The referee checks Darren is okay; he is. But his head and chest are now red from the impact of the blows. The round resumes. His opponent continues to keep his distance and Darren struggles to get near him.

The fighters come out for the second round and Darren appears to be gathering momentum in the early stages, landing a few punches to his opponent's head, each blow bringing loud cheers and more enthusiastic encouragement from the crowd: 'Go on Darren', 'Come on lad' emanate constantly from various sections of the crowd. However, Darren is unable to capitalise, as his opponent is clearly a skilled boxer and quickly moves out of Darren's reach before more blows can be landed. In a brief melee of punches Darren's nose is left bloodied; he runs his glove along his nostrils to wipe the blood away, which is left smeared across his face. Darren catches his opponent with a blow to the head much to the delight of the crowd; his opponent retorts with his own brand of sarcasm, wobbling his knees together and rotating his head to feign being 'punch drunk'. A roar of boos erupt from the crowd in response to his unsportsmanlike behaviour. The lads stood in Darren's corner, clad in Stone Island jumpers and polo-neck t-shirts, shout abuse and threats at his opponent.

The round comes to a close. Darren is breathing heavily and his face is red from the physical exertion and the impact of the blows. The third round starts with both fighters continuing in a similar vein to the previous two. The skill of his opponent begins to show and he lands a few punches to Darren's head, which forces Darren into the corner. His opponent advances, reining blows on Darren who raises his guard to defend himself. Darren's gum shield is knocked from his mouth during the melee and the referee temporarily stops the fight. Consultation takes place between Darren's trainer and the referee, and his trainer takes the decision to retire Darren from the fight. Darren's frustration and disappointment is obvious; he shakes his head and is clearly keen for the fight to continue despite the amount of punches he has taken. After the decision is announced his opponent walks over to Darren's corner, they embrace and he holds Darren's arm aloft. Sections of the crowd, particularly the young men stood around Darren's corner, continue to boo and shout abuse at his opponent.

The lights go up, the music is turned back on, and preparations begin for the final fight of the evening. The lads I'm with talk among themselves about the fight; much of the conversation is dominated by the context of the encounter, as one of the lads feels that had the fight been outside the ring the other fighter's boxing skills would not have counted for much:

> Darren's a brawler, not a boxer. If it was a fight in a pub or a street brawl that kid's skill wouldn't have meant anything, cos Darren is the sort of lad that doesn't give a fuck and will just physically dominate you, jump on you, and bite your face or fucking ear off.

I stand amid the incessant chatter of the crowd, listening to the lads' conversations about the fight while sipping my beer, and I try to imagine how Darren must be feeling about this defeat; his first defeat as an amateur boxer. I am reminded of previous conversations where Darren described occasions when he had taken a beating (outside the ring) and how important it seemed to him to be able to take something away from an encounter that seriously undermines the self-image he projects to others. He had reiterated to me that even in the face of superior opposition you cannot show fear and that it is better to keep fighting – to, as he put it, *stand* in front of them and *trade* punches with them, even if you know you cannot win. From Darren's perspective he did this tonight: battered, bleeding, exhausted, he continued. But I wonder whether his display of stoicism will be enough for him. And I also wonder if Darren too is reminding himself of the controlled context of tonight's fight and that when you are outside the ring where there are no referees, no trainers with white towels, no ropes, and no 'rules', it's how far you are prepared to go, rather than skill, that matters most.

Discussion

The purpose of providing an in-depth case study of one participant is to provide the reader with a whole life narrative of an individual man with an extremely violent biography. Importantly, Darren's life history provides a series of important analytical threads that will be drawn out in the next three chapters in relation to the biographies and experiences of other men who participated in the ethnographic fieldwork. Through exploring Darren's life history, several reasons for his persistent involvement in violence are detectable, which are permeated by varying motivations: desire for thrills, excitement and a 'buzz' feature strongly, as does a sense of identity. But violence also represents a means for Darren to elevate himself above others.

Importantly, his biography reveals how violence emerged during his childhood and youth as something that fascinated, excited and, importantly, made sense to him; the sense of awe and wonderment he possessed for his reputed and respected late father and Darren's near emulation of him; the emotional exhilaration Darren experienced during confrontations as he released his rage; and the early fledgling reputation he gained within his community from his willingness to use serious violence. All of these confirmed to him that violence is a potentially useful resource which 'can be adopted and made one's own' (Winlow, 2012, p. 209), and violence representing something for 'one's own' is an important analytical point here. Darren attached great significance to several incredibly traumatic events that occurred during the latter stages of his youth. These appeared to signal a subsequent transformation and shift within him and his positioning within his immediate milieu, towards extreme volatility, a 'nothing to lose' mentality, and an intense desire to be recognised and feared as 'somebody' within his community and beyond. Violence, and the ability to wield it competently, gradually became a defining feature of his self-identity, a self-identity that is founded partially upon narcissism. Violence is something to which he can make recourse with little restraint and a minimal amount of genuine critical reflection.

Clearly, from simply observing him, Darren identifies strongly, and has done since his youth, with a masculinity that is embodied in powerful, virile physicality and violent potential. These are traits and qualities that had been possessed by his late father and the other 'hard men' that Darren admires, and that are associated with the durable 'visceral cultures' (Hall, 1997) that linger in the economically defunct ex-industrial community from where he has emerged. Darren has striven to emulate this iconic image of the respected and feared hard man, who wields violence in return for a particular form of cultural capital that is granted to those few men who are successfully violent (Hobbs, 1995; Winlow, 2001). We can detect in Darren's narrative the melding of this 'archaic' masculine imagery and cultural capital with wider hegemonic cultural currents which increasingly promote and inspire individuality, social distinction, narcissism and interpersonal envy (see Hall *et al.*, 2008). Certainly Darren's biography is indicative of the changing life and identity trajectories of some working-class men in post-industrial Britain, where work, violence, crime, entrepreneurialism, and consumerism, can meld into hybridised identities (Hobbs, 2012; Treadwell, 2010; Winlow, 2001).

Yet, this exterior image of intimidating, powerful, dominant masculinity and aloof narcissism is ambivalent, as it belies a catalogue of evident vulnerabilities and insecurities; the violent victimisation he has experienced, as well as the emotional difficulties and traumas that Darren has grappled with during his adult life. Indeed, trauma, anger, bitterness and resentment seem to drive his uncompromising rage and violent potential, which seems to be a crucial prop in a façade that conceals this background static of troubling emotions. Certainly, such insecurities are dominant themes in Darren's life course – in a very *real* sense through the threat of violence from others present in his immediate environment. Although a desire for dominance and self-elevation can be detected, his violence has evidently been stimulated by an intense desire to avoid a terrifying abyss of insignificance, indignity and humiliation that he believes awaits those men who will stand by passively while others attempt to dominate them: men who will not *stand and trade*. By his own admission Darren is an exemplar of a form of masculinity that is closely bound to a subjective structure intimately connected to violence and its competent usage against others.

Darren's story presents a highly complex picture of one man's biography, identity and his relationship to interpersonal violence across his life course. The complexity of his life course and evident subjectivity should alert us to some of the limitations of much existing criminological/sociological theory (see previous chapter) that has developed to explain male violence. In particular, perspectives that have at their centre a rational, calculated subject (see Wieviorka, 2009), or an unfortunate, misunderstood, impoverished subject who is a product of a draconian state and media-induced moral panics (Hall and Winlow, 2012). Despite some indication of performativity through his physical appearance and occasional bravado, neither does violence appear to represent an alternative means to 'do' masculinity with other avenues thwarted (Messerschmidt, 1993); being in fairly stable employment, married, and a father, Darren possesses many of the means that are deemed necessary to 'be' masculine legitimately. Nor does his violence seem to represent a subjugated 'protest' that enforces the structured relations of patriarchy and that allows him to reap the 're-worked dividend' spoils that benefit him and his male counterparts (Connell, 2005a). Violence for Darren is highly personal and individualised, but clearly mediated by context. So the question of masculine subjectivity and violence, in this case, is I suggest far more nuanced, complex, and is informed through drive, emotion, biographical experience, memory, and their interaction with broader culture and economy.

It is at this important juncture that the book will now begin to assemble the main theoretical framework via an exploration of the experiences and lives of the other men involved in the ethnographic fieldwork. These are outlined in Chapter 4 to Chapter 6; in Chapter 7, I return to theory.

4 Born to fight

Chapter 3 provided an in-depth case study of the life history of one of the participants who I referred to as Darren. Darren spoke extensively about aspects of his childhood and youth, in particular, his experiences with violence during these phases of his life course. This chapter now deals with this broad theme, drawing on data gathered from some of the other men involved in the ethnographic fieldwork. What this data reveals is the significance of facing violence early in the life course and the legacy this leaves in terms of its emotional impact and subsequent formation of masculine identity.

Stand up for yourselves: Gary and Paul

Brothers Gary and Paul are not what criminologists might call 'persistent' or 'dangerous' violent offenders. Their biographies are not characterised by the more frequent and serious forms of violence that some of the other men in this study have been involved in, particularly those who have come into contact with criminal markets. For the most part, their everyday lives are fairly passive, with the threat of violence only an occasional possibility; but nevertheless possible. And the brothers are known among their peers as men who are prepared to engage in physical confrontation if required to do so.

Like their father, both brothers invest heavily in physicality, spending hours in their local gym to maintain their impressive physiques. Gary possesses a lean muscular build and tattoos cover his upper body. Paul is slightly broader across the shoulders and a little bulkier than his brother, but he is also in very good physical condition. They grew up together on a housing estate that borders what had once been one of their hometown's most significant industrial arteries and an abundant source of local employment. Their father had worked in local heavy industry since leaving school, but like so many other men, lost this employment when local extractive and associated productive industries declined during the area's accelerated de-industrialisation in the late 1980s. Their community is predominantly white and staunchly working class. Particular sections of the community possess a reputation locally for being known as 'rough' and containing a number of men who are prepared to use violence. The British National Party (BNP) has in previous elections been able to garner support from some sections of Gary and Paul's community.

Although Gary and Paul have experience of violence and are fairly adept at deploying it, they do not actively seek notoriety for this. In contrast to Darren, whom we met in the previous chapter, they do not seem particularly interested 'in riding the waves of dread and sycophancy that excessively violent men can generate in their locales' (Winlow and Hall, 2006, p. 143). In quiet conversation they regard the use of violence as a last resort, but a necessity nevertheless. Their relationships with violence are bound up with their familial history and a stubbornly durable masculine habitus that informs this (Hall, 1997). Early on in their childhoods, Gary and Paul were encouraged by their father to 'stand up for themselves' and to not hesitate to resort to violence if the situation required it:

> **Gary**: I think it goes back to how we were both brought up . . . my dad told us to like stick up for ourselves. Like, don't be afraid to get involved if someone is in your face giving you some shit and you can't get out of it, don't be afraid to deal with it. And from then on . . . me and Paul have always had a good handle on those kind of situations . . . obviously me and my brother have both been in our fair share of scrapes, and I think it's just the way we've both been brought up . . . not like a tough upbringing but kind of like a straight one. So like if someone's in your face, someone is bullying you, pushing you around, shit like that, don't be afraid to stand up for yourself. And if it means you have to get involved then don't hesitate.

What emerges strongly from Gary's narrative recollections is the sense of value he feels at his father's influence in his early life, particularly the psychosomatic abilities this has endowed him with. Paul discusses in more depth the influence of their father:

> **Paul**: My dad always used to say, if you are getting bullied or anything like that it's like, my dad would never have condoned me for hitting anyone, my dad always used to say [impersonates his dad's voice] 'Well if they deserved it then they deserved it' and that would be it, that's all you would get out of him. Now he would never sort of say 'I want you to go and hit people', but he would never say surely there's a better way of solving it. He'd say 'well if you hit them they'll not come and do it again' sort of thing, that was always my dad's approach. My mum was always the exact opposite she'd say to my dad 'You shouldn't be telling them this, you shouldn't encourage that kind of behaviour' know what I mean? So very different schools of thought from my mum and dad . . . I just felt like I didn't want people to get away with like wronging me or pushing me about. So that's what I would do, I would lash out. And then if I got into trouble for it like at school or anything like that, what I would do is I would tell my dad first . . . Cos I know he would then say 'Well if they had it coming then they had it coming' sort of thing. And it was like a protector from my mum's bollocking then, cos I know my dad agrees with that . . .

Gary and Paul's discussions of their father and his advice to them during their early lives are somewhat ambivalent. His advice is certainly underscored by a strong air of ambiguity with their father appearing to neither strictly encourage, nor entirely discourage, the use of violence. Rather, their memories of his advice are woven into a set of injunctions and personal sentiments that have at their core vague notions of deservingness, as well as self-defence, self-preservation and protection when faced with threats of violence. Some readers may find the injunctions instilled in Gary and Paul by their father during their formative years somewhat perverse, and, as some scholars have suggested, potentially a form of violence in itself (see Hearn, 2003). However, it is important to acknowledge the complexities of these cultural injunctions and their grounding in the pragmatic, habitual day-to-day lives of working-class males, where violence is occasionally a visible and potential feature (see Hobbs, 1988). In contrast to some of their peers, who the brothers felt were poorly equipped to deal with physical confrontations, Gary and Paul saw this inheritance as a matter of practical necessity; a significant advantage in what they perceived was a competitive and at times unforgiving milieu.

> **Gary**: I can just tell when like a situation is going south [becoming violent]. Like just walking about you can see people eyeing you and stuff like that. Like, it doesn't happen with me so much now cos obviously I'm a pretty big guy. And I know I can handle myself, so I like, walk with a lot of confidence and some purpose about things . . . when me and my brother go out we're both physically big guys, and we're both pretty good at reading situations . . . So we can tell when guys are eyeing you up and stuff like that and looking for trouble . . . I always keep a look out for things like that where situations can get nasty and then if it does you kind of just deal with it don't you?

Their discussions relate strongly to interlinking issues of pride, self-dignity, self-worth, and their recognition by others. What they are attempting to convey is both theirs, and their father's, intense desire to not be dominated and to ensure that those aspects of the self, which are a source of pride and dignity, are not threatened or denigrated by others. In their accounts, self-dignity and self-worth are strongly connected to their ability to react appropriately to those individuals who attempt to dominate and impose themselves. Their father's insistent exhortations to physically defend yourself and to use violence if the situation requires it, emanate from his own fears for his sons' personal safety and an intensely felt need to adequately *prepare* them for an outside world that is believed to be potentially dangerous. And his exhortations were/are not the result of entirely paranoid imaginings or nihilistic cultures of thuggery. They are considered to be pragmatic *necessities* that possess genuine utility in the immediate locality in which he, and they, are situated.

The injunctions that Gary and Paul describe here around being prepared and willing to react to domineering aggressive individuals, generally do tend to be elevated in significance within working class and marginalised male cultures (see

Winlow and Hall, 2009). Violence represents a distinctly masculine resource in working-class communities and a means with which to defend oneself that is often relayed from father to son(s) (Hobbs, 1994). As Paul's humorous impersonations of his father suggest, his, Gary's, and their father's logic, is based upon an assumption that a demonstrable willingness to defend oneself, or a competent display of physical prowess and power, will inspire both respect and trepidation in equal measure in the eyes of others, therefore, deterring anyone who might attempt to become unduly dominant, or to humiliate, denigrate and wrestle from them their sense of self-dignity and worth. Some of the brother's abiding memories from their childhood are of their father's potential volatility and his willingness to defend both himself and them:

> **Gary**: I remember when I were young and he came home once with a black eye [Gary laughs]. I think he'd been out in the pub, got drunk, gobbed off and got hit.

> **Paul**: He wouldn't take no shit off anyone from the estate . . . one time we were playing football in our back garden and the bloke from next door said something. And I were right cheeky with him and he starts gobbing off at me saying he were going to give me a clip, so dad comes out and says 'what you been saying to my lads?' And this bloke started shitting himself and my dad walked round and went into his garden . . . And this bloke like ran in his house and locked the door and [Paul starts laughing] my dad were proper banging on the door going 'Come on, get yourself out here now' and this bloke's wife come to the door and were telling my dad to go away and saying she were going to call the police, and my dad just wouldn't let it drop going 'tell your bloke to be a man and stop hiding behind his wife and get himself out here'. But he just wouldn't let things drop though . . . And when he went off on one he were proper intimidating.'

The durability of Gary and Paul's early socialisation within this particular gendered habitus (see Hall, 1997; Winlow, 2012) is fairly self-evident and from within this familial context violence was first experienced and enacted.

> **Gary**: . . . one time my dad were arguing with my mum, and my mum were right and I were just saying 'listen you're wrong' and he wouldn't have it. And he were stood on the door step in the kitchen and he took a step towards me, so I just pushed him out of the front door and I says 'fuck off'. So he just went for a drive somewhere to cool off and then he came back. He was right enough, but like I say we're all in a similar vein all three of us.

Many of Gary and Paul's early experiences of being violent were with each other and, on occasions, would rapidly escalate into quite pernicious violence:

> **Paul**: . . . me and our Gary have always been like best friends, more than brothers. It were strange . . . I think we've got a really good relationship for

brothers, but we did have some really bad fights . . . and it would start up over the most ridiculous of things . . . we started fighting and I remember Gary hit me with a cricket bat, it split my head open, I had to go to hospital and get it glued . . . he ran off cos he saw my head bleeding. I chased after him and I had him in a headlock that hard that it burst the blood vessels in his eyes, cos mum were trying to split us up and I remember all his eyes went red . . . I don't really understand why, cos we never hated each other, we were always like best mates . . . I can't explain it. I guess we are both pretty intense individuals and nobody wanted to back down.

Gary elaborates, with a distinct air of fatalism, on the violence that occurred between them during childhood:

Gary: I stabbed him in the knee with a fork once and he stabbed me in the neck with a pen . . . So we had a lot of fights and, they were just like childish squabbles. But obviously with us both being the way we were, it escalated really quickly and we just fought. But, there were never, kind of any real animosity to it, but we fought. [laughs]

AE: You said the way you both were, what do you mean?

Gary: We were both the same kind of, quick to flare people, quick to lose our tempers and unfortunately we both had the same kind of reaction. Like, he'd push me, I'd push him, I'd push him harder, he'd hit me, I'd hit him back and that were it. That was just kind of the way it went. It weren't kind of like rooted in anything, it weren't like we got beat up as kids or anything like that, I think it just goes back to how we were both taught to defend ourselves.

Gary and Paul's descriptions of the occasionally extreme manifestations of their sibling rivalry are accompanied by a mutual bemusement at the frequency and sheer intensity of the violence they inflicted upon each other. Despite an awareness of the occasional excessive gratuity of their violence, both believed it was simply a normal part of a gendered life course (see Hobbs, 1994) and felt the violence had been, to an extent, beneficial:

Paul: I don't think it shocked my dad that much . . . my dad's never been someone who's sat us down and said 'You shouldn't be doing that you are brothers'. My mum would go mad, she'd get upset, she'd cry, she'd split us up, scream at us, whatever. I mean my dad's always come across really thick skinned, I'm sure he wouldn't be happy with the fact that we were doing it . . . but it never really seemed to upset him, my dad used to fight with his brother all the time . . . So I think for him it's not maybe that shocking, you know to fight with your sibling to that level. So he might have been 'oh well that's what boys do' or whatever, but my mum it used to really upset her.

Gary: I've always thought it's just what brothers do. If someone told me they didn't fight with their brother, I'd be like 'What? Why?' I just thought it was what was supposed to happen . . . It [violence] kind of breeds a bit of a mutual respect, cos it's like you think, yeah he's a decent lad, he can handle himself . . . It's just what we are supposed to do, what lads do innit? Growing up getting into scrapes with each other . . . it don't mean you don't like each other, it just means we are brothers.

The 'toughening up' process Gary describes here, that began within the context of his familial home and through the relationships he developed with his father and brother, is one that is often present in the biographical narratives of men who have used violence, where both mental and physical toughness are believed to be important forms of cultural capital (Winlow, 2012). His socialisation within this general atmosphere brought Gary close to violence in a way that meant he was able to summon the will and ability to deploy it with relative ease, while giving little consideration for the consequences:

Gary: . . . when I were younger I had a really bad temper, like I would be really quick to boil. And I just kind of lose it a bit and that got me in trouble. First time in junior school, probably like, my last year before Comp [Comprehensive School] . . . Just one of my friends . . . it got a bit carried away like, just pushing and shoving. And I thought, this is getting a bit out of hand, I best deal with it. So I just chinned him [Gary laughs] . . . it was just a flash and I just kind of lost it for a second.

AE: Can you remember what it was like?

Gary: Trying to think of a response without glorifying it . . . a bit of an adrenaline rush isn't it? It's kind of like flight or fight response. You either like leg it [run away] or you think right let's deal with it and I obviously chose to deal with it. So I got a bit of an adrenaline rush. And at the time I didn't think I had done anything wrong. In retrospect when I had time to calm down I thought, shouldn't have done that, probably didn't deal with that in the best way, but it's past now.

As Paul also described, he too could become easily enraged in a manner similar to that described by his brother. Many of his early experiences of violence outside of the family home were relayed as humorous anecdotes; passed off as inconsequential and normalised as a typical aspect of a young working-class male's upbringing, although this was in stark contrast to some of the more serious violence he experienced later in adulthood (see next chapter). As appears to be the case for many young people contemporarily, the night-time leisure economy is a context in which much violence is now encountered (Tomsen, 1997; Winlow and Hall, 2006), and Gary and Paul's experiences are no different. Local bars and night-clubs became something of a gladiatorial arena for them and their peers, where the possibility of violence was a thrilling, yet mundane and accepted prospect within this social setting:

> **Paul**: . . . one of the lads started scuffling with this kid . . . we all saw it so we were like 'fuckin hell' so we all just jumped in. Loads of bouncers just came out from nowhere, like pinning people, twisting people's arms up against the wall, and they said they were going to phone the police so we just ran off . . . I were rolling around on the floor with someone . . . I remember my mate got pinned to the wall by this female bouncer and we all took the piss out of him for ages cos he was the only one who got pinned by one of the bird bouncers.

Despite the sense of adventure and thrill that characterises Paul's memories of some of the violence encountered during his youth, his recollections of being dominated by an older, physically superior male while he was still a child were articulated rather differently. Paul attached quite immense significance to this particular event during which he was quite badly beaten in what was an unprovoked attack on the street near his parents' home. Although Paul's inferior physicality in comparison to his more mature attacker was acknowledged by him and he accepts there was nothing he could do to defend himself, this does nothing to alleviate the anger he felt and the concomitant bitter resentment and feelings of persecutory torment it left him with:

> **Paul**: . . . it were obviously upsetting when it happened. It's more that you couldn't get your own back that bothered me more than anything else . . . it's always been that you feel like someone's got one over you and you are like, oh I can't leave that, I can't just let it be like that, do you know what I mean? I used to hate him, used to always think I'm going to, I don't know, hide behind his shed and just throw a brick at him or something like that when he comes out of his garden, but I never really had the bottle to do that.
>
> **AE**: You imagined yourself doing that?
>
> **Paul**: Yeah yeah, that would be something I would think like, I hate him I really hate him I'm going to do him one day just when he comes out of his garden or something . . . I would imagine it and toy with it.

The benign texture of this setting suddenly mutated into something quite horrific and unimaginable. Paul's initial response was to freeze in shock at the sudden eruption of inexplicable and unfathomable anger in his more mature attacker; a bewildered, disturbed response common when a child is confronted with aggression it cannot understand or even comprehend (Bollas, 1995). The shock and trauma of this event has remained with Paul throughout his life and, as he describes, became a source of painful regret and rumination because of his failure to act in his own defence.

Killing the kid: Brett and Liam

I look around towards the entrance of the pub and see Brett emerge into the bar area. We make eye contact and I nod in his direction; he returns the gesture and slowly makes his way over to the table where I am sitting. He walks gingerly; I later find out this is because he is suffering with bruised ribs. He is dressed in a black t-shirt, tracksuit bottoms and Nike trainers. Brett stands around 6 feet 2 inches and possesses a large, heavy-set frame. His head is shaven and his weathered, scarred visage immediately suggests this is a man who has experienced extreme violence. The bridge of his nose is distorted and has clearly been broken several times. Beneath his t-shirt lies heavy scarring across his stomach and rib-cage. Brett is a serious and committed criminal of considerable repute. From humble beginnings working as an apprentice with a construction firm at 16 years of age, Brett rose to become a major figure in the drug trade. Now in his forties, his current life is something of a contrast to these former heady days of gangsterdom. From a life of regular parties, attractive women, money, recreational drugs, where, as he put it, 'everything he touched turned to gold', Brett now scrapes together a living selling amphetamines and cannabis as well as doing occasional cash-in-hand construction work for friends and acquaintances. We shake hands and he takes the seat opposite me. I ask him if he would like a drink:

Brett: Pop please.

AE: What kind of pop?

Brett: Anything mate, any kind of pop will do.

I head to the bar and fetch two glasses of Pepsi. Brett thanks me and immediately proceeds to take several large gulps of the sweet brown liquid. He places the half empty glass on the table, hunches forward, and stares straight at me. Before I have a chance to get into the brief pleasantries that often initiate interviews Brett announces:

You want to know about violence yeah? For your University course or something isn't it? Well, I reckon I'm violent cos of my dad, he was an horrible bastard, a right bully, he used to knock me about, and I think that's why I get so angry, I just flip out and get into a rage over stuff.

As I listen to Brett unload, bombarding me with horrific tales of his childhood and adult life, I sense this is a conversation he's been waiting to have his entire life. His success as a large-scale supplier of illicit drugs came at a price. Lifting up his t-shirt he says:

Here look at this.

He points to a large thick line of white scar tissue that extends across his stomach and then to smaller pink-tinged markings on his ribcage:

> . . . a machete did that . . . he stuck it in with two hands this lad, it went all the way down to me bowel. I were in hospital for 2 weeks, had to have my organs stitched up . . . lost one of my lungs, fucking knife in the ribs did that . . . I knew it were bad as well cos I could feel the blood coming out and it were red hot.

Returning to the brutality of his childhood:

> I were adopted when I was kid. I never met me real fatha like. My adopted mum told me when I was about 7 year old like that I'd been adopted. And I remember my fatha got right angry about it, that I'd found out. I told all my mates like, the little gang of mates I knocked about with, and they didn't believe me. They were going like, 'no fuck off you are not adopted' so I took them to my house, opened the door and shouted to my mum like 'tell them I'm adopted like, I'm adopted aren't I mum?' And I just remember my fatha went mental, saying 'oh you've fucking told him now haven't you' and all this.

Brett spoke fondly of his adopted mother, but had a difficult relationship with his adopted father who would occasionally physically abuse him. The physical abuse could on occasions be particularly brutal. Brett described once eating gravy from his plate using a knife instead of a spoon, his adopted father became, in Brett's words, unfathomably enraged at this and stabbed Brett's cheek with a table knife before instructing him to eat his gravy with a spoon:

> I mean what the fuck? Why the fuck would you do that to a kid? . . . he was a complete fucking bastard. We moved away when I was young and we'd not been there long and my mum's parents and family started interfering like telling her to come home, not letting her settle properly, so we ended up coming back and I think he was pissed off about that.

When describing violence he had committed against others Brett would always infer a loss of self-control at the point of executing violence, with a narrative preamble to this loss of control that was characterised by a build-up of an unbearable sense of humiliation and betrayal. These internal, intolerable feelings would then explode outwards in a brutally destructive rage:

> . . . not long back I went fucking mental at this kid cos he had ripped me off, he'd betrayed me, you know like doing all this shit behind my back . . . so I fuckin lost it with him and proper fucked him up.

Brett hospitalised this individual, who has been left with lifelong physical injuries because of the attack.

In the brutal and horrific biographical narratives provided by Brett, strong links were established between his past and present, particularly the way in which he believes the former informs the latter. Brett's description of his relationship with his adoptive father, and his childhood in general, was unrestrained and replete with anger, bitterness and resentment; these feelings appeared to be targeted at the image of his father, who seems to have become in Brett's mind an approximation of a tormentor – a spectral reminder of a time of utter weakness, helplessness and powerlessness at the hands of a dominant other. In this sense, Brett's anger also seems to be targeted at the memory of his child self and his concomitant naïvety and vulnerability. In particular, his weakness and powerlessness to stand up for and defend himself from his adoptive father's beatings has remained with him and are habitually returned to, memorialised through a lens of regret, rueful impotence and humiliation (see Winlow and Hall, 2009). The legacy of this traumatic upbringing seems to frame Brett's interpretation of some of his other relationships during adulthood, in which he views himself as being constantly taken advantage of and an object of ridicule to others. Brett's schizoid account of himself presents a down-trodden, dominated, pathetic, weak, loathsome individual, who has consistently failed to prevent his own humiliation. Yet, simultaneously, he describes himself as an incredibly visceral and uncontrollable force, capable of descending into blind rage and of inflicting extreme destruction.

Liam's childhood also featured a father who was, at times, volatile and dominant; but one whose abuse was targeted towards Liam's mother, rather than directly at Liam. Until he was around 11 years of age, Liam had lived with his parents only a short distance from the deprived council estate where he currently resides with his girlfriend, their son and a ferociously territorial dog that wrapped its enormous jaws around my foot one afternoon when I stepped through the front gate of Liam's garden. I used the backdoor from then on. Liam is aged in his early 30s. He stands around six foot in height, is slim in build, quite pale skinned, with short hair, which is usually covered by a branded cap or a woolly hat. He is a recovering drug addict, who for most of his adult life has struggled with his addiction. From his late teens onwards Liam has oscillated between prison and a life of drug use, violence and low-level acquisitive street criminality, from which, apart from a few scars, he has little to show. At the time of writing he is unemployed and has recently been released from a short-term prison sentence.

Liam's account of his early life contained a quite striking ambivalence. He initially spoke quite positively about this period, describing himself as happy and as having many friends. Yet this contrasted with, and belied, his mother and father's tumultuous and occasionally abusive relationship:

Liam: My earliest memories of violence, thinking really is my dad hitting my mum obviously . . . Cos that used to kill you as a kid . . . Horrible. [I] Remember sitting at top of the stairs listening to them arguing and smashing things, it's awful . . . I just remember hearing it all . . . I don't think I'd ever actually seen it. I possibly have to be honest, I know he did have a temper, think it was the drink that used to do it. Quite mean as well. I remember he came into the kitchen once and me and my mum were watching TV, cos they'd been arguing . . . think my mum were doing a bit of cooking . . . and my dad came in and cut the plug off [off the TV] and walked back out . . . He's not like that now, he has changed, but that's what he was like.

Liam's parents divorced when he was around 11 years of age and he and his mother moved to a house located on a large council estate.

> **Liam**: Really difficult age looking back and I hated it, hated it. Always hoping you know that they might get back together, living in hope . . . when we moved there it was like my world had just ended. Cos I had no local friends, I was travelling all way up to school on the bus, which was a major mess about. And when I was coming home . . . I'd got no friends there . . . we used to go up and see my dad and he'd have another bird in there, other kids playing with my toys. Honestly, terrible time it were, honestly . . . When you are young like that it does affect you and you do need someone strong in your life. I mean my dad, he's a good man don't get me wrong, decent bloke, but no father material. Played no father role with me whatsoever . . . Cos I know that when you're a child, you want a strong relationship with your dad don't you? Especially a male, any male, cos if your dad is not there, what I'm saying is your kind of uncles sometimes step in don't they? Grandads . . . So you've got a male figure in your life. But I didn't, so that has 100% contributed towards why I've ended up with a criminal record. Definitely.

Liam's first experience of using violence was in school when he was identified by his peers as 'cock' and subsequently coerced by several older male pupils into a series of fights to test his supposed credentials:

> **Liam**: . . . you always get these little trouble causers don't you? And they were all going round all different groups of lads who'd come from various junior schools finding out who were cock like, that's what they called it. 'Whose cock of your school then?' 'Oh it's him.' 'Whose cock of that school?' 'Him.' 'Right all cocks fight and let's find out whose cock of the first year.' And I thought oh god I'm not cock, don't anyone tell them it's me. Everyone just presumed it was me from my school, don't know why.

The school had arranged a disco to welcome its new cohort of pupils and it was after this event that the fight to decide 'cock' of the school year had been arranged by the older pupils:

> **Liam**: So yeah, they arranged a fight . . . I've gone up to the disco scared to death, heart going, adrenaline going cos it's mad that adrenaline rush you get when you are fearful. I know it's only nature really to make you prepared for the worst, so I was scared stiff. Gone to the disco, disco's finished . . . started fighting with this kid, before I knew it he'd given up.

AE: How did you find people reacted around you?

Liam: Oh brilliant, oh aye they think it's fantastic don't they? That's why all the older ones were saying 'Come on now do Jones in next, let's go and get him', they love it don't they? As long as it's not them doing it, or things like that, I mean you don't know if you are dealing with a grudge they've got against this person. Yeah reactions were probably good, suppose it made you feel good in a way.

Liam's experiences were typical of the 'peer pressure' and cultural expectations which can weigh heavily upon males who are *expected* to use violence in particular situations (see Anderson, 1999; Armstrong, 1998; Winlow, 2001), even if they are reluctant to do so themselves. But here Liam also touches upon the sudden feeling of transformation experienced by the individual after using violence and the way this is reflected in, and acknowledged by, the sudden change in behaviour and conduct of those around them. This sudden transformation dovetailed with a growing reputation he was gaining on his housing estate. Despite some difficulty adjusting initially to living with his maternal grandmother in the wake of his parents' divorce, Liam became friendly with an older male from the estate who came to represent, for a period, an approximation of a mature role model. Liam spent periods of his youth living with him and began associating with a group of young men from his estate who were well reputed and feared locally:

Liam: I was living with this bloke I used to stop there a lot . . . I looked up to him not as a dad but like just as a good friend really. But he used to let me get away with all sorts, like drive his car when I was only like 15, he gave me money to buy a motorbike . . . So everything got a lot better once I'd got used to the situation . . . And then my downfall was, you know [says name of several local criminals]?

AE: Don't recognise the names.

Liam: These guys were proper nutters, everyone was scared of them and looked up to them. These were like my new batch of friends.

Liam's new friends were occasionally violent, habitual shoplifters and drug users, who regularly went 'grafting' in large retail outlets and shopping centres across the region. Liam left school at 16 with few formal qualifications. For around a year he held several jobs for brief periods: predominantly low-paid, low-skilled, manual forms of employment. By his own admission, he struggled to commit himself to the routine of legitimate employment and found he was unable to last more than several months in any of the jobs he held during this period. Not unexpectedly, Liam gravitated towards 'grafting' and habitual drug use with the men from his estate. Following a dispute with a group of local men which ended with Liam chasing them armed with a baseball bat, he received his first criminal conviction at 16 years of age and was given a community order. Liam consistently failed to comply with the order and following a court summons was given a short custodial sentence in a Young Offenders' Institute.

> **Liam**: I got sent to prison . . . a proper shock let me tell you, I didn't think I was going to prison that day. Never been before had to do two months. It was like a lifetime mate. Did my time, got out . . . started back smoking heroin. Soon as I got out it was like, I don't know like a magnet just pulls you towards it. You just don't see no hope, you've lost everything, you've just got out so you want to celebrate, so I just started buying heroin again . . . But I got out that first time and that's when the rollercoaster started properly, with heroin, you know thieving to support your habit.

The prospect: Neil

The atmosphere in the bar is one of anticipation. It is early in the new football season; match day, against local rivals. Optimism is high and with an abundance of alcohol and cocaine, so are most of the lads. The bar is one of several favourite haunts for the local men who associate with the football firm. Guarding the door is a nervous looking bouncer and two police officers, one with a hand held camera filming everyone who enters. A large group of around 10–12 young men appear on the opposite side of the road, which attracts the attention of some of the lads who have spotted them from the window. A loud rallying cry of 'their fucking youth firm are here' goes up, and around five to six lads immediately head towards the doors; Neil among them. I watch proceedings from just inside. They spill out onto the pavement, chests puffed out, gesturing to the rival lads across the road:

> 'Come on then you fucking cunts' and 'Let's fucking have it then' are issued in the direction of their rivals.

Most of those inside the bar have now noticed the developing confrontation, some shouting encouragement to Neil and the other lads who are trying to get past the police cordon. A police officer stands in front of one of the lads from the firm and mouths something at him. The lad continues to gesticulate aggressively and attempts to push past the row of luminous green coats and black hats. A police officer grabs him and drags him away from the bar up the street, shouting aggressively in the lad's face, much to the amusement of the other members of the firm in the pub who cheer, laugh and shout 'go on [name]'. The rival lads are swiftly moved on by the police towards the stadium, while the other lads from the firm who have avoided arrest come back into the bar, Neil among them, swaggering confidently.

Neil is aged in his early 20s and works full-time. In his spare time he associates with the same football firm as Darren, who we met in the previous chapter. At around 5 feet 8 inches in height Neil is not the tallest of men, but he possesses a solid, bulky frame, and as indicated, will not hesitate to involve himself in violence, particularly within the context of the football firm. Like Darren, his evident 'gameness' has earned him a healthy amount of respect from his peers and some of the older members, including Darren who, before introducing me to Neil, likened his enthusiasm and appetite for violence as similar to his own. Neil possesses a reputation for being 'switched on' (intelligent) and for knowing when and crucially when not, to 'kick off' at opponents. This is in contrast to some of the other young men involved in the faction known as the 'youth firm', who have attracted the disdain of some of the older more established men and are frequently referred to derogatorily as – 'retards', 'wannabee hooligans', 'dressers' – for their recklessness, eagerness for recognition, and tendency to over exaggerate their experiences with violence. Neil however, appears to be highly conversant with the complexities of the football hooligan culture and the personal distinction that is available to those who engage in it competently. This approach to using violence has earned him a healthy amount of respect and admiration from peers and has made him something of an unofficial 'top lad' among the younger men that associate with this network.

Neil spent the early years of his life on a deprived housing estate close to what has slowly become an industrial wasteland of a few functional, but now mostly abandoned or demolished, steel mills, forgeries, workshops and warehouses.

> **Neil**: I'm from a working-class family, typical sort of working-class upbringing really. You know fuck all to do when you are young, nowhere to go, so I just hung around on the streets with all my mates, inevitably got into trouble, fighting with people and that . . . where I lived up until I was about 10 was proper fucking rough . . . Most of the kids round there were into all sorts, always in trouble, taking drugs and that, in and out of prison all the time. To be honest I reckon I would have ended up that way if we hadn't moved when we did, probably best thing that happened to me getting out of there.

Neil and his mother moved a short distance away to where they now currently reside. However, as he indicates, although the move distanced him somewhat from the drugs and crime that plagued the estate, this did not extricate him from encountering violence during his youth and now during adulthood:

> **Neil**: They were fighting up our end only the other day, this kid from our end had a fight with this paki kid from [housing estate] in the [local pub] car park, me and my mates were watching from the window and the lad from up our end was beating him, so this paki lad ran to his car, pulled out a gun and fired it in the air. We were all shitting ourselves in the pub, all fucking getting under the tables and that [laughs] . . . I was out in town other week up near Top Bar, and this lad I know got into a fight with this kid, got him up against the wall outside this bar and was stabbing him with a drill bit [Neil performs a stabbing action].

The presence and possibility of violence continues to inspire feelings of fear and dread within the individual but this can become mundane and somewhat 'normalised' (see Winlow and Hall, 2006), manifesting in a way of 'being' that seeks to deal with such threats in a stoic manner. Charlesworth (2000) discusses the internalisation of such a way of 'being' in the world when living in threatening and marginalised circumstances:

> . . . it may be necessary to walk in a certain way, a way that exudes strength and a capacity for violence . . . one comes to know how to comport oneself in urban space so as to efface the threat of actual physical harm
>
> (p. 21)

Earlier, Gary described a way of 'walking' and 'reading' other men and specific situations that for him possesses the dual function of being both a deterrent to others as well as akin to a 'sixth sense'. This way of 'being', in Charlesworth's terminology, is indicated by Neil with his juxtaposition of both genuine fear and amusement at having to hide under the table from a volatile individual wielding a firearm. Underneath its presentation as a humorous anecdote, one can detect the ulterior function of such 'black humour' as a mechanism to manage and disguise fear and the grinding sense of insecurity and threat that must be confronted by individuals occupying these contexts (see Winlow and Hall, 2006). Winlow (2012) has suggested that close proximity to violence can engender an appreciation of the benefits and rewards that it can offer those willing to use it. As Neil and another young male involved in football violence explained to me, while we sat drinking in The Fox – another favourite haunt for those who associate with the football 'firm' – their overwhelming sense of awe and desire amid the fear of violent men:

> **Neil**: I started going to the matches at 15, 16 [years old]. Me and him [Neil's mate] started going together with a few other lads. We used to see the older lads like Darren and that, and I remember when I saw them like I thought I want to be like them, I want to be just like them, didn't we? That's how we were weren't it?
>
> **Neil's mate**: Oh yeah definitely. [smiles and nods his head enthusiastically]

By this point in his life course Neil was already familiar with violence and its enactment; very much like the men who have been discussed so far who also encountered it early on. Like some who have been discussed, and will be discussed later, Neil often found himself gripped by an uncontrollable sense of rage that seemed to evade effective articulation and understanding:

> **Neil**: I can remember my first fight actually . . . It was with this kid who lived on the same street as me. When I was growing up I was best mates with this lass who lived next door to me, we were about same age. And this kid had hit her, so I hit him. I fuckin pushed him off a wall that were about 5ft high,

gave him a right beating, I had to be dragged off him. That were the thing with me when I was younger I used to be so angry, just wanting to fight all the time with anyone, and I never understood why.

Fair lad, doorman, hardman: Vince

The first time I met Vince he told me that he was an ideal participant for my research as he had had more fights than hot dinners, had knocked out two million people, and had been knocked out a million times himself. Despite his rather exaggerated self-description, he is a man who is well-versed in violence and has forged a career out of his own reputation and that of his large family. At nearly six feet five inches, heavily tattooed, with few teeth of his own, and scarring at the base of his back from a bullet, Vince possesses the kind of physique and aura that makes you want to avoid making eye contact with him. He works as a night-club doorman and has done for over 20 years; an occupation that has opened up a variety of 'opportunities', or 'fiddles' as Vince calls them, with which to supplement his income.

The first few months of Vince's life were spent in a block of high-rise flats, before his family moved to a large council estate where he spent his childhood and now lives. This estate became a new home for many families that were re-located during the post-war clearances of the dilapidated slum housing that had mushroomed up around the city's industrial arteries. Vince, along with his five other siblings, was raised by his mother – his father left the family when Vince was very young:

> **Vince**: . . . we used to have this policeman who worked our community. Little fat cunt he were, but I respected him. Me and my best mate used to be fuckin bad you know, getting in trouble and that on the estate all the time, and this copper used to come round and give us a right hiding though. He'd see us and he'd shout over 'Now then you two, what you been fucking doing?' He used to make us stand to attention as well, hands by sides and the lot, and if we'd been misbehaving he used to give us a right belting. Then he'd take me home, tell my mother what I'd been doing then I'd get a clip off her an all [laughs]. I were terrified of him . . . But if you were good he'd take you to the shop and buy you a piece of fruit . . . I believe that if it hadn't been for him I wouldn't be where I am now, I'd probably either be dead, a drug addict, or doing life.

Vince's narrative of his early life was replete with such nostalgic, and somewhat romanticised, references to the solidity of working-class culture and the loss of this in the wake of social and economic transformation. Despite this, he was one of the few participants who genuinely possessed a language capable of articulating so strongly the sense of change and transformation within his community and native city, and the politico-economic driving forces behind them (see Charlesworth, 2000):

Vince: . . . thing is now, it's not like that round on the estate anymore, its changed loads. There's no community, you know what I mean? It's like everywhere now across this whole country, there's no community anymore. Everyone's suspicious and fearful of each other.

AE: So what was it like to live on the estate back then?

Vince: It was good, sound like. Everybody knew each other, my family knew everybody on our street and it was proper safe. Nowadays you only know people who live next door to you, back then, we knew people who lived 10 doors down from us. We had pubs and working men's clubs back then and everybody used to go there. All the blokes would go there after they'd finished work, have a few pints and go home. In summer all the family would go down. Problem is they've all closed now, and there is nothing to replace them.

Vince is attempting to communicate, through such rhetoric, the profound sense of change that he has lived through and the palpable sense of uncertainty that such changes have generated in his immediate environment. The degradation evident on the large housing estate where he grew up, and still resides, in the shape of boarded-up pubs, broken windows and run-down communal areas, is the visible evidence of this change and the slow decline of what had previously been a more unified and thriving community. Ironically though, Vince is very much the epitome of mutating forms of working-class masculinity that meld the residue of 'hard' industrial physicality (Hall, 1997) with the same market conditions that hollowed out the institutional and symbolic structures of which he bemoans the loss (see Winlow, 2001).

Vince began working on a fairground when he was 11 years of age, neglecting his formal education. He was not born into affluence and the material comforts this brings. Growing up in a large, single parent family, he had possessed little in the way of material goods and took his opportunity to earn money from an early age while most of his peers attended school. By his own admission, Vince held an acute fascination with money and fashionable clothing during his youth, especially the symbolic capital imbued in these material products (Hall *et al.*, 2008). By 13 years of age he had left home, living and working on the fair as it travelled around the UK. During his early youth Vince was thrust into a communal life of physically demanding manual work, autonomy and independence. He learned quickly to look after himself and developed a keen entrepreneurial acumen (Hobbs, 1988) while living within a transient working community that is often vilified, has little contact with the state, and maintains an active presence in the 'informal' economy (see Okely, 1983).

Vince: We had to look after ourselves. The traveller community is a proper community, you know, together. Like it used to be on my estate when I was growing up. You look out for each other. And the traveller community sorts its own problems out, they don't go to the police, not like normal people . . .

when I was about 11, 12 years old the fair was using a local racecourse . . . and we allowed this gypsy bloke who had some donkeys to give donkey rides around the outside of the fair. Problem was a load of other gypsies turned up, wanting to park their caravans on the site and offer their services to the fair users . . . Thing is we didn't want them there, cos once they are there that's it, you can't fuckin get rid of them. So we ended up having to fight all these big fucking gypsy blokes, proper big fucking gypos man. I got battered all over, but I didn't have a choice, had to fight them, cos we couldn't let them camp on the site.

From a very early age Vince was exposed to environments that severely threatened his physical and emotional well-being. His description of having to defend himself against more experienced and physically superior attackers is enveloped by a strong sense of fatalistic fortitude and stoicism in the face of genuine and unavoidable physical danger (see also Winlow and Hall, 2006). It is devoid of any sense of agency or potential for choice. Vince seemed to regard his early life as an important precursor: a hard, brutalising, but nevertheless important period that moulded him into a resourceful, capable and morally rounded individual. There was never a detectable shred of resentment or bitterness about his upbringing whenever I discussed it with him. On the contrary, Vince believed the physical discipline, violence and communal values he was subjected to, made him the man he is now.

Vince: I was brought up properly. I was taught manners, respect, that's why I'm okay. I got hit with the slipper, the belt, never did me no harm. It fucking hurt, especially leather belt with the metal buckle on it, fuck me . . . I didn't have a father growing up, I'm alright though. It's this generation that's the problem, they know the law better than the police do, they know what they can get away with. All these fuckin do gooders have come along and made laws so parents can't touch their kids no more, they've never been beaten, they don't have any respect or manners.

Turning point: Shane and Carl

Shane keeps a pickaxe by his front door.

'It's just in case anybody comes round,' he tells me with a smile.

His brother Carl, who is sat next to him on the sofa dressed in biker leathers, laughs to himself while shaking his head. Shane stands around 6 feet 3 inches. He is slim, but his height gives him an imposing physical appearance. He is employed full time in a manual, but skilled, occupation. At just under six feet, Carl is shorter than his older brother. At the time the research was conducted Carl was unemployed and had been for almost 12 months. He had left his previous employment.

following a long-running dispute with a senior colleague, which ended with Carl having to be physically restrained by fellow co-workers as he tried to attack his superior with a screwdriver.

The brothers spent the first few years of their lives in a small village located in a town that lies on the periphery of a sprawling conurbation. Just before Shane reached schooling age the family relocated further north, where the brothers' parents began working for local government to provide support and temporary accommodation to young people who were leaving prison or were in the care of the state. For much of their childhood and youth the brothers lived and socialised with young men, and a few young women, who had emerged from severely abusive and neglectful circumstances; and some of whom were regularly involved in crime and violence.

Shane: . . . they [young people] were all kind of like fostered and all this weird crap. But yeah we used to sit and watch TV and mingle with like armed robbers, fucking thugs, burglars, you name it. And invariably it rubs off on you doesn't it? . . . I think that was the catalyst for what happened. I mean I'm not blaming anyone cos you make your own choices don't you? But at that age you are impressionable aren't you? So, up until that point I'd never met someone who'd hit someone, and so that's when things started to change.

AE: And you said that you felt that was a turning point, what did you mean?

Shane: I think so personally yeah, I mean you think about it going from being a quiet lad who to a degree had been pushed around at school, and bullied, tried to fit in and stuff. And all of a sudden you find yourself in a house full of people who would rather knock somebody out than talk to them, know what I mean? You start to think, well it's alright this, I like this idea of being in control of everything, you know the way they were. And you start being like that don't you? You start feeling like that.

Following the family's relocation, Shane had struggled initially to adapt to his new lifestyle and described how he quickly found himself isolated and bullied in his new school by other pupils who poked fun at him for not being local and for his accent. Carl was also a frequent target for bullying by groups of young males who attended his school:

Carl: [I had] pretty much half the [school] year [them] coming up to me every day and kicking the crap out of me. I mean it didn't bother me really, cos they never hit that hard anyway . . . And I think my dad was in hospital [at the time] . . . And they started taking the piss and I just couldn't think straight, and I went for them, but got someone else, you know they got in front, and then they started then.

There is a strong sense, particularly from Shane, of disdain and revulsion at the weakness and vulnerability displayed during those early formative years, similar in some ways to that described by Brett. The brothers spoke extensively about the importance of loyalty and mutual support for one another in the face of a cast of hostile individuals that they described populating the various contexts they had inhabited during childhood and since then. Their familial home was a tense kernel of potentially volatile individuals and for Shane in particular, the sudden presence of these young people in his life who were the antithesis of meek submissiveness seemed to catalyse his orientation towards aggression and violence. By their teens Shane and Carl had matured into young men who were, in their own words, 'running the place' as their own personal reputations for using serious violence gave them status among the various young people who shared their home. The hard man discourse can be appealing to some marginalised men, particularly for those whose immersion in it represents a potential means of vanquishing the indignities and humiliations of previous victimisation at the hands of others (see Jefferson, 1996). Shane described his first experience of committing violence during secondary school and the epiphany-like feeling this invoked within him (Goodey, 2000):

> **Shane**: . . . the first time I ever did anything was when somebody had had a go at our sister on the bus on the way home from school . . . I would have been about 13 or 14. And I went in the next day and battered him . . . it was the first time I'd ever done anything, ever in my life. Know what I mean? And that was . . .

His brother Carl interjects to reinforce the point:

> **Carl**: . . .the turning point wasn't it?
>
> **Shane**: That was it, that's when you think to yourself. . .
>
> **Carl**: . . .Once you've done something like that you tend to think, well I quite like this feeling, and you know, it's weird.

Carl described his earliest memories of committing violence through utilising the commonly used phrase 'seeing red' to communicate the sense of losing control of his body during this encounter. Carl emphasised his loyalty to a friend who he perceived to be weak and in need of his protection and during this incident required physical intervention from someone else to actually restrain him:

> **Carl**: I stuck up for someone at school. The kid who I was mates with at the time was diabetic like I am now, but he was a lot worse than me, and the school bully took his insulin off him . . . So I walked over to this kid, asked him for it, and he wouldn't give it me so I just saw red and I thought my friend could die here . . . I just saw red and just knocked him out basically and got dragged off him . . . I just saw my friend getting picked on and that's what triggers me, if someone's getting picked on and he's a close friend who can't

do anything about it, then I'll try and get something off them first, but when you start getting pushed and punched yourself, I just snapped basically. I've got a very short temper.

Early encounters

In this chapter I have paid particularly close attention to the early biographical experiences of some of the men who were interviewed as part of the ethnographic research. These men grew up in what were once staunchly working-class industrial communities where, despite considerable fracture and transformation, elements of the visceral cultures of the industrial period of capitalism (Hall, 1997) still persist contemporarily. The men's early lives were evidently shaped by the immediate presence of individuals (fathers, brothers, peers, significant individuals within communities) who possessed these 'durable' masculine qualities common to such cultures and in particular contexts, these individuals encouraged violence and aggression. These significant, mostly male, individuals provided evidence of the cultural benefits that can be accrued by those who are willing to be violent. And crucially, they encouraged these men to not 'walk away' when threatened, insulted, slighted or humiliated by another.

Evident within the men's biographical narratives was a nonchalant acceptance of the presence of violence during their early lives and subsequently into adulthood. Violence was not posited so much as a choice, but as an enforced circumstance that simply had to be faced and dealt with. There was little sense that violent and threatening individuals could be completely avoided. For as far back as they could remember the participants discussed here appear to have possessed an acute sensitivity to the possibility that others may attempt to dominate and humiliate them. And this sensitivity extended into what was described by them as a specifically gendered experience of shame, indignity and humiliation that awaits those who are on the receiving end of another's violence. However, the occasional gravity and rapidity of their violent responses to situations that were deemed to be threatening seemed to perplex them. Their explanations for occasional unrestrained rage were very often elusive to them. Commonplace expressions such as 'I lost it', 'I saw red', and others similar to this, were fairly typical and were employed in an attempt to communicate the feelings and emotions associated with becoming violent. Yet simultaneously, there was also a real poverty of language and articulacy to explain motivation beyond the immediacy of the circumstances and stimulus, while the general feelings of seemingly persistent anger that were described had a vague objectless quality that struggled to find effective vocal articulation in language (Hall, 2012a).

Certainly there does exist, at particular times, an incredibly primal, almost atavistic, logic to forms of sociality between males in the local community contexts where these men were raised and continue to live. The messages and specific injunctions that the men interviewed here received during childhood and youth conjure up an apocalyptic-like image of dangerous and ultra-competitive environments where the individual is constantly under threat and must always be prepared to *defend* themselves – a theme that Winlow (2012) has also identified in violent men's biographical narratives. In such contexts, there is a palpable feeling that one must remain constantly vigilant and be ready to use violence, while feelings of persecution, contempt, humiliation and self-loathing evidently await those who do not abide by this logic, or confront this atmosphere of perceived interpersonal competitiveness with a violence that ensures recognition of the self by others and the retention of self-dignity. Importantly, the general atmosphere described here rather than remaining a mere apparitional background static, actually ruptured the early lives of these men in quite a brutal fashion.

The next chapter will develop these incipient analytical threads in more detail, by exploring in more depth these and some other men's experiences of violence as both perpetrators and victims.

5   Handy lads

In Chapter 3 'Darren' talked at length about the emotional and subjective experience of committing violence. He emphasised in particular the thrilling, exhilarating aspects of confrontation; but also a sense of 'wounded pride', the humiliation of this, and the uninhibited rage that must be summoned in order to attack. In the previous chapter I discussed some of the other participants' early lives and experiences with violence, which echoed these experiences. This chapter now explores in-depth experiences of committing violence against others and also of being victimised. It is comprised of two main substantive sections.

The first substantive section explores men's views on how they approach and deal with potentially violent and threatening situations. Part of this discussion draws on ethnographic data of the interactional dynamics of confrontational situations. The second substantive section delves beneath the surface of the interactional context of violent encounters between men and focuses more on subjectivity. This section is comprised of three 'case studies' of particular contextualised violence, although, as will be discussed, these are not mutually exclusive categories that comprise a 'typology of violence'. These case studies are used to begin to excavate the motivations and emotions that lie behind violence and the masculine subjectivities that perpetrate it.

Know thine enemy: negotiating the semiotics of threat

There was remarkable consistency from the men when they described reacting to confrontational and threatening situations, both real and hypothetical. Their views were underscored by a powerful sense of fatalism and cynicism about the motives and intentions of others. They were both firm and unmoveable in their convictions that violence is inevitable and unavoidable in particular situations. They felt that it was better to learn and accept this *fact* and to be prepared to use violence against an opponent first before they had the opportunity to do so. Hesitancy, attempting to negotiate or placate, backing down, walking or running away were simply not viable options in some situations:

> **Liam**: . . . sometimes you get into a situation where you know damn well he's going to swing for you . . . So I always get in there first me and head butt

them straight in the face and it proper fucking knocks them for six, you know it gives you a bit of time, it's quick and swift you know what I mean? . . . I always think that you have to get them first . . . Cos if you think about it, it might be too late. You haven't really got time to assess the situation sometimes.

Shane and Carl were equally unanimous in the view that a swift, but powerful first blow is vital in any confrontation; as is bodily stance, positioning and an awareness of the surrounding environment:

> **Shane**: I know exactly how to stand and where to stand . . . always expect the worst . . . if something starts in the street, or in a pub . . . you've got one punch really before it turns into what you don't want it to turn into, and that's a wrestling match. And if you don't make your first punch count then more fool you, cos people do not stand toe to toe with each other in pubs and box. You are going to get a chair or a bottle or a glass aren't you? So you've basically got one punch to put them down. That's how I've always looked at it.

> **Carl**: . . . your first punch is most important in a pub fight. Cos if he's with a load of his mates and you can guarantee if you don't hit him hard enough they'll jump straight up, it all kicks off and you are going to get a good hiding.

> **AE**: . . . always hit them first?

> **Shane**: Oh yeah, don't stand there arguing with them, fuck that. Cos you know where it's going anyway . . . It's going off one way or another.

Vince elaborates further on the semiotics of imminent violence by focusing upon the corporeal signals that one must be aware of and be able to read in order to react appropriately:

> **Vince**: . . . the split second before someone hits you they will always look down at the hand they are going to hit you with. It's a natural reaction. So you've got a split second to get in there and fucking bang them [Vince thrusts his left fist into the open palm of his right hand to emphasise the point]. If you don't, you are getting hit. So I know if someone is invading my personal space then they are threatening me . . . Anyone comes within that area they are trying to threaten me and are intending to hurt me. So I'm going to react.

Such sentiments emerge from pragmatic experiences and understandings of violent and confrontational situations. These men are acutely aware that in most cases confrontations and fights are short, swift interactions, and that the individual who lands a powerful enough first blow stands a good chance of being victorious (see Collins, 2008). They are also acutely aware of, and accustomed to, the tense, fearful emotions elicited during confrontations and that the vast majority of people in such circumstances will seek a non-violent resolution (Collins, 2008; see also Winlow, 2012). What you say and how you act are important in determining the eventual outcome of a confrontation.

Such fatalism should not lead to conclusions that every confrontational situation these men encounter will inevitably descend into violence. What these accounts reveal, is a partial representation of the idealised images these men harbour of themselves. Lacan (Zizek, 2006) refers to this as the ideal ego, which reflects how the subject wishes to be and desires to be seen in the eyes of others. These men see themselves, and wish to be recognised, as competent fighters, who will react to any personal slight made against them. These internalised self-conceptions are moulded by a wider socio-cultural environment and its injunctions, which connect notions of self-worth and dignity with a willingness to confront such threats with competent displays of physical aggression, stoicism and fortitude (see Winlow and Hall, 2006 and discussions in previous chapter). They also emerge out of acute pragmatism – experiencing first-hand the physical pains of being violently assaulted and the psychological pain that can remain long afterwards.

During the ethnographic fieldwork, I was able to observe on several occasions the interactional context for violent confrontations. Some confrontational situations arose, involving the men I was observing, that did not result in actual physical violence. Instead, elaborate displays were enacted which ensured recourse to violence was not required. Such displays and posturing, I would argue, are operationalised within the broader cultural context of 'saving face' and narcissistic interpersonal dominance that characterises male-to-male violence. I will provide two examples to illustrate this.

Flexing reputation . . .

It is early on a Saturday evening in a busy city centre bar some distance from home. As daytime activity draws to a close the city is now in transition. Large numbers of shoppers, tourists and football fans are taking part in an exodus; leaving a void that will be eagerly filled by a deluge of mostly young people who will colonise its bars and clubs until the early hours of Sunday morning. I, along with several other lads who associate with the football 'firm', are among the few sticking around for the night. We congregate around a table with our drinks, shouting loudly, with expletives regularly thrown in. With most of us dressed in casual attire associated with the hooligan sub-culture we stand out among the bar's other clientele, who appear to be largely students of the local University. The drinking began in the morning before our arrival in the city, and it has been relentless since. The lads are taking the piss out of each other and focusing much of their piss-taking on each lad's fighting skills. Wayne is instigating much of the mockery. It is the first time I have met Wayne and I do not know much about him; he seems to be well liked by some of the lads. Full of alcohol and growing in confidence, I feel relaxed and comfortable enough to join in the banter; but remain careful not to offend. I make a veiled comment to Wayne about my fighting skills, which is clearly self-mocking. Wayne smiles and seems to appreciate the joke; the other lads laugh too. The mood remains quite jovial, until Wayne, unexpectedly, takes exception to a joke Billy makes at his expense. Staring intently at Billy from directly across the table he says:

> You've been playing at being the fuckin big un all day Billy and I'm fuckin pissed off with it. So we'll fuckin sort it now if you want?

There is a brief moment of disbelief and shock when the group realise that this is not a joke and that Wayne is serious. An uncomfortable silence descends on the group as everyone averts their eyes towards Billy. Billy's body language becomes immediately submissive. Hands stuffed in his coat pockets, shoulders drawn slightly forward and inward, his head drooped forward, he cowers into a mere shadow of his huge and imposing 6 feet 5 inch frame. The apology that emerges from his lips is total anathema to the deep guttural voice that utters it:

> I'm sorry Wayne, I didn't mean to offend you, I was just having a laugh.

Wayne retorts aggressively, at no moment does he break eye contact with Billy:

> Well you've been doing it all day and it's doing my fucking head in. You got a fucking problem with me or what Billy? Cos I'll fucking lay you out pal.

The rest of the lads remain silent; some stare into their drinks, clearly too afraid to intervene. I glance at Billy again, who now looks genuinely fearful for his safety as he squirms under Wayne's unflinching stare and accusations. I begin to feel incredibly sorry for him. I glance around the rest of the group again, and begin to hope that someone will intervene on Billy's behalf. Then I feel something else: guilt. This is what I am here to study. Here it is unfolding before my eyes. And it is so difficult to watch. I have been in the position that Billy is in right now. I begin to feel the horrendous amalgam of humiliation, terror and helplessness that I know he is feeling. The nauseous feeling that grows in the pit of your stomach when you feel as if every ounce of your dignity is being stripped away, and the whole world is watching. I want to intervene, but being new to the group and occupying a covert role I know it is better not to. My personal experience of such situations is that you are likely to become a target if you intervene and appear to be taking sides, particularly if you do not possess sufficient influence to placate the aggressor. With feelings of guilt and helplessness reverberating in the pit of my stomach, I do what the other lads are doing and what past experience has taught me, I keep my mouth shut. I glance over at Jez, a popular and respected lad in the group, who places his hand on Wayne's arm to draw his gaze temporarily:

> **Jez**: Alright Wayne, leave off him pal, he's only fucking about with you.

Billy seems to sense a window of opportunity has opened to escape what is likely heading towards a physical conclusion. Seizing this moment of brief respite following Jez's intervention, Billy reiterates the apology:

> Honestly Wayne I'm sorry mate, I wouldn't do that to you pal, you know I wouldn't.

I hold my breath for a moment as Wayne processes Jez's reasoning. His shoulders drop slightly, he breaks eye contact with Billy, and the tension seems to be slowly easing. After reiterating again that he is not happy that Billy had been taking the piss out of him, Wayne appears fairly content with the apology and Billy's quite evident submission. Much to my relief the atmosphere gradually becomes less intense, the laughter and banter quickly returns to the group. Unsurprisingly for the rest of the night, Billy remained quiet and kept his distance from Wayne. Conscious of not attracting attention and knowing the time to ask questions about this incident was inappropriate, I waited several weeks before raising it again. At a more relaxed evening at one of the lad's houses, when large quantities of alcohol and cocaine had lubricated their cogs of sociability, I used the opportunity to find out more about the confrontation. With loud music blaring from the speakers, and Billy not in earshot, I ask Jez about what happened:

> **AE**: So what's Wayne into then mate? Because I remember when we were in [city] and he started having a pop at Billy, Billy proper backed down.
>
> **Jez**: Billy is handy, I've seen him lay out some pretty hard lads before in town. But Wayne can be a bit of a headcase. He's a proper sound guy, got a good heart and that, but he's been involved in some proper serious shit. He's been to prison a few times.
>
> **AE**: For violence?
>
> **Jez**: Yeah and for other stuff as well, he got caught in possession of a shitload of blow. Thing with Wayne and Darren, and a lot of the other lads we know who come from that end of town, they just don't give a fuck, know what I mean? I mean they are good lads, but if you piss them off or fuck with them that's it, they don't care, they don't have any remorse.

Squaring up . . .

It is late on a mid-week evening at the end of December and I am out with Gary, Paul and several other men in a large city centre. I have not been able to shake off an illness that developed over Christmas. With a headache, blocked nose and aching limbs, a night spent wandering from bar to bar in single figure temperatures is something I could do without. Not wanting to attract mockery or dampen the jovial mood I keep quiet and continue drinking to try and ease the pain. After frequenting several pubs it is approaching midnight as we walk through the streets seeking a livelier venue. The piercing December winds feel like knives stabbing me as they cut through my thin jumper. I force my hands into my pockets in a futile attempt to keep them warm. We arrive at a busy venue with loud music and a large contingent of people standing outside smoking. We make our way in, pushing through the crowds. A few of the lads go to the bar to fetch drinks. One returns with two plastic cups containing a suspicious looking red liquid. He hands one to me.

'What's this?' I ask.

'Treble vodka and Vimto,' he replies.

I give a wry smile and take a gulp. The sickly sweet taste of Vimto comes first; the burning intensity of the vodka on the back of my throat second. My face contorts as I strain to hold back the contents of my dinner, which feels like it is preparing to make a swift exit from my mouth. The other lads find this hilarious. We stand around for several minutes. The conversation revolves mainly around the 'standard' of women in the bar, remaining brief and superficial; the atmosphere is not conducive to anything more. Shortly we are joined by Gary, Paul, and the rest of the group, who have also gone for the vodka with a splash of Vimto. We stay in the same spot for a while at the bottom of some stairs that lead up towards a large seated area. The bar becomes progressively busier. The nearby dance-floor is awash with bodies, which in the rapidly reducing amount of space begin to gravitate closer to where we are congregated. Groups of young men and women begin to spontaneously form around us. The increasingly crowded and claustrophobic atmosphere creates more regular physical contact, as people have to literally squeeze past one another when moving. It feels like every few seconds someone shouts 'excuse me' in my ear, which is then followed by the feeling of warm, clammy flesh against my jumper. A drunken young male walks past and bumps into the back of Gary. He walks away, seemingly unaware that he has just collided into a six-foot shaven headed man covered in tattoos. Crucially, no apology is offered. Gary shouts after him:

Watch what you are doing mate!

The young male is not apologetic and, in what seems to be an attempt at defiance, grins and sniggers at Gary. Furious, Gary shouts at him:

You what? Bump into me you little cunt? I'll knock you the fuck out.

Without putting his drink down, Gary squares up to the young male. Gary towers over him; and is physically superior. Gary lowers his head to engage some eye contact. The fore of his shaven head is almost touching that of his opponent's, as he attempts to colonise as much of his personal space as possible. Gary's tightly fitted t-shirt displays his tense muscular physique and heavily tattooed arms.

As he seemingly senses that the dynamics of the situation have altered the young male's facial expression changes to a look of fear. He tries to turn away in what is clearly a submissive manoeuvre, but Gary is in no mood to let it go as he continues to issue threats, remaining only ever a few inches from his opponent's face. In that moment Gary had the chance to let his opponent walk away, in a means that would not be construed as undignified. He did not. I have witnessed Gary's physical power before and it is utterly uncompromising. I now know violence is imminent. Gary is totally fixated on his opponent, in an almost trance-like state, as if there is no one else present in the room – just the two of them. The music, noise, myself and the rest of the lads are momentarily a distant background static, barely registering on his senses, which are now primed for physical action. If Gary's opponent makes eye contact, alters his facial expression, or makes a sudden move, Gary's next move will probably be physical. And physical intervention from someone else is now the only means of halting the escalating situation. Seemingly sensing this too, a member of the group intervenes. As he slips between the two of them he tells Gary's opponent to

Fucking do one. [go away]

The young male obliges without a moment's hesitation and heads for the exit. Gary's shoulders drop, his internal tension easing, he mutters something to himself along the lines of

Little fuckin prick.

I ask him what happened:

Gary: The little cunt banged into me. It wouldn't have been a problem if he had just apologised, but he just fucking laughed at me.

Showing restraint? Aggressive displays and effective intimidation

These two examples demonstrate the volatility and unpredictability of men prepared to use violence and the rapidity with which seemingly innocuous inter-actions and occasions can descend into aggression. Personal reputations and bodily displays during interaction are powerful weapons, which can negate the requirement to revert to actual physical violence. Data gathered during the field-work suggests that resorting to violence is not inevitable, even for those who value violence, as Collins (2008) has discussed at considerable length. Yet, Collins' work does not situate confrontations within a requisite analytical and theoretical framework that explores underlying motivation and subjectivity – the combination of life history and observational data gathered during this research offers an opportunity to situate these incidents within such a framework.

A personal reputation for violence and the cultural capital that accompanies this have been discussed at length within the literature (see Winlow, 2001). However, what has not been discussed are the ways in which reputation and masculine corporeality can be used as symbolic weaponry during the immediacy of confrontation. It is my assertion, based on the data gathered, that escalating situations to *actual* violence is the result of a complex exchange, during which individuals will attempt to manoeuvre themselves into positions of dominance that ensure the maintenance of their own self-dignity, and crucially, the avoidance of terrifying humiliation (see Winlow and Hall, 2009). Willis (1990) recognised that during confrontational encounters:

> Respect is gained by negotiating with an antagonist. This is part of 'standing your ground' and is preferable to fighting. None of this works, however, unless you are prepared to fight *in extremis*.

> (p. 105)

Crucially, this moral economy is vulnerable to breaking down, as it is difficult to ascertain clearly how much opportunity should be afforded to the opponent to 'walk away' before physical action is required. Repeated threats that are not then carried out with physical violence after a certain threshold is reached are in danger of becoming highly undignified attempts at appeasement, which these men are greatly attuned to. It is at this point that men's reputations and identities seemingly come under severe threat.

In each of these incidents both Wayne and Gary quickly manoeuvred themselves into positions of dominance, both morally and physically. Wayne immediately pointed to Billy's distinct lack of respect, citing this as justifiable reason to use violence. By phrasing his initial threat as a question, rather than a statement or description of his intent, Wayne imposed upon Billy the *illusion* of agency. This gave Billy, ostensibly, the option to escalate matters or back down. Yet, in reality, it left him in an unenviable and impossible situation facing a dangerous, volatile individual with a fierce reputation, whom Billy knew it was unwise to challenge. This unfolded under the watchful gaze of a judging audience of male peers, highly conversant with the moral dramatic economy that frames these interactions. It was blatantly obvious given Billy's body language and verbal responses that he was not going to retaliate and had immediately submitted. Yet, Wayne continued to issue threats, in a manner which continued to reinforce his utter moral and physical supremacy. It quickly became incredibly uncomfortable and humiliating for Billy, as Wayne prolonged Billy's discomfort and reaffirmed his interpersonal dominance over the encounter and among the other men present.

Gary was unable to make recourse to his reputation with a stranger. He gesticulated aggressively, 'squaring up' face to face with his opponent in an embodied manoeuvre that in marginalised male cultures is symbolic of willingness to fight. This was a more risky manoeuvre by Gary, as he had no knowledge of his opponent's fighting prowess. The initial impetus was to secure a dominant position over the unfolding encounter. Under pressure and clearly physically inferior to Gary, either by getting a severe beating or walking away, Gary's opponent had to accept the indignity of defeat, and surrender to a superior opponent.

Men who are versed in the interactional rituals of physical confrontation immediately seek to secure a position where they minimise the possibility of experiencing indignity and humiliation. If possible, they will project onto and incite such internal suffering within their opponent who threatens their physical integrity and symbolic identity. It is this incredibly powerful drive (Hall, 2012a) behind the *immediate* response in each incident, which reflects a clear and highly conversant understanding of marginalised masculine culture. Wayne and Gary could both walk away fairly satisfied, dignity intact, having successfully intimidated and deterred their opponent in front of an audience of male peers, without the need for physical action. This violates the other's identity by deliberately appealing to notions of pride, dignity and self-worth. As discussed in the previous chapter, these men have been socialised in climates that equate dignity with one's ability to react appropriately to those who attempt to dominate and denigrate. As these examples show, their opponents' failure to respond placed them in an undesirable and dominated position, invoking feelings of personal inadequacy, failure and humiliation, while for Wayne and Gary the momentary possibility of humiliation detected in these perceived threats was swiftly transformed through an aggressive reaction, returning them, for a time, to a state of pride and personal aggrandizement.

Exploring contexts and subjectivities

This second substantive section presents a selection of violent incidents involving some of the men who participated. Three 'case studies' of violence are presented, each occurring in different spatialised contexts. The first focuses upon violence within the night-time economy. The second focuses on violence committed within localised communal social networks, consisting of acquaintances, peers and family members. The third case explores violence within the context of the serious crime community. I do not present here a 'typology' of violence. There are contextual differences between them, but they overlap and converge in some respects and are therefore not mutually exclusive. The intention here rather, is to excavate the subjective convergences between these examples despite their contextualised differences, particularly when explored from the perspectives of the perpetrators. It is at the nexus of the motivations and emotions that lie behind violence that this section begins to explore further the subjectivities of men willing to use it.

A decent war story

> **Paul**: . . . this kid were squaring up, so I went in and pushed this kid and says 'look leave it'. They all started surrounding me and it were pretty bad cos I thought I'm definitely going to get hit here, you know when it's sort of dawning on you? . . . somebody sneaked around the back and bottled

me on the side of the head, I went down, I couldn't do anything and I just remember our Gary shouting 'Paul do one' so I just got up and ran off cos I couldn't see anything.

Gary: Paul went down . . . (I) just started hitting people . . . I just started leathering them . . . I could feel my hands hitting stuff and then I got hit from behind, fell to the floor, got kicked on my ribs, but kind of just covered my head . . . I managed to pull myself up and then I just started hitting . . . one of the kids I hit I think I might have broken his jaw. I hit him so hard on the side of his face his jaw was just like wobbling . . . He couldn't say anything he was just making right strange noises.

This incident happened late at night in a city centre after Paul and Gary had been out drinking. The bottle that hit Paul broke his nose and left shards of glass in one of his eyes. As he frantically ran away, partially blinded, he managed to phone their father who immediately drove to the scene armed with a baseball bat; but their assailants disappeared before he arrived:

Gary: . . . it were quite a scary situation cos you never know what's going to happen. You never know what people have got on them, knives and what not . . . it just kicked off. One minute I were stood there, next minute just hitting people . . . I got beat up a little bit, but it was still a big rush . . . when it's forced upon you, there isn't anything you can do about it. You either get beat up or you stand up for yourself. So it were quite an adrenaline rush, quite exciting at the time . . . I just thought fuck it, get stuck in . . . I can kind of laugh about it now . . . got a couple of scars from it . . . it's a decent war story.

Gary was pleased with how he had conducted himself. The rapidity with which this incident descended into serious violence might have induced an immobilising sense of fear and shock in others, but not in Gary. His hyper-vigilance and readiness for violence allowed him to react immediately to defend himself and his brother. This event plunged Gary into adversity, against a numerically advantaged enemy that he refused to back down from and, in his opinion, faced stoically. As he explains, Gary reacted in accordance with the cultural injunctions of the marginalised male habitus (Bourgois *et al.*, 2012), and therefore, from his perspective, admirably.

Paul's feelings in the aftermath were anger and bitter resentment at having been victimised and the acute sense of helplessness that his attackers had subjected him to and had induced within him. These feelings persisted for some time until several months after the attack when Paul was on a night out with a friend and, by pure coincidence, spotted one of his assailants:

Paul: . . . waiting for a taxi and this bunch of kids walked past. And I thought that's that kid that done me in and it definitely 100% was him . . . I just saw him walking further and further off and then I thought hang on a minute, these fuckers did me in . . . So we walked after him and I said 'Oi' he turned around and I went 'crack' [imitates punching the man in the face] just banged him. I was furious with him . . . I hit him and he went down, my mate was kicking him, and I gave him a boot as well, and we just left him on the floor . . . he was on his own, so I thought no you can fucking have it now, like I did.

AE: How did you feel after you had done it?

Paul: I felt like right shaky, like full of adrenaline, almost like I can't believe I've done that. I regretted it instantly I thought that's bad that. But afterwards I thought no he probably deserves that cos they did me . . . I don't condone like jumping people, but he did it to me and he got what he deserved, I do believe that . . . I hated that they had got away with doing me in, I hated it. I hated that I didn't know who they were, I hated that I never saw them anywhere. I felt like they had one over me and then when we saw him that night it seemed too good of a chance to turn down really.

There are clear resonances here with the event in Paul's childhood when he was physically assaulted by an older male (see previous chapter, p. 65) and left feeling bitter, helpless and unable to extinguish these feelings. This more recent event returned him to that state, leading to a vicious return of repressed feelings associated with past experience and a powerful sense of failure connected to that previous similar event within his biography. History repeats itself, in a cruel and uncompromising fashion. As Paul watched his attacker walk slowly into the night, the window of opportunity closing agonisingly, it was as if his sense of dignity was leaving with his attacker. Paul envisaged the persistence of his humiliation and regret at having failed, once again, to react and seize the opportunity. Determined to not 'fail' again, Paul reacted and inflicted an attack of tremendous personal significance that seeks to redirect himself onto a path different from that which occupies his memory and that he would remain on if he did not act. An appreciation of the significance of traumatic experiences scattered throughout a biography as *interconnected* and their humiliating effects as potentially cumulative, is vital, and something that will be returned to later in this and subsequent chapters.

Bonded by blood

By the end of his teens Shane had been stabbed with a screwdriver, a knife, and had received his first criminal conviction for violence. Carl's youth had followed a similar trajectory. Before reaching his 20th birthday, Carl received his first conviction for violence and was ordered by the court to have weekly meetings with a psychologist to address his anger.

Carl: . . . it's got to be something that annoys you [to use violence]. Like bullies, I detest bullies, because I got bullied at school.

Shane: . . . the trigger for me is betrayal, humiliation, bullies, it's them things. Nothing else, never has been anything else.

Both Shane and Carl had been the victims of bullying while in school (see previous chapter) and their narratives were upheld by a belief in the moral sanctity of their violence, which was rich in reactionary and defensive tones. The incident with the screwdriver had arisen out of an abusive relationship Shane experienced with a violent, yet clearly vulnerable, young woman who was adopted, for a time, by his mother and step-father:

> **Shane**: . . . you are not talking about your average girl here. She was over 6 feet tall. I've seen her knock out lads. You wouldn't think she was a girl, she didn't look like a girl. Hard as nails, lads were terrified of her. She'd fight with her fists, know what I mean? She was a proper hard girl.

Despite getting along well initially, their adopted sister developed what Shane described as a 'weird infatuation' with him, which became abusive when Shane refused to acknowledge her affections:

> **Shane**: [She] started wrecking my clothes . . . then she got a lad to stab me . . . she terrorised me, and then she left, moved out of our house, and then the windows were getting broke . . . And all kinds of stuff for about 12 months after, until we found out who did it and sorted him out. And then that stopped.

Several years later she confronted Shane one evening:

> **Shane**: . . . she was always going to have a go at me when she saw me, it was inevitable . . . she just started gobbing off about this that and the other, can't even remember in detail. And I just started thinking about all this shit she'd put me through, and put my family through. So I just smacked her, cos I thought I'm not listening to this crap, cos if I hadn't she'd have hit me anyway, cos she was tapped.

Shane's account of committing what is considered within masculine culture to be an incredibly shameful and 'unmanly' act (see also Gadd and Jefferson, 2007; Jefferson, 2002), was primed with justificatory allusions to her (masculine) physique and aggressive behaviour, which had transgressed expectations around appropriate traditional femininity. When Shane talks about violence, feelings of humiliation emerge strongly and this was something that regularly permeated his and Carl's biographical narratives. These are emotions that both men have struggled to cope with during social interactions where they are likely to resurface:

> **Shane**: I broke a lad's jaw cos he was laughing at me . . . in front of all my mates . . . Just taking the piss . . . calling me a dickhead and everything, so I got into a rage cos I was embarrassed . . . when me and my wife split up and she ran off with the kids and I didn't know where the kids were . . . I lost the

plot then. Beat up the new lad she was with . . . I beat him and his brother up in a pub.

Later, Shane's ex-wife met a new partner and they moved away from the area. Upon finding out her new partner had been physically abusive towards Shane's children, he swiftly intervened:

> **Shane**: Me and my mate went over there and I had a gun. Had this gun and went over there in the night, she [ex-wife] let me in cos she was scared of him. I went upstairs cos he was in bed, I sat on the bed and pointed this gun at his head I said 'wake up'. He woke up and I had the gun pointed at his head . . . I threatened him about the kids and he was sat in bed crying. I went and got in the car and my mate was pouring sweat [starts laughing] shitting himself cos he thought I was going to do something . . . then he left the next day, left her.

Shane has recently retired from amateur boxing having trained regularly and fought amateur bouts since his early 20s. Carl also attended the same gym. Not that many of the other men who trained there would get in the ring with either of them, especially Shane:

> **Carl**: I was the only one that would spar with him. No one else would spar with Shane.

> **Shane**: . . . it's hard to hold back I think you know if you are doing something like that. For me it's all or nothing, I can't do none of this soft contact shit it has to be proper . . . I used to get, and no one's ever properly got their head around it, I used to get like a mad adrenaline rush if somebody hit me, I used to buzz off it . . . just like someone just switching a switch, it would be like bingo, and that's it I would go then and that was it. And I wouldn't be arsed, you could hit me all you wanted and it wouldn't even phase me, I'd just get more and more pumped off it.

As one might expect given their early lives (see Chapter 4, pp. 76–79), 'bullies' became a frequent target for Shane and Carl's violence. When a friend of Carl's was being extorted, Carl felt obliged to intervene on his friend's behalf. But the intervention quickly escalated to violence:

> **Carl**: . . . he was picking on him, and I just, again I can't stand bullies, I hate them and so that's how all that started . . . he started mouthing off at me, from inside his car. And I just couldn't cope with it . . . I put my hand through his window, dragged him out, knocked the living crap out of him . . . and smashed his car up.

In the aftermath of this assault, friends of Carl's victim had been attempting to intimidate and goad Carl into further violence, knowing that the police were keeping a close eye on him:

Carl: I kept my nose clean, started to walk away from fights . . . But everything was still going on anyway between the lad I'd had the fight with and his mates trying . . . to goad me into doing it, but it didn't work.

The threats and intimidation came to an abrupt halt after Shane attacked one of the ringleaders. With his willingness to use uncompromising and often extreme violence, Shane's reputation as a local hard man grew within the community. A friend of Shane's, who had been working for him, was being intimidated and extorted by a local criminal. Shane hospitalised this individual after attacking him with an iron bar. Later, Shane discovered that this same friend had stolen money from him while they were working together:

Shane: . . . this mate who I'd helped out, he stole money off me . . . I put his hand in the vice and asked him if he trusted me, he said 'yeah', so I tightened the vice around his hand and I said 'yeah I used to fucking trust you' and I broke all his fingers.

Shane's volatility and rage was often so unrestrained it had unintended consequences:

Shane: . . . we went round to this guy's house, knocked on the door, soon as he opened the door my mate punched him . . . And I'll never forget, his wife was in the kitchen and his kid, was only a little boy, he started screaming 'mummy mummy they're killing daddy'. And that was the most horrific thing. It played over and over in my head for weeks and weeks afterwards.

AE: . . . did you stop?

Shane: Instantly stopped . . . there was a moment where everything starts being like slow motion and that weird distant, everything's a background noise and that strange shit going on in your head, where everything, the world stops turning. And then I remember my mate pulling up in the car and I remember just getting in the car and we went straight to the pub, and I remember just getting absolutely wasted. Cos I just felt like shit honestly . . . But, you know, you can't do stuff like that, can you? You can't behave like that, he shouldn't have done what he'd done is my point. Had he not done that, that situation would never have arisen. I was just enjoying a normal day and then that happened, and as far as I'm concerned you've got to deal with it. Cos otherwise you just give people licence to take the piss, don't you?

Recently, Carl's daughter had begun seeing an older male who she worked with. Carl was enraged upon finding out about the relationship and threatened violence against the man. At the behest of his wife and threats from his daughter to never speak to him again, Carl refrained. Despite my questioning and further probing, Carl and Shane were unable to explain to me the specific nature of the pair's relationship. There was a vague ambiguity to their responses, and instead the focus of their discussion was upon the inappropriateness of the age gap, the man's rumoured predatory and perverted sexual intentions, and the need to protect Carl's daughter from this with violence:

Shane: I kidnapped a lad who was taking the piss out of my niece . . . he was just too old to be going out with her.

Carl: I promised my daughter I wouldn't hit him, she begged me not to hit him . . . And I couldn't go back on my word . . . she said if anyone hits him, she won't speak to me, and I didn't want to risk losing my daughter . . . It bugs me to hell that I couldn't do anything, but at the end of the day I still see my daughter every week.

Shane: He was just a sicko and he was trying to get into her.

Carl: . . . he was grooming her, but he was turning her against me and her mum . . . Anything that we said about him was wrong . . . It was just weird, he was grooming her and it annoyed me that I promised her I wouldn't do anything. But I wished to god I had done. And if I do see him I will do it now, now I speak to my daughter and he's gone, cos he shouldn't have done that to my daughter . . . he kept giving her lifts home and he'd finish work at 10pm, but she wouldn't get home until 1am.

AE: Did you ever have an idea where they went during that time?

Carl: No idea, she won't speak to me about it . . . she's always been close to my wife and she swears that nothing ever happened. And my wife believes her, and my wife can tell when she's lying . . . she's going out with someone now in his 20s, but she won't tell me, I'm not allowed to know. But my wife knows about everything, so as long as someone knows what's going on I don't mind . . . if anything does happen, my wife will tell me and I'll step in then. But until then I'm going to leave it, as long as she doesn't get hurt I don't mind.

AE: What did you do to him?

Shane: . . . we locked him in the house and wouldn't let him go . . . Took his phone off him and that . . . just roughed him up a bit, made him realise what would happen if he went near her again. And then he packed his job in . . . moved away from the area.

Gary and Paul's experiences described in the previous section demonstrated how spontaneous random violence between strangers can invoke and connect with previous humiliations and experiences within an individual's life course. Yet, quite evidently, these previous observations are applicable here in the shape of a similar legacy of repressed emotion, humiliation and fear of weakness that is present in the life courses and violence of Shane and Carl.

Shane and Carl's violence is underscored by an almost paranoid desire to protect and defend those closest to them, often with extremely violent consequences. Interestingly, with the exception of an occasional crude tendency to resort to women-blaming (see Ellis *et al.*, 2013; Wykes and Welsh, 2009), male-to-male violence and masculinity more generally, has often been discussed and theorised in homosocial terms with little requisite discussion of men's relationships with women (Collier, 1998). Yet, quite clearly here, themes of protection and, as subterfuge, possession of women and dependants, feature quite strongly in Shane and Carl's violence towards men. Their sentiments of protection, paternalism, and desire for children, partners, wives, friends and their wider family to be safe are understandable and to be expected; an absence of these would be concerning. However, the willingness to resort to sometimes extreme violence in the name of 'defence' and 'protection' hints at the presence of fears around imminent loss and the rupturing intrusion of existential threats. The motivations for their violence have not always arisen out of direct threats to them per se, but Shane and Carl view those close to them, particularly women and dependants, as extensions of themselves (see Gregory, 2012) – an attack on these, is an attack on them, and a challenge that must be confronted without hesitation. To not do so indicates weakness. For the brothers, showing weakness is simply not possible or acceptable in some situations. They are terrified of weakness, because within the context of their biographical histories and pragmatic experiences, weakness will be exploited without mercy.

Robbing smack, thieving crack and fighting back

'And there's been another goal!' cries Sky Sports presenter Jeff Stelling on the cinematic 50 inch flat screen TV mounted on the wall. As the clock approaches 4:45 on a Saturday afternoon the tension in the living room is palpable, as is the pungent earthly aroma of marijuana. Out of the window the winter sun slowly slips behind the trees that overlook the rear garden, creating a sombre atmosphere that is penetrated only by the glare of the TV screen and the warm red light from the gas fire. The owner of the house, Derrick, is a drug dealer. He fetches me a cup of tea and shows me a brand new pair of designer jeans he recently purchased:

> Alright them Tony aren't they? Brand new jeans, £100 in the shop, only cost me a tenner.

'Who did you get them off then?' I ask.

'Mate of mine who's a shoplifter' he replies.

Ian, Derrick's friend, is sat across from me; perched on the edge of the sofa, staring intently at the TV screen while the drama of the afternoon's football fixtures begin to reach their climax. I too am sat forward in my chair as I monitor my own team's progress, sipping my cup of tea while (passively) inhaling the smoke that emanates from the joint nestled between Ian's index and middle fingers. Now and then

Ian shoots me a glance with his dark eyes as we talk about the contrasting fortunes of our respective teams. The several mobile phones on the coffee table next to packets of Drum tobacco, Rizla, small transparent bags of marijuana, and unopened letters, ring at more regular intervals, as Ian and Derrick's punters begin to place their orders for the evening. Suddenly Ian leaps to his feet thrusting his fist into the air he shouts 'Fuckin get in there!' an added time goal for his team, which proves to be the winner. Apart from this animated reaction, that I've found tends to happen when Ian watches football, he generally speaks quietly and calmly. He does not possess the imposing muscularity and physical stature that defines some of the other men described in this book. A superficial glance reveals nothing remarkable or threatening, no outward signs of menace; only a veneer of banality that belies Ian's potential for violence. The only visible signs of his violent history are the little, inconspicuous scars on his hands.

Ian was vague with the details concerning his early life, despite my attempts to gather information on this during our regular conversations. From the shreds of information I was able to pick up I learned his stepfather had been a habitual gambler who had a habit of accumulating large debts. His spiralling debt problems had forced the family to relocate to the area Ian now resides in. The manner in which Ian discussed his stepfather suggests their relationship had been poor. Ian's mother had died some years ago and he has siblings who he does not see regularly. Overall, I sensed from Ian's reticence that this was an aspect of his biography that he wasn't too comfortable discussing. I followed my instincts and did not pursue this line of questioning too much, focusing more on his criminal career and his experiences with violence, which he was more willing to divulge.

Since his teens Ian has displayed an unwavering commitment to serious criminality. His first encounter with the law was in his late teens, when he was given a custodial sentence for his involvement in a burglary. After release he renewed contact with several individuals he met in prison and began a successful stint as a distraction thief, targeting medium and large-sized retailers. With shrinking opportunities due to the introduction of CCTV and increased security measures in the retail industry, Ian's career trajectory altered to drug distribution. Ian is part of a network of serious criminals who have maintained a sustained presence over the past several decades in the area's local criminal markets. He was involved for a time in the trafficking of large quantities of illicit drugs from Europe, later becoming a key figure in the heroin trade that exploded in marginalised sections of the rapidly de-industrialising North. But his success got him noticed. Several years ago Ian was nearly murdered by a local gangster who attempted to rob him of drugs and money:

Ian: It happened at my house, this woman I was with at the time was with me . . . I had a look through the door window and saw these lads on the doorstep; they weren't my regular buyers so I was suspicious. I had a knife and my gun wedged in the back of my trousers, opened the door slightly and says 'Alright, what do you want?' This kid says to me 'We wanna buy some gear mate' . . . I just said 'I'm sorry mate, I've no idea what you're talking about'. As I'm shutting the door he threw himself against it . . . I'd got my shoulder behind it so he didn't manage to push it open very far . . . his arm was coming through the gap and he had a gun in his hand and was trying to hit me with it . . . he ended up firing the gun . . . I fell on the floor and this kid brushed past me and into the house . . . his mates had run off and left him so I grabbed my knife and gun and ran into the living room. He'd got my missus by the hair on her knees and was pointing the gun at her head saying 'Give me the fucking gear and money or she's dead.'

In the struggle that followed Ian was shot several times.

Undeterred by his flirtation with death, Ian continued to supply heroin, among other substances. His aptitude, entrepreneurial zeal, and willingness to use violence, enabled Ian to become one of the largest suppliers of heroin in the area. Armed with better quality 'product' and muscle, small time drug dealers were, literally, brushed aside as Ian began to attain a large segment of the localised drug market.

> **Ian**: . . . slowly we began to establish a presence. It was a great opportunity for us, cos there was only a couple of guys selling gear . . . and it was pretty shit quality. I'd . . . been getting some good quality stuff from my suppliers . . . word got round to all the smackheads that we were selling gear and it was fucking good quality, better than the shit they had been getting anyway . . . as you can imagine they [other dealers] weren't very happy about it, but they didn't have a say in it, cos there wasn't really anyone with much of a rep [reputation for violence].

For a while business was good but when Ian was betrayed by a local criminal he mercilessly beat him, leaving him with life threatening injuries.

> **Ian**: . . . his head was like a fucking basketball [after the beating]. To be honest I don't know why we gave him such a beating, he was terrified of us and realised that he had made a big mistake. I don't know if it was cos some of the other lads were there, and that's what made me keep beating him, you know like egging me on to do it . . . Everyone knew what a dishonest little cunt he [victim] was, he couldn't be trusted, he was the type of lad who would rob your house if he knew you were on holiday or out, know what I mean?

Ian has recently been released from prison for a violent offence and is attempting to resurrect the success he had achieved prior to his sentence. From a large and severely deprived council estate, Ian continues to supply his clients with a wide variety of illegal substances.

As we watch the football Derrick enters the room with an associate, who has arrived back at the house following a delivery of drugs to a regular client. His associate joins Ian and myself in front of the TV, shaking our hands and exchanging brief pleasantries. I watch Derrick from the corner of my eye as he produces a fat wedge of notes from his pocket and begins counting them. I estimate that he must have at least several hundred pounds in his hand. As Derrick returns to the kitchen to make more drinks there is a knock at the front door. I hear Derrick answer it and the visitor steps into the house. After several minutes of hushed conversation with Derrick in the hallway, the visitor timidly enters the living room; it is a young woman. She slowly makes her way over to the sofa, swaying in a disorientated fashion. In the dimness of the room the brightness of the TV sheds light onto her. She is holding a can of Special Brew and that is when I notice the marks on her face. As she steps closer I am quite taken aback by what I see. Her face is severely swollen and beginning to bruise. There is dried blood around her mouth and on her clothing; scratches on her neck, and her mascara has been smeared by tears. She takes a seat in one of the chairs and asks Ian and Derrick if they can sort her out with some 'phet'. Nobody seems to notice, and even if they have, they do not seem particularly interested in the fact that the young woman has clearly been badly beaten. I feel angry and upset by what I am witnessing, but keep my mouth shut and maintain the occasional façade of nonchalance that has got me through the research so far. Ian and Derrick retreat to the kitchen to talk. Ian announces he is 'popping out', I presume to get the young woman what she has asked for. Tired and upset I make my excuses, thank Derrick, and leave to return home.

For Paul, Gary, Shane and Carl who were discussed earlier, issues of morality and justification began to emerge, and Ian's narrative account was also rich in a narcissistic self-righteousness. In it there is an inverted morality that disavows the harsh, totally excessive brutality of his violence and that elevates his own suffering, indignity and humiliation over his victim's. It represented a narrative of arduousness, victimisation and struggle, at the lengths he had to go to, to ensure that 'justice' was done (see Arendt, 2006). Such brutal and uninhibited violence should not surprise us. On those occasions when violence within criminal markets does erupt, it is very rarely restrained (see Hall *et al.*, 2008; Pearson and Hobbs, 2003; Winlow, 2001).

As was discussed in Chapter 4, Brett's criminal career has also been punctuated by extreme violence. Recently he was embroiled in a feud with a rival criminal. Brett believed this individual had orchestrated a robbery, during which Brett was forced to hand over drugs and money at gunpoint. Brett was convinced this individual, and his associates, wanted him 'out of the way' and they began to target something they knew would goad Brett:

Brett: I trusted a woman. Honestly mate, never fall in love with a woman . . . never trust a woman.

The specific contextual setting here is illegal drug markets, but careful analysis reveals deep subjective motivations and emotions that drive Brett's violence in this context. As was present in the case study of Shane and Carl, discourses of love and protection, but also an accompanying sense of insecurity, are interwoven into Brett's description of his eruption into rage. It took some considerable time before Brett would open up to me about the intricacies of this intimate relationship, which undoubtedly is a source of tremendous threat to his exterior appearance and projected identity of 'hard' impenetrability.

The woman in question was Brett's ex-partner, who he had begun seeing again after a period of separation. When they first met she had worked as a sex worker, but stopped when they began a relationship. It seemed she had returned to the trade during their separation, or was perhaps coerced by some of the men involved in the feud, as Brett suspected:

> **Brett**: . . . we'd been together previously . . . and then started seeing each other again. And I fell in love with her and I shouldn't have done, it was stupid. I mean she would lie to me all the time, and it took me ages to figure out what was wrong. We'd be together and she would get phone calls and she'd be upset but wouldn't tell me what was going on, she'd say it was nothing and don't worry. But I could tell it wasn't right . . . sometimes she would tell me the truth, but she would lie as well, so it took me about 3 months to piece it altogether and eventually I realised what was going on. I think she was in on it though, I can't be sure, but I think she was part of it all. She used to be on the game [prostitution] years ago and when she met me she stopped and while we were apart I think she'd gone back on it, I don't know really.

As was discussed in the previous chapter, Brett's description of this relationship resonates with the betrayed, humiliated, dominated, 'walked all over' individual who emerged from the dualistic description of his biography (see previous chapter pp. 66–68). Brett was at pains to describe the love and support he believed he had provided this woman during their relationship and struggled to vocalise this to me during conversation. His body language and general demeanour as I encouraged him to talk were indicative of internal distress and discomfort, in contrast to his joviality and the bravado that often characterised our meetings. He tried changing the subject at one point before returning to it later when he clearly felt composed enough to express his feelings about it. Brett remains unsure whether the woman had actually colluded with his rivals, but when he 'figured out' what was going on extreme violence followed:

> **Brett**: I think she was kind of part of it, but I think they forced her into it as well and I think she did want help . . . I mean I did three people in over that. Shoved a shooter in one of the lad's faces for threatening her, hit another kid, like beat him up.

Brett's violence ended with him attacking the individual he believed had orchestrated the robbery:

> **Brett**: . . . these lads are proper fucking scumbags mate . . . we were arguing and he was giving me shit, so I just thought fuck you like your fucking having it.

Brett described, as alluded to in the previous chapter, how he 'flipped out', lost control of himself, descending into an uncontrollable rage. Brett attacked his opponent with a hammer. Afterwards he described 'coming round' to find his opponent lying on the floor unconscious and covered in blood.

Liam was more than willing to target the vulnerabilities of those involved in the drug trade (see Jacobs, 2000). Liam would use intimidation and if necessary violence to 'rip off' or 'tax' dealers and vulnerable drug users:

> Liam: . . . if they've just got their drugs then people were probably rattling, not feeling up to it, can't be bothered with it, they're wimps, something like that. Don't forget I weren't picking on big lads. I'd be picking on all the small fry, all the vulnerable ones. That's what a predator does isn't it?

Liam, aware of who he was actually robbing but seemingly indifferent to the potential consequences, targeted a small-time female drug dealer who was selling crack cocaine on behalf of several violent gangsters:

> Liam: . . . [drug dealer] gave us 50 quid and a little bit of crack . . . But I didn't want to get caught in that flat by them gangsters . . . cos there was only one way in and one way out, and the windows didn't open properly in there, didn't fancy jumping through a double glazed window [laughs]. So this girl I was with were saying to me 'she's got it in her knickers'. And I were going 'No no, forget it, we've got some cash and some gear, we are sorted'. So we'd got a few quid, I had a quick blast on a pipe they'd already got out, I grabbed this pipe, stuck the crack on and smoked it [laughs] fucking crazy man. So this lass I was with wanted to take her into the bathroom and strip her like, cos she was saying 'She's got to have more than this'. And being the total idiot I am said 'forget that, we are going'. And all the time she had 4 grand down her pants . . . fuckin hell it's not nice thinking back to that. So what she did then, clever bitch, blew all the money didn't she, blew all the gear and told them [gangsters] that I took the lot . . . couple of days later we are in this drug house . . . front room were packed out with people . . . And then slowly but surely it just emptied the room, they'd all just gone into the kitchen, and there was this lass sat at side of me and she goes to me 'Liam, get out of this house now, it's a setup' . . . Guy [gangster] with the claw hammer came through from the kitchen . . . I just dove for the door as quick as possible . . . opened it, and there was the other bloke [gangster], there like with an axe . . . I landed in the middle of the street, cars were beeping at me, so I was just waving my hands about basically going 'Help me, help me somebody . . .' . . . next minute I'm being taken to hospital cos there was all blood coming out of my head, he'd got me on head with the hammer.

Earlier in the day, prior to being set-up and attacked by the gangsters he had robbed, Liam and an associate had visited a drug dealer operating from a block of flats in order to 'tax' him. They dragged the dealer from his flat, held a kitchen knife to his throat and repeatedly beat him with a piece of wood until his terrified friends, who had locked themselves in the flat, gave Liam and his associate a bottle of Temazepam.

Discussion

Real violence, as opposed to its mass-marketed sanitised Hollywood variant, is ugly, often clumsy, desperate and brutal. It bears little resemblance to the clinically executed 'designer' violence (Pearson, 1995), which we are accustomed to seeing on television (see Collins, 2008). Real violence, which has been a feature of these men's lives, is driven by raw brutal determination and a willingness to inflict damage with little regard for the consequences. Martial arts training, bulging muscles, physical presence and stature, can only take the individual so far before uncompromising rage, ferocity and a lack of restraint must take over (see Hobbs, 1995, p. 50–51).

Confrontational interactions do not always inevitably lead to physical violence, but this should not be construed simply as showing restraint: indicative of succumbing to the 'fear and tension' that characterises confrontations (see Collins, 2008). These confrontations are of course mediated by spatial context. Space and context is important in the perpetration of violent crime, where broader 'socioeconomic processes are realized and structured' (Ray, 2011, p. 193). These confrontations occurred in places that have strongly felt the effects of de-industrialisation and concomitant economic decline. Some of the violence presented occurred in the liminal night-time economy, a commercialised space that has burgeoned in response to the aforementioned broader crises brought about by economic change (Hobbs *et al.*, 2003), but in which ostentatious individualism, hostility, interpersonal competition, crime and physical violence, are largely normalised (Winlow and Hall, 2006). Yet, we cannot simply assume that the characteristics of such spaces and contextual settings will automatically produce outbursts of violence. The conditions of such spaces following neo-liberal economic restructuring are important features here, but we must also consider the masculine subjectivities present in such spaces and the motivations and emotions implicated in the violence that occasionally erupts there (see also Hall and Wilson, 2014; Ray, 2011).

The violence presented here is permeated by a general sense of injustice, betrayal, victimisation, desperation, entitlement, humiliation, and an intensely overwhelming fear of ruminating over what could have been done, or what might have been. These men are engrossed in conceptions of themselves that reflect an acutely insecure desire for recognition. Confrontational situations are approached in a manner which ensures, as much as possible, the maintenance of self-dignity and avoidance of persecutory humiliation associated with having been dominated and a *failure to act*. What the men who feature in this book do 'possess' they protect fiercely. As discussed, money and illicit market opportunities, personal status, reputation and respect, as well as females, dependants and friends, featured heavily in accounts of violence. When the latter were felt to be under threat they were defended and protected with, sometimes brutal, consequences. The evident sense of fear and troubling emotions in these narratives seem to be partially anchored in certain past events that characterise these men's biographies, representing a traumatic subjective collision of the present and past that transforms, albeit not always instantaneously, into rage. Interestingly, despite the proclivity within much scholarship to account for male-to-male violence as homosocial in motivation and nature, the data presented here suggests that issues concerning relationships with women, usually intimate, can on occasions be at the forefront of some violence that takes place between men. Some men, as described earlier, become enraged in response to feelings of threat that are rooted in a strong attachment to, and obsession with, maintaining paternalism, protection and proprietary over female intimates. A desperate desire to extinguish or avenge, through harming others, these feelings was clearly evident. In their desperation to extinguish traumatising and persecutory feelings men's violence is often subjected to a minimal amount of restraint. In some cases it can be incredibly primal, predatory, and not bound to any rigid notions of 'rules', 'codes' or appropriate 'engagement' (see Emsley, 2005b).

This chapter has engaged analytically with the complex motivations that lie behind aggressive violence and provides a clearer picture of the subjectivities of men that perpetrate it. What also accompanied this violence was a powerful sense of self-righteous entitlement and moral sanctity that will be explored in the next chapter.

6 It's 'not me' . . . it's 'them'

Violent reflections

In the previous chapter, issues of morality and justifications for violence began to emerge during some of the men's discussions of violence they have committed against others. Returning briefly to Chapter 3, Darren's case study also alluded to several significant thematic issues relevant for the discussion in this chapter. First, the issue of 'deservingness' and how he felt that those he has physically harmed *deserved* it. Second, his emphasis upon a lack of choice around violence, which emphasised that being aggressive and violent, is sometimes absolutely necessary and unavoidable. Finally, what seemed to unite these sentiments was both a sense of personal absolution in relation to the doing of violence, but also disdain for those who misunderstood these sentiments and thus failed to acknowledge the complexities of his life and of using violence.

This chapter explores and analyses such justifications and how they are related to the self-identities of these men in more depth. In doing this, the chapter alludes to the men's varying reflections upon several issues: the morality and appropriateness of their violence against others and their attempts to justify this; the 'types' of men they considered themselves to be – their 'masculinity', self-identities and how this is related to violence; and, lastly, their perceptions and understandings of their roles as father figures, in particular to young boys within their families, and how issues of morality, violence and masculinity inform this.

Morality and defensive justifications

> *all violence is an attempt to achieve justice*, or what the violent person perceives as justice.
>
> (Gilligan, 2000, p. 11)

> The availability of languages of justifiable violence, as revolutionary or self-defensive, offers perpetrators in general a view of themselves as powerless victims.
>
> (Ray, 2011, p. 14)

As both Gilligan and Ray have argued, instances of interpersonal violence are rarely without some attendant justificatory explanation, even if these justifications have little genuine or reasonable foundation. Like much violence for those who perpetrate it, the participants heavily justified to me their use of violence and were at pains to point out the justifiability of their behaviour. Some of the men were able to reflect more deeply than others upon the morality/appropriateness of this behaviour. Some even felt their behaviour had at times been excessive and said they felt guilt and shame at this. Generally though, from their perspectives, and as was intimated by them in the previous chapters, their violence was committed in response to a perceived sense of injustice or victimisation that justified inflicting, occasionally serious, harm upon others. Violence was always felt to be *deserved* by those who were on the receiving end, however obscure, perverse or unfounded this may appear in the eyes of the reader.

For example, Gary reflects briefly upon an assault he committed against a male acquaintance who he found had been 'bad mouthing' him to others while he was not present:

> **Gary**: . . . he didn't get anything apart from a busted nose and a red face . . . I didn't like the kid so I didn't really feel any sympathy for him . . . I just thought well you deserve it. If he didn't want to get punched he shouldn't have been so cocky, bad mouthing people behind their back. So [I] think he got what he deserved.

While Ian focuses upon his own perceived sense of victimisation after attacking an individual with a knife, who then committed the cardinal sin of 'grassing':

> **Ian**: . . . the fucker grassed on me, couldn't believe it. I spent a lot of time in prison thinking about what he did to me, how he'd grassed. I heard off a few people . . . that he'd been done in a couple of times cos of what he did to me . . . I remember being sat in prison fuming about it, I thought a lot about what I would do to him when I got out. I considered many times going round there and fucking doing him properly, got time [prison sentence] for that cunt.

In the next example, Liam talks more generally about the necessity of being able and willing to defend yourself, with a specific emphasis upon having to use violence while in prison:

> **Liam**: I've always been right with people if they're right with me, I'm right with them. If someone tries stealing something off me, or confronting me, things like that, you've got to haven't you? [use violence] Cos if you don't in prison, you'll soon become a muppet, and that's when your life does get difficult in prison . . . You have got to look after yourself though, don't get me wrong, cos I mean you have to look after yourself cos they'll take you for a right idiot, they'll be doing all sorts.

Similarly, Shane offers his more extensive and generalised reflections on his violent history, which shift between various justifications and denials:

Shane: I've done some horrific things, but, really, you know, at the time, I felt like, [it was] . . . the right thing to do. And in my head now if I try to analyse it today I still think it was the right thing to do, even though it was over the top, I'd still think well you shouldn't have done what you did should you. Shit happens doesn't it? I've got no remorse for anything I did . . . Cos at the end of the day I wouldn't have done what I done if I wasn't put in the position to do it, because if someone wrongs you, then you have to straighten it don't you? That's the way I look at life anyway. And I've never hurt anybody who didn't . . . deserve it. I've never gone after anybody who didn't deserve me to go looking for them and I've never ever bullied anyone, picked on anyone, made a fool of anyone or anything, so, I aint got no regrets. I regret that I wasted a lot of my life doing stupid things . . . I have got regrets, but no regrets that revolve around stuff like that [violence] . . . because I'm not what I would call an aggressive person.

Research that has gathered narratives from men who have committed violent crimes has found that they tend to be devoid of a sense of personal agency (see Hearn, 1998; Stein, 2007). The accounts from the men minimise agency in two important ways. First, by indicating that they were given little choice or option but to use violence to defend themselves and to ensure they would not be targeted with further violence and humiliation. And second, by shifting agency onto the victims, who are designated as responsible and somehow at fault for making them behave violently. In short, the victim should have known better, realised what the consequences would be, modified their behaviour, or simply stayed well away.

Other participants were not so firm in their convictions that their violence is, and has always been, totally warranted and justified, acknowledging feelings of guilt, regret and shame. However, these were not aired or discussed without recourse to some justification, which still imparted blame upon the victim or was done through reference to an incident in the past in which they themselves had been victimised.

In the following extract, Paul reflects on attacking another male in a nightclub. Paul's opponent knew Paul's girlfriend and had had a brief relationship with her several years before she and Paul had met. Paul said the history between the two of them did not bother him and had not been part of his motivation for the attack. However, Paul felt his victim still harboured some feelings for her and described how on this particular evening this individual had been attempting to goad him. Paul's girlfriend was not present during the assault and does not know about it. I asked Paul to consider how she might feel about it if she were to find out:

Paul: She would be disappointed with me, I mean she knows what I'm like . . . I think she'd see that I was being picked on, she'd say 'Oh you can walk away from things like that, you don't need to do that' and she's right you don't, but . . . I were drunk as well, so that's why it happened basically. It wouldn't have happened if I were sober, I would probably have just said 'Come on let's stand somewhere else'. But cos I were drunk and he was

. . . just generally mugging me off I thought, no that's enough, know what I mean? It changes how you think when you are drunk but you are still sort of sober enough to move about. It's like you haven't got as much of a problem with doing it, you just think no fuck it. But I regretted it right bad, right bad the next day. I remember saying to my mate 'I'm right sorry that that happened'. I felt like I'd ruined our night out, I felt right bad.

AE: And what did he say?

Paul: He just said 'No no he deserved it'. But I mean I were happy that they weren't annoyed at me, but I did feel bad for hitting this kid, cos he was nothing, he was like you know your stereotype student? You picture them just like they'd never be, sort of able to look after themselves in that kind of situation, you know what I mean don't you? . . . I'm not saying students are like that but there's a stereotype isn't there? And he were like one of them and I just thought, there were no challenge whatsoever to walking over and hitting him and I do feel bad about it.

Paul, like the other men involved in this study, has emerged from a cultural context in which self-worth and value are intimately connected to one's ability to defend oneself and react appropriately to challenges and attempts by others to achieve or exert dominance. The measure of the man is often taken from his ability to *react* to such circumstances. Historical research focused on England highlights the existence of unwritten rules of engagement and comportment during male violence, particularly notions of 'fighting fair' (Emsley, 2005b). Men's violence is often constructed around notions of a 'fair', honourable fight between two well-matched opponents during which *real* men, who have earned the right to call themselves *men*, engage in confrontations to reaffirm idealised images of themselves (Whitehead, 2005). Recent work drawing on ethnographic data suggests these informal governing injunctions may be dissolving though, amid atmospheres of extreme interpersonal competitiveness (see Winlow and Hall, 2006).

Certainly, from Paul's narrative, we can detect remnants of something which might be construed as a set of informal governing injunctions around interpersonal combat that linger as a vague background static, particularly the sense of shame at his violent actions, as he did not see his victim as 'fair game'. Paul's allusions to the other male's inability to fight and his general lack of masculine credibility in the aforementioned sense of being able to defend oneself, created a situation in which Paul had dominated what he considered to be an inferior opponent; although, one may also construe this as blatant narcissism on Paul's part. As was discussed in the previous chapter, the moral economy of male violence can easily disintegrate under pressure and an attempt at appeasement through offering an opponent the opportunity to walk away can very quickly threaten the individual male with a loss of face and self-dignity, particularly if such dignified appeasement fails (see Willis, 1990). Later on during this particular interview, Paul responded in the following way to a discussion about himself and his brother Gary, and when they consider it is appropriate to use violence:

Paul: I think we both think that if it needed to happen then there would be no issue. Like say if one of us were in trouble or looked like we were going to get hit or something, like for instance in the takeaway,[1] if that lad had made a move to hit our mate, there would have been no standing and thinking oh what do we do? We'd have been straight in.

AE: So if it needs to happen you won't hesitate?

Paul: Yeah if it needs to happen. We don't go looking for it and I always feel bad after but it's like that night in town all over again.[2] If I think, you know one of us is going to get hit, or has been hit, or whatever then it needs to happen, then there would be no, there's not a problem, it's not a problem to get involved.

The image conjured up from Paul's narrative is of an individual who occupies a social space where the possibility of violence is always present, even if you 'don't go looking for it'. Paul constructs himself, as do some of the other men whose justificatory discussions are cited, as an approximation of a reluctant fighter. He does not want to be violent, and Paul describes feeling regret, guilt and shame at having to do so, but simultaneously feels there is little choice in the matter. Being taunted by someone Paul considers a stereotypical 'soft' student, raised in a safe and secure environment and thus unfamiliar with the need for violence and self-defence, represents no genuine threat or challenge to a *man* like Paul. However, his allusion to his previous experience of being attacked with a glass bottle is core to his justificatory mechanism for violence against an inferior opponent he considers to be unworthy of the effort and physical exertion. As discussed in Chapter 5, Paul's more recent experiences of being attacked and left feeling helpless and vulnerable, resonate with his earlier childhood experiences of being physically dominated by an older male from his local estate (see Chapter 4). Pragmatic experience and memories of these events has forced Paul to reconsider and reappraise aspects of his self-identity in light of past circumstances where he has *failed* to react in a manner commensurate with immediate cultural expectations and which left him physically and psychologically scarred. This reappraisal, and its attendant moral justifications, shapes his ongoing social engagement with others and the social world (see Winlow and Hall, 2009).

What emerges from the examples explored is what Hall (2012a) has identified as morally flexible selves that are capable of engaging with moral and ethical frameworks that instruct individuals not to harm others in a calculating manner. These men are not pathological as is so often assumed in media, political and some academic commentaries of violence (see Ellis *et al.*, 2013). They do not suffer from a mental affliction that renders them devoid of the ability to empathise or express care and concern for others' well-being. They recognise the moral and ethical injunctions against violence, but believe these to be totally out of touch with the 'realities' of everyday life (see Winlow, 2012). Rather, everyday life in the more marginalised sections of advanced capitalism, is perceived to be occasionally highly pressurised and morally challenging, requiring a flexible engagement with ethics that transcends the simplistic dualism of 'right' and 'wrong'. Thus, violence is neither wholly right, but nor is it entirely wrong in particular circumstances. And this ambiguous, context-bound understanding of the morality of violence that these men display is a crucial analytical point in understanding their relationships to violence and which I will elaborate upon later in this chapter.

Hearn (1998) describes how the men he interviewed who regularly abused intimate female partners attempted to minimise their violence as only a minute part of themselves that did not represent the 'core' of who they actually were. In a psychological sense, such manoeuvres represent the process of dissociation: of psychically separating-off experiences from the self and consciously denying any association with them in an attempt to deal with experiences and behaviour that threatens the coherence of the self (see Stein, 2007). Abby Stein (2007) discusses this at length in reference to acts of serious violence. She argues that perpetrators of violence slide along a continuum of points away from the 'good me' and the 'bad me', towards the 'not me'. The 'not me' is the extreme dissociated part of subjectivity, which hosts rage and is seen as responsible for perpetrating violence and harm. Thus, it is only through the subject's dissociated 'not me' that an association with their infliction of serious harm upon others can actually be made. Hall (2012a) extracts Stein's thinking from this individualised framework, locating it within a socio-cultural analysis. Hall describes this process in response to the systemic demands of life under advanced capitalism, suggesting that individuals in significant nodal positions within the system invoke the 'not me', doing what is 'necessary' at that time in order to fulfil these demands.

What these narratives indicate are attempts by these men to psychically deal with the harm they inflict upon others. Under intense feelings of threat, when the idealised self is felt to be on the brink of disintegration, the sadistic, but completely necessary, 'not me' fulfils the function of annihilating the threat in order that the self can avert feelings of shame and be restored to a state of pride (Gilligan, 2000; Hall, 2012a), not always and not necessarily through actual violence, as was highlighted and discussed in the previous chapter, but in a manner which successfully re-elevates the self over the other and wrestles back a sense of dignity, however fleeting and ephemeral, from contests with other men within much wider social contexts of shame-inducing marginality (see Hall, 2002; Ray, 2011).

The men we are: self-identity, pride and respect

It seemed crucial to the men I spent time with to be able to justify their violence through narratives like those explored earlier on, which uphold and are intimately connected to their self-identities. These narratives, despite some subtle variations, generally contain allusions to pride, self-dignity, respect and recognition by others, which they valued highly and were alluded to during Chapter 4. As one might expect, the participants did not feel that their self-identities adhered to media generated or commonplace stereotypical images of individuals who have committed, or possess a genuine capacity for, violence. They strenuously denied any possibility that they were 'bullies' or 'thugs'; such derogatory labels were vehemently rejected. Crucially, the men involved in this research do not actually perceive themselves strictly through the lens of violence. Of course a *potential* for violence informs their self-image, but in a manner that is bound up with contemporary notions of what some authors have called 'male honour' (Spierenburg, 2008), as well as a sense of respect, 'ethics', dignity, and other sentiments and injunctions defined by defence and protection of both the self and of 'vulnerable' significant others (see Anderson, 1999; Winlow and Hall, 2009).

Living the right way

Shane: I've spent many nights on the observation ward in hospital because I didn't walk away. But you just get up the next day and go home, my self-respect is intact isn't it? But if I hadn't I'd torture myself over it, and I'd go over it and over it in my head . . . I've always respected everybody else, other people's feelings, other people's wishes, other people's beliefs. You know, I've never put anybody down, bullied anybody, taken something off someone, nothing. So no I don't have, I can't sit here and say I've fucked my life up cos I haven't, I've lived it, bit crazier than most people, but I've lived it you know, I've lived it according to what I think is right. Even though what I've done is, in the eyes of the law wrong, it's still how I perceived things to be at the time.

AE: Do you ever think that, in the eyes of other people, that they might have seen you as bullies [referring to him and his brother Carl]?

Shane: No.

AE: No?

Shane: No not at all . . . people know that the trouble is because such and such has done something, not because Shane is a dickhead . . . so no I don't think that, you know, not at all. Because if you do something to someone you have to expect it back, that's life isn't it? . . . if you want to hit my mate and he won't hit you back cos he's not that kind of person, then I'll do it for him, know what I mean? You go and steal something off my friend, well I'll come and take it back off you. And that's not bullying, that's a form of defending the people that are around you . . . You protect your kids, your missus, your house, and you extend it beyond that don't you? To your work colleagues, your friends, you know your wider family, and that's just how it is I think, that's how I've always been anyway.

In the discussion, Shane attempts to communicate the hypothetical sense of self-loathing and worthlessness he would feel had he not reacted violently to events during his life that he believes have in some way threatened him or those he cares for. He would have, as he explains, literally 'tortured' himself through ruminating constantly over the memory of not reacting, of remaining static when he felt action was required, and mourning the loss of the opportunity to catapult himself on a different path towards unbridled satisfaction and security at having ensured that his 'self-respect is intact'. Threat of personal failure and a sense of expectation are themes that have been explored in much of the masculinities literature reviewed in Chapter 2 and are theorised as weighing heavily upon men who assume responsibility for protecting and providing for others and suffer in the pursuance of this (see Jefferson, 1994; Kaufman, 1994; Kimmel, 1994). As Shane intimates, stoically, violence has at times been necessary in order for him to fulfil these expectations. He has paid a hefty price physically and psychologically to be in the hallowed, enviable position of being a proud, ethical man. A man who has done what is right by defending himself, those close to him, and those more vulnerable than he is. Ultimately, Shane believes that his violence has left him able to peer at his reflection and to be content with the image that is reflected back: a man who takes no 'shit' from anyone, has respect for others, is respected by others, but crucially, a man who is able to have respect for himself because of this.

Liam's account of recently 'standing up for himself' by offering to fight a former work colleague who had been verbally abusive and who he perceived was attempting to exert authority and control over him, evokes many of the specific qualities alluded to in Shane's self-reflections on how he has comported himself in relation to others around him:

> **Liam**: . . . he were a normal worker, just like I were, but he were telling me what to do. And he'd been pushing and pushing, honestly Tony I have to be pushed and pushed and pushed [to react violently]. Started shouting again so I basically offered him out, says 'come on get outside if you want to talk to me like that, try it out here'. He shut up and it totally revolutionised our relationship, after that day he were totally sound with me, and I thought I'm really glad I did that, cos he respected me then.

> **AE**: Do you think he was scared of you?

> **Liam**: [objects quite strongly] No, no no, I don't think he was scared of me, he were a decent lad. But what it were, it sort of, it really helped, it sorted everything out for me, cos he just acted like a totally different person with me then. And it were much better, the environment were much better, you know the working environment was a lot nicer for me, cos he'd been on at me all the time, but he like respected me.

> **AE**: What, cos you'd stood up for yourself?

> **Liam**: Yeah, I stood up for myself, yeah definitely. If I'd not stood up for myself he would probably have just been the same as he'd always been, a total fucking nob. Basically having an axe to grind . . . it were like all the time, and you're thinking hold on, if I do that is he going to have a go at me?

You know one of them, and you can't have it like that . . . it were getting to a stage where I'd just had enough, you need to stand up to them . . . and like I said it was totally different, he were totally sound after that, we were like best mates man after that, honestly Tony man, like best mates.

A subsequent confrontation with another colleague resulted in Liam being relieved of his duties and he has been unable to find employment since his dismissal. Significantly, the emphasis within his narrative is not upon a sense of regret or shame that he had lost his job through being unable to control his anger, but more upon the positive effects of his actions through standing up for himself and not allowing what he perceived as his colleague's bullying and intimidation to continue.

The self-identities of these men are enveloped by qualities associated with aspects of the gendered, visceral habitus that places the ability to retain and to be imbued with a sense of respect and dignity from others at the core of identity (see Winlow, 2012). As has been intimated already, the sense of value, self-worth and dignity these men seek to possess and to be recognised in them by others, does not lie completely in their potential and willingness to physically harm. Rather, in a highly complex and somewhat contradictory fashion, it lies in their ability to ensure others are not unduly dominant during interactions. The aim here is to ensure that others recognise their presence and give to them respect, which in turn, enables these men to feel they are entitled to have a particular form of respect for themselves. Liam argued vehemently that he was not given respect out of fear and was, as intimated through his strong objection to my question, rather horrified by the idea that the man in question was frightened of him. Acknowledging that he inspired fear in others would have plunged Liam into the mould of the 'bully' – the despised 'other' the participants are so desperate to not be identified with. Contrarily, for Liam, he gained respect because he refused to be passive and to accept someone else's attempts to exert dominance and control without a reasonable claim to legitimate authority. Like Shane, Liam does not consider himself a 'bully' whose mere presence inspires fear and dread in others, because he has *reacted* to the conduct and behaviour of another that offends his moral sensibilities. For both men then, *reactivity* to stimuli considered threatening is the line that separates them from the bullying 'others' they loathe and despise.

This process of 'othering' in the construction of masculine identity is important and has been discussed in some literature addressing the construction of male ethnic identity through race hate and violence (see Treadwell and Garland, 2011). At a broader level, some masculinities literature has usefully highlighted hierarchical competitiveness and homophobia between men as constitutive of masculinity (Kimmel, 1994), yet, not in the context of the dialectic between identity and violence, as I discuss here. These attempts at 'othering' in relation to one's own violence are vital for making sense of these men's constructions of their identities, but they rely upon a contradictory, false dichotomy, which I will discuss in the remainder of this chapter.

'Safe man'

The field notes I present in the next paragraph are taken from an incident I observed while in the presence of Vince, develop the arguments I have made in the previous section. On this particular occasion I was able to witness the power of Vince's reputation in action. What was interesting about this was that this social encounter appeared on the surface to be quite cordial and was constructed by Vince afterwards as an exemplar of the type of respect he is frequently granted by others. The event was seemingly non-violent. Yet, simmering beneath was recognition by all involved that violence, and its possibility, was very much a structuring force for the interaction.

Vince and his friend leave the bar for a cigarette and ask me if I want one; I decline as I don't smoke, but I tell them I will join them regardless. As they head towards the doors to leave the bar I pay a visit to the toilet. As I am returning to the doors I see Vince talking to a man who I do not recognise. I am unsure whether to approach, but I am starting to feel sufficiently confident to be more assertive around Vince, and decide to join them. As I approach, the man talking to Vince turns his head in my direction and shoots me a brief nervous glance before he continues talking; he seems slightly on edge. Vince does not avert his gaze from the man, nor does he say anything to me, he just continues listening while maintaining unceasing eye contact with him. I sense that Vince does not have a problem with me hearing this conversation. It becomes clear that they know each other and the man is apologising:

> **Apologetic Individual**: . . . yeah I'm sorry about other night mate. You know me I don't want to cause any trouble, and I didn't want you to think that I was being disrespectful, just one of them things you know?

Vince extends one of his huge tattooed hands out in front of him and clasping the man's outstretched hand he shakes it firmly. Vince tells the man not to worry and that he is welcome back anytime. The man replies:

> **Apologetic Individual**: Yeah well you've bought enough cars off us anyway, so don't want you to not come back.

They both laugh and the man shakes hands with Vince's friend before leaving. Vince turns to his friend, they smile at one another. Vince then turns to me:

> **Vince**: See what I mean pal? That's a good example there of how I run things. That bloke is a decent lad, but when he gets some drink in him he's a problem, know what I mean? Starts causing trouble and he's done it a few times. He was doing it other day and I asked him to leave and told him to come back when he'd sobered up and apologise to me. As long as people do that I haven't got a problem. I ask people to go away on the night and give them the opportunity to come and apologise to me. If they don't, it's quite easy for me to find out where they live. I can quite easily pay them a visit and teach them

some respect. Few times I've kicked people's front doors in on a Sunday afternoon while they're having their Sunday dinner with their girlfriends or wives. Bit of a shock when I burst through the door and give them a good hiding in front of their missus. Wives and girlfriends will be going mental, but I'll tell them as their other half is knocked out on the floor: 'Control your husband then, teach him to respect others and I won't need to come round and do it for you.'

I lost count of the amount of times that Vince reiterated to me the importance of respecting other people, but, more importantly, ensuring that he was respected by others and the leverage this gave him within the community where he lives and works. Vince is a man committed to violence and a self-image that is built around this, more so than many of the other men involved in this research as Vince must adhere to and continually invest in this self-image and the reputation that goes with it. There is so much at stake for him, because reputation is what enables Vince to engage in the post-industrial marketplace. Without it there would be little else available to a man with no formal qualifications and who can barely read or write. For this, Vince receives an immense amount of what he interprets and construes to be respect from others.

As Winlow (2012) argues, men prepared to use violence often mistake the fear and dread they can inspire in others as a form of respect, as others will often structure their behaviour in ways that avoid incurring the wrath of men known to be prepared to use violence. This was discussed in relation to Liam and Shane previously, who were unable, or perhaps unwilling, to recognise their own aggressive dominant behaviour as having an intimidating effect. The individual, keen to offer his apologies for his previous misdemeanours while under the influence of alcohol, knew it was potentially unwise to not return and offer Vince an apology out of fear. In all likelihood nothing would come of not offering an apology, despite Vince's stern, and slightly exaggerated, rhetoric of the amount of times when he has 'kicked in people's front doors' and disrupted a pleasant afternoon dinner in order to teach respect. It is the lingering uncertainty that not apologising to a man such as Vince would leave. The fear of how Vince might interpret this and how he may act in a future encounter; it is this sense of uncertainty that such men are able to inspire in others that is crucial.

Social encounters with men who are and have been violent, like the one described in my field notes, are often incredibly cordial, with plenty of hand-shaking, conversational pleasantries, ego-inflating compliments, and general sycophantic 'sucking up' that, to the individual, appears to be borne out of a genuine affection and sense of respect for them. Yet, underlying this is trepidation, uncertainty and wariness about how they will act and their potential for violence. No matter how much men like Shane, Liam and Vince may attempt to deny it, it is inescapable that their self-identities are partly informed and defined by other's perceptions, knowledge and memories of displays of physical aggression towards others – no matter how justified or justifiable. In the communities where these men have grown up and live, such raw displays of brute physical aggression can very quickly alter the way an individual is perceived and are likely to remain etched into the collective memory of those who witness or hear about it (see Hall *et al.*, 2008; Winlow, 2001).

'Listen to your Dad': fatherhood and preparing sons

Discussing fatherhood with some of the participants revealed a contradictory tension that lies at the heart of these men's relationships with the children in their lives, particularly sons. Those men who had sons and talked about them with me were caught between a desire for their sons to stay out of trouble, but to also be able to adequately 'look after themselves'. None of them wanted their sons to experience what they had, or behave as they have done. Yet, they were acutely aware of the very real potential that exists for their sons to become embroiled in confrontational situations, and this was a cause for concern, confusion and uncertainty.

Like father like son?

Carl's son has already been in trouble for fighting with other young males at his school and seems to be displaying a temperament similar to his father and uncle:

> **Carl**: He's [Carl's son], it's a bit hard to describe it, he's not like we [Carl and Shane] were, but he'll have a go at anyone . . . He got into a fight with someone at school and apparently he knocked him out by banging his head against a wall . . . And I said to him 'did you really do that? Or did you just take the blame for someone else?' And he wouldn't answer me. So I presume he did do it, but both me and my wife sat him down and said 'look why did you do it?' And he said the other lad was picking on his friend. And once I heard him say that I thought well that's the kind of thing I've been through. So I tried to get him to stop and he said to me he wouldn't do it again. And since then he's not been in trouble, I mean he was getting in trouble pretty much every week for fighting, but nothing serious, it was just minor things . . . I hope to god now that we've had the talk he'll not do that. Can't guarantee it but we hope to god he doesn't. He wants to learn boxing to teach him a little discipline, cos both me and Shane did boxing. So we started teaching him that . . . Since that incident with the head on the wall he's been alright. Since we spoke to him about it and told him the possibilities that could happen, you know through the experiences of me and my brother, since I told him about it and what could possibly happen, I think he's stood back and thought, hang on I shouldn't be doing this maybe dad is right. I mean he won't admit it to me cos he's like that, but it seems to be that he's behaving himself, he's not getting into trouble. He gets in trouble with my wife, just silly little petty arguments, but he's a kid growing up, it's what they do. But other than that he seems to be getting his head screwed on now. We told him that if he gets into trouble to try and walk away from it, if he can't walk away from it,

don't take it on. If you can't, if you're in school, there's going to be plenty of people who you know, just walk to them. And if you've got more people with you than they've got with them picking on you then they'll disperse and leave you alone. And he says that has happened, he's walked over to a group of friends and the ones that have been mouthing off to him have walked off. They've left him alone now cos they know he's got a lot of friends, it's sort of school yard rules isn't it? My gang's bigger than your gang sort of thing, don't actually get involved in the violence, but it's actually learning him to keep his temper under control, cos he does have a bad temper my lad.

Their interventions seem to have been somewhat successful in curbing their son's anger, who has managed to remain out of trouble while in school. But, as Carl explains, he remains concerned about the future, as he knows what will be expected of his son should he encounter trouble again. Carl himself cannot help but expect it from him:

Carl: . . . if we're not careful with it, he might go down a similar sort of route that me and Shane have gone down, if I'm not careful with him.

AE: And if that was to happen how would you feel about that?

Carl: I would be upset that he's getting into trouble, but at the end of the day he's my son. But I just hope to god it doesn't get that far. I want him to be able to look after himself, obviously every parent does don't they? Their kids to be able to look after themselves, but I don't want him to end up in prison for doing something stupid. You've got to defend yourself . . . You've got to be prepared to look after yourself, but not to take it too far. Self-defence yeah, but don't take the piss out of it and I think he's getting that into his head. Yeah it's okay to fight if I have to, but not unless I have to. He's alright he still wants to box with me all the time when I come home, when I pick him up from school and he comes home he starts going like that [Carl puts his fists up] . . . We have a bit of a laugh about it and then he goes and plays on the Xbox or something. So he's alright with it, but I just hope whenever it comes to the time it stays how he is at this moment.

Do not follow in my footsteps

Liam: I want to start working again, don't want to be one of these that makes up the numbers of unemployed anymore. I need to stop smoking cannabis as well, got to kick that it's no good . . . I mean I'd even do like factory work, just need to do something, it's more for my boy, cos he deserves better. I mean I don't want to be getting involved in any violence, hopefully I won't do anymore and that's the end of it.

A surface reading of Liam's narrative here might indicate a positive will to engage in self-transformation. However, a more careful and considered reading conducted within the context of his biography, reveals a painful awareness that his ambitions to gain employment, to 'kick' his drug habit, and, importantly, to bring an end to his regular physical confrontations with other men, lack absolute certainty. In his narrative, Liam *hopes* to avoid violence, leaving a distinct lack of certainty regarding his actual ability to do so. This uncertainty and his own frustrating inability to control his occasional rage were expressed quite aptly to me:

> **Liam**: . . . even right up to this time in my life, I'm still doing it, I'm still headbutting people.

A recent altercation with a local man in the presence of several children and women left Liam with superficial injuries. Following an arrest no charges were brought against his attacker. In the aftermath of this incident, Liam himself escaped arrest and charges after he beat a local man until he was unconscious:

> **Liam**: . . . with him being a big guy, once they grab hold of you, honestly Tony, basically you've fucked it if they grab you, big man like that, yeah so you've got all these things whizzing through your head and I'm thinking hold on, it were only a couple of weeks ago that I was thinking to myself no I'm not retaliating, if he hits me he hits me, I'll get the police involved. That didn't work out very good for me did it? Made me look a chuffing idiot, even our lass takes piss out of me still.

Amid palpable feelings of uncertainty concerning his future, as well as the haunting presence and possibility of humiliation and utter social insignificance, Liam has remained committed to his relationship with his young son:

> **Liam**: I like to spend a lot of time with my son, and if there's anything on at school where parents can go into class and take part, I do that because I can remember when I was a kid how much I would have loved that. You know or even for my mum and dad to watch me play football, they never used to come, never . . . So that's why I try to do that with my boy, try to fill the gaps, you know get on floor and play cards with him and that, you know you might feel daft but you're spending quality time with your kid. So in that regard, I do think back and try to make his life a lot better in that sense through having a relationship with his dad. Cos I've never had a relationship with my dad, never, never once . . . I give him advice about school. I always say to him 'If anything happens to you just go straight to teacher'. Anything like that he goes straight to them, and he does, he listens to me . . . when I went to parents' evening, the teacher said she didn't have a wrong word to say about him, and that he gives 100% in everything that he does. Honestly it was fantastic hearing what she said.

Despite his young age, Liam's son already has a scar on his face from a piece of wood that was thrown at him by a local boy while they were playing on the street together. The impact left a deep gash in his son's cheek, which required hospital treatment. Whether he intended to hurt him is unclear. Nevertheless, Liam paid a visit to the boy's home and threatened his father with violence. When I asked Liam more about his son and the possibility that he too may continue to encounter violence as he matures, like Carl previously, Liam expressed deep concern, fear and anxiety:

> **Liam**: I do worry yeah, I do. Because it's going to be a situation where there isn't really going to be a right or wrong answer is there? If you know what I mean. Like you said, it's almost inevitable that he'll be put in a confrontational situation, that's going to be quite, hostile as well . . . to be honest if you analyse it properly you wouldn't want to bring your child up in this town. You wouldn't want to bring your child up on an estate like this . . . I mean it's getting worse round here, you're taking him to school there's rubbish everywhere, so like you are saying you are stuck in a place aren't you? And you can't really escape that, you could do I suppose, but even so you still aren't going to escape all the devil's armoury, the problems are you? No matter where you go. So yeah as far as advice goes to my son, going to have to be to try and do your utmost to not get yourself in the position in the first place. That's got to be first and foremost, and then after that who knows.

When the father to son relationship has been discussed within literature in relation to violence and masculinity, the emphasis has tended to be upon when fathers encourage and teach sons about violence, or when they subject sons to actual abuse (see Hobbs, 1994; Winlow, 2012 for example). This was discussed as a theme present in some of the men's childhoods in Chapter 4. Yet, there has been little acknowledgement in literature of the complexities of this and the specific reasons why some men's relationships with their sons are connected to violence.

What emerges from Carl and Liam here is an acute set of anxieties, uncertainties and concerns that appear to be borne out of a natural and understandable, yet highly idealistic, desire for their sons to be protected and to remain free from intimidation and threats. Neither Liam nor Carl has had the luxury of being able to avoid violence and intimidation, and, unfortunately, it is hard to imagine their sons avoiding them completely either. For Carl and Liam then, pragmatic experience features strongly in their parenting, as does a strong sense of fear. And this fear seems to emerge from a recognition and realisation of the dependency of their children, who must learn to become conversant with this immediate milieu; conversant enough to retain dignity in it, but not to the extent that it will lead to arrest and conviction or serious injury. As fathers, they experience a strong sense of responsibility and duty (see also Goodey, 1997) to adequately prepare their sons for this, to 'toughen them up' to the extent that they are capable of negotiating threats adequately. Carl felt that violence, albeit in the controlled form of boxing, will help to instil discipline in his son and teach him to regulate his aggression.

Neither man wants their sons to dominate others, or to become involved in serious violence as they themselves have. Yet, simultaneously, they do not want others to dominate their sons and both express an anxious desire for them to be able to adequately 'look after' and 'defend' themselves. This does not represent a brutal, unreflexive approach to instilling a form of hardened 'protest' masculinity – a blunt instrument for reproducing a dominant hegemony (see Connell, 2005a). More accurately, it represents an anxiety-ridden approach to fatherhood, and the attempt to cultivate the young male's identity, that is caught up in an ambivalent struggle to instil respectful, moral behaviour, as well as a capability to deal with very 'real' threats adequately. Importantly, what envelops this is the same strong sense of paranoia, fear and insecurity about what exists 'out there' beyond the immediacy of the familial home that emerged within these men's accounts of their own childhoods in Chapter 4.

Corporal punishment

Like data presented earlier from interviews conducted with Carl and Liam, Vince discusses his role as a father figure to both his niece, who I met during fieldwork with Vince, and his other nephews. Like Carl and Liam, Vince discusses the role of violence in his nephews' lives, but in contrast outlines his firm commitment to physical forms of punishment and intimidation as a means to discipline his nephews and their occasional 'challenging' behaviour.

I am sitting in Vince's living room, sipping a cup of tea while watching the early afternoon news on TV. Vince is sitting to the right of me. He is slouched at the other end of the sofa, one leg crossed over the other, with his tattooed stomach hanging slightly over his jeans while he smokes a cigarette and drinks his tea. His twenty-something niece, Kerry, is seated in the chair opposite him, legs tucked under her, occasionally taking sips from her cup while thumbing the keypad on her mobile phone. Vince points to a framed picture on the wall behind her. It contains a young man dressed in a black shirt. Either side of him stand several women smiling for the camera, his arms draped around them:

> **Vince**: That's our Kev, my nephew, when all the family went up to visit him for the day.

Kev is in prison, serving a long sentence for a serious violent offence.

> **Vince**: . . . they [police] basically wanted him off the streets for as long as possible . . . He's not a particularly big lad, but he's just not bothered. There are two things that will happen if he is after you, you'll go to an early grave, or you'll spend a lot of time in hospital.

Vince has no children of his own, but has helped his sisters to raise their children in the absence of their biological fathers, especially Kerry who lives with Vince and whose father left her and her mum when Kerry was very young:

Vince: I raised her you know [pointing at Kerry] I did a good job as well. Brought her up proper, that's why she's never been in no trouble.

Kerry: Oh yeah, he were right strict with me, him and our Kev. One time I was going out with my friends to a party and before I went they called me into the room to check what I was wearing. [laughs]

Vince: What's up with that? That's a good thing, kids need that in their lives. There isn't enough of it nowadays, especially not round here. [the estate where they live]

One of Vince's younger nephews is already developing a fledgling reputation locally for his aggression and volatility. And Vince is attempting to curb his nephew's aggression with a brand of discipline that had been a feature of his own childhood:

Kerry: It's proper funny when Uncle Vincent's around though you don't hear nothing out of him. [laughs]

Vince: That's cos he knows I'll give him a clip if he starts getting mouthy. He's a bully my nephew and I can't stand bullies. None of my mates can stand bullies. Other day I had to bollock him for mouthing off at some lass.

Kerry: He goes about with all of his mates in a big gang, that were funny when you saw them outside the shop the other week.

Vince: Him and all his mates were stood in a gang outside the shop up the road. I was in my car with my mate [local gangster] and I pulls up at the side of them, soon as I did my nephew went right quiet and put his head down. I says to him 'You cause any trouble tonight round here and I'll give you a right hiding, and that goes for all of you, I'll crack fucking lot of you if you cause any bollocks round here and I'll crack all your fucking fathas as well if you want to fetch them down.

The family suspects one of Vince's other nephews may have ADHD. Vince is not convinced. The behaviour of his nephews when he is present is proof enough for him that they do not have a condition:

Kerry: He's like my brother is though when you're around [laughs] he daren't move.

Vince: We had the nurse round a bit back to observe him. I came in the house and says 'Hey up love, what you here for?' She says 'I'm here to observe your nephew for his ADHD.' I goes 'ADHD? He hasn't got ADHD love, I'm going to sit here and show you.' So my nephew came back from the shop and sat in the living room with me and the nurse, and I'm telling you, he sat there for an hour and read the newspaper cover to cover without moving once. I goes to the nurse 'Are you still trying to tell me he's got ADHD love?

Kerry: I don't get it when people say you shouldn't hit your kids? Why? They're your kids. I was hit when I was naughty growing up and I've never been in trouble.

Vince: I'm telling you, there's nothing wrong with giving a kid a good hiding now and again.

For Vince, violence makes perfect sense. It is something that he has learned to hone and deploy in a competent fashion. Violence represents a pragmatic and commercial resource within his life course that, for him, is a ready-made solution to any situation where there is an absence of 'respectful', 'disciplined', socially acceptable behaviour. And that is regardless of whether it is on the night-club doors and streets that he protects, or to *beat* the *bully* out of his nephews. Contrary to Carl and Liam's more cautious and ambivalent approaches, Vince is more robust and confident in the utility of physical punishment as a socialisation strategy. However, in a similar vein to Carl and Liam, it is not for the crude purposes of ensuring his nephews are dominant and superior over others, rather, albeit misguidedly, for ensuring his nephews become what he perceives to be disciplined, moral and respectful individuals.

We do what we want

What emerges strongly from the men's reflections and accounts in this chapter, and which has been hinted at in previous chapters, is a general point of consensus and agreement among them that their everyday lifeworld is threatening, potentially dangerous and morally ambiguous. What these men describe being confronted with since their childhoods is a social context that is often highly pressurised and, from their perspectives, appears to be populated by atomised, highly competitive and aggressive individuals who lack basic moral principles and who will harm others to further their own ends. Marooned in such morally and ethically vacuous circumstances, these men present themselves as facing a deep, complex and unavoidable quandary that requires them to adopt a 'flexible' approach to legal and moral sanctions around appropriate behaviour and conduct towards others that they *themselves* must decide upon. Pragmatic experiences and memories of previous social encounters that have been highly traumatising and humiliating seem to provide much of the guiding principles for negotiating this. For those men who occupy a 'father' role, this complexity and personal experience informs their approaches to fatherhood. As discussed, the moral principles that they are attempting to instil in children – particularly young males – are not to actively seek to harm others in order to achieve dominance. As we saw with Vince, ironically, effective intimidation was considered an appropriate means of preventing his nephews from becoming unduly dominant and disrespectful towards others. The emphasis is upon fostering a 'toughening up' process in which qualities like fortitude and resilience are instilled in young males to ensure they are able to defend, protect and 'look after' themselves.

The men themselves decide what is 'moral' and 'ethical', which is informed by allusions to possessing, but also giving, 'respect' and underpins their own conceptions of their self-identities. There were vaguely similar sentiments articulated and aired by the participants around moral behaviour and their own 'maleness', which tended to emphasise qualities like self-defence, reacting to threats from others, 'taking care' of oneself as well as those you care about, and protecting those who are 'vulnerable'; who in most cases are women and dependants. As discussed, these identities are always constructed in relation to the imagined 'other' who bullies and intimidates those weaker than them without justification.

Fundamentally, these are well-meaning sentiments that are defensive in nature and mirror gendered discourses that equate maleness with control, power and protection (see also Gadd and Jefferson, 2007; Winlow and Hall, 2009). Yet, the violence of these men, as discussed in the previous chapter, does not always fit neatly into such a framework, despite their claims and exhortations that it does. These men's attempts at 'othering' in the construction of themselves as men are therefore based upon a rather false dichotomy between 'them' and the 'other'. Any individual who does transgress this vague set of moral and ethical values, in the eyes of the participants, *deserves* violence, as this is considered the only form of suitable and *just* punishment. To quote Zizek (2008b), the men who participated perceive their violence as righteous and *divine*, which 'stands for such brutal intrusions of justice beyond the law' (p. 151). Such 'transgressions' committed against the participants provide ripe justification for them to transcend prohibitive psychosocial restraints against harming others. The result being they can then 'do as they wish' to those who have transgressed. This is complemented by a concomitant air of narcissistic self-righteous entitlement and absolution that nobody else can question or criticise, what Hall (2012a) terms 'special liberty'. This returns us to the discussion of the 'not me' that arises in violent encounters that is, in specific situations deemed to be threatening, seemingly able to by-pass a prohibitive symbolic order that demands individuals do not physically harm others. The 'not me' can *handle* himself and others, transgress moral frameworks, and although acknowledged as *bad* by some is actually capable of doing what is occasionally considered *necessary* within the challenging socio-cultural contexts these men purport to occupy.

To summarise, engagement with issues of morality and ethical behaviour are done in often contradictory, confusing and calculated ways. That does not mean these men are immoral, on the contrary, they were extremely keen to moralise their violence through their attempts to situate it within discursive frameworks that they felt made their actions justified and *right*. But in such a context, we are confronted with a situation in which 'what is ethical and unethical, is essentially a decision for the individual and therefore nobody else's business' (Winlow, 2012, p. 208). And clearly, for these men, *righteous* and *justified* 'divine' violence (Zizek, 2008b) represents, as others have suggested (see Winlow and Hall, 2006), a means to enforce something appropriating a moral order.

Notes

1   Paul is referring here to an incident that happened several days prior to this interview, during which one of his friends was involved in an argument with another male which did not lead to violence
2   See Chapter 5, pp. 89–91.

7 Shadow world

> Many young males are receiving brutal treatment . . . to 'toughen them up',
> for what are they being toughened up?
>
> (Hall, 2012a, p. 192)

This chapter responds to the pertinent question asked by Hall in this quote. In Chapter 2, I reviewed a large amount of criminological literature that has addressed male violence. At the end of that chapter, I emphasised the importance of using incipient psychosocial approaches in order to provide more nuanced accounts of masculine subjectivity within the immediate and broader hegemonic contexts in which they are formed. I deliberately departed from theoretical debates at this juncture and presented throughout Chapters 3 to 6, data gathered through conducting in-depth ethnographic work with men who have experienced and are involved in serious violence and crime. Following this lengthy, but necessary, detour, I return now to theory in this chapter.

I want to begin by briefly outlining what I consider to be a fairly obvious set of observations about the men presented in previous chapters. An undeniably unifying factor among them is that violence, both as perpetrator and victim, has been a core feature of their early lives and something that has persisted into adulthood. Some readers may no doubt have detected, correctly too, some scalar differences among this group of men both in terms of the amount and severity of violence they have been exposed to and personally experienced. Nevertheless, it is incontestable that encounters with physical forms of violence and aggression have been enduring features. And, in conjunction, the marginalised masculine cultures into which these men have been interpellated broadly valorise the ability to physically defend and protect oneself from others. Additionally, some of these men have been subject to quite difficult, traumatic experiences in both the formative and adult years of their lives. Strained familial relationships and periods of estrangement from family, bereavements, tumultuous relationships with intimate female partners, physical and psychological abuse and problematic drug use, are features of some of these men's life courses. And these are lives that are situated in quite marginalised localities defined by a recent socio-historical legacy of de-industrialisation, economic decline and de-politicisation. The significance of violence, deprivation, marginality, as well as cultures of masculinity, were all identified within the existing literature that was reviewed in Chapter 2 as important for understanding the reasons behind male violence. Yet, very few theorists have attempted to weave these various factors together into an integrated approach, while simultaneously, anchoring this approach within an analysis of in-depth empirical data. Of course, tying together these various experiences and conditions is a complex task, but one which I will attend to in this chapter. Importantly, I posit here my ontological position on the nature of marginalised masculine subjectivities through utilising a fusion of theoretical and conceptual ideas drawn from theoretical psychoanalysis, continental philosophy, gender studies, and critical criminological/ sociological theory.

Within criminology today, and for much of the discipline's history, the dominant liberal canon around the ontology of the human subject oscillates between two positions. On the one hand, a rather crude reductionist interpretation of the 'I' in Descartes' cogito – the rational, self-interested individual that emerged from early modern Utilitarian philosophy; and, on the other, a human subject determined by socially constructed symbolic systems of meaning, culture, language and constitutive discursive frameworks that has its roots in the 1960s cultural/linguistic turn within academia (see Winlow and Hall, 2013). Importantly, these dominant ontologies do not map neatly onto the data I have presented in previous chapters pertaining to the lives and experiences of this group of men, and men like them. My ontological position on subjectivisation is influenced by an incipient theoretical framework that is predicated upon an acknowledgement that subjectivity is formulated in the process of emerging out of a pre-social state into a symbolic order, or a state of culture: that of transcendental materialism (see Hall, 2012a, 2012b; Johnston and Malabou, 2013; Winlow and Hall, 2013).

A key ontological point here is that the human subject begins life in a pre-maturational pre-social state, confronted with the terrifying void of its material existence: base corporeality, conflicting drives and emotions, while being in a state of utter dependency and helplessness. The process of subjectivisation, of transcending this terrifying void of early biological material being into de-materialised forms of subjectivity, is an inevitable and unavoidable process. Humans crave insertion into an effective symbolic order to counter this chaos and the overwhelming anxiety it produces. This is the point when the human subject can formulate relationships with others, construct identity, and make sense of its experience of the material and social world. Once in this state however, we are not suddenly divorced from our early lives, our 'feelings' or emotions; rather, we remain 'anxious human subject(s) shot through with tense, conflictive emotions and desires' (Hall, 2012a, p. 192) and our experience of these is mediated by the hegemonic socio-economic cultural contexts of our lives (see Hall, 2012a).

An acknowledgement of these important and fundamental ontological points is not incompatible with the evident fact that humans are capable of making decisions and that our uniqueness as a species lies in our ability to harness language and to construct quite complex and sophisticated systems of meaning that are capable of shaping interaction and our behaviour. Crude forms of biological determinism, first promulgated by the Italian Positivist School and that were discussed briefly in Chapter 2, were rightly abandoned. I am not positing here a deterministic argument and position. What is important, however, in the transcendental materialist conception of human subjectivity, is that our ability to transcend our basic corporeal materiality is the only determinism we, as social scientists, have to accept. Importantly, for transcendental materialism, human neurological constitution is not determined, but rather it is potentially flexible, plastic and malleable at the material level in accordance with the socio-economic and cultural conditions in which it is situated. And contrary to much conventional criminological thinking, it is the order of symbols that organises the socio-economic and cultural realm that is liable to become rigid and fixed, even those who claim 'plurality' and 'diversity' because they accept the same underlying socio-economic model of consumer capitalism and its associated symbolism (see Hall, 2012a, 2012b; Winlow and Hall, 2013).

This is the ontological foundation for the critical psychosocial perspective that I will now develop in this chapter. What I provide here is an analysis of masculine subjectivities that are formulated in micro contexts of occasional brutality, marginality, hyper-competitive masculine cultures and advanced capitalist cultural hegemony.

Violent trauma

How are we to use this framework to make sense of some of the horrific violence and the forms of masculine subjectivity that have been described in the previous pages of this book? As has been effectively established, violence, of varying degrees of seriousness, has been recurrently encountered throughout the lives of the men described in this book and has remained a genuine possibility. But why is this? Why are these men willing, in certain situations, to harm others? And willing to risk serious harm to themselves in the process? These are important questions that I will explore here. To begin to provide detailed and convincing answers to these questions though, we must begin with the concept of violent traumatic experience and its potential consequences in terms of masculine identity and engagement in violence.

Before continuing, I want to offer a brief pre-emptive defence of this analysis. I am not positing here an analysis that suggests victimisation *causes* an individual to become violent and to victimise others; nor that victimisation precludes perpetration. Neither am I attempting to somehow justify men's violence through drawing attention to their personal experiences of victimisation. It is important to bear in mind the benefits of adopting a 'victimised' identity for some men who will use it to justify certain behaviours (Gadd, 2004; Hearn, 1998).

As the previous chapters indicated, these men certainly do not fit into the narrow mould of 'ideal' and 'co-operative' victims that lie at the heart of victim reform agendas (see Hall, 2010). Nevertheless, it is inescapable that these men are both harmful and harmed, and we must address analytically this complexity. Criminology has tended to think in a restrictive dualism that separates *offender* from *victim* and sees them as distinct from one another, perpetuating 'the myths surrounding criminality in general and the victimization of men in particular' (McGarry and Walklate, 2011, p. 913). Criminology, if it is to better understand the lives of those men who inflict serious harms upon others, must first accept that the typological categories of 'offender', 'perpetrator', 'victim', that it obsessively attempts to impose upon what are incredibly chaotic and complex lives, actually make little sense when we attempt to apply them to the lives of the men, and other similar men, who feature in this book. Their lives do not fit neatly into such categories and, as I intimated in the previous chapter, even when these men do commit violence against others they rarely see their actions through such a simplistic lens of being 'the perpetrator'. Fundamentally, a complex paradox lies at the core of the lives of the men involved in this study: they are potentially *dangerous* and simultaneously *vulnerable*. This potential dangerousness and vulnerability arises in relation to other men who are similar to them. Like particles caught in a raging vortex they circulate and collide with other men. Collisions that often result in pointless confrontations over meagre and largely worthless cultural resources and capital that are fairly insignificant in a material and broader political sense (see Hall, 2002).

Trauma represents an unfathomable and terrifying rupturing force that is experienced as profoundly emotionally disturbing. Traumatic encounters leave individuals with a profound sense of loss, disturbance, inarticulacy and betrayal that may linger for a considerable, potentially infinite, period of time. For Freud (1961), trauma represents a source of external stimuli that ruptures the protective barriers of the brain. Working from Freud's conception of trauma, Zizek (2006, p. 73) elaborates:

> [trauma] Intrudes into our psychic life and disturbs its balance, throwing out of joint the symbolic coordinates that organise our experience . . . the problem is how to symbolise the trauma, how to integrate it into our universe of meaning and cancel its disorienting impact.

Zizek's discussion is helpful here, as it raises several important issues in relation to traumatic experience and its consequences for the formation of the kinds of masculine identities described in previous chapters. The 'disturbing of balance', which Zizek alludes to, highlights the potential for traumatic events to change the subject's internal experience and to alter subjectivity. In relation to this, Zizek hints at the subject's attempts to try to deal with the destructive trauma – to essentially *accept* its presence within their psychic life, so that they might live with it and temper its disturbing, disorienting impact. In more specific and focused terms with reference to the men discussed here, how has traumatic experience with violence been integrated and psychosocially addressed by them?

Zizek's discussion of trauma is located within Lacanian psychoanalysis, which theorises physical violence and abuse like that described in previous pages within the realm of the terrifying *real*. The *real* exists outside or apart from what we experience as our 'reality' and represents something that is yet to be symbolised, or which actively resists symbolisation (see Fink, 1996). This resistance is what gives the real its traumatic impact, as it is a force utterly 'other' and alien to the symbolic order that provides the meaning to our experience of the world. The symbolic order functions to smooth out encounters with the real to bring the subject into a state of culture and language in which relations, meanings and identities can be forged. For Lacan, the infant's early experiences of life are within the realm of the real; its body and behaviour is subjected to training over time to assimilate it into the rules, values, expectations and behavioural codes of the symbolic. The symbolic cancels out the primitive experience of the real, overwriting its base corporeality and nothingness with signifiers. It attempts, as much as possible, to 'smooth' out the real in order to try and repress and mitigate its traumatising impact; however, traces of the real will remain as a residuum which is always present (Fink, 1996). The real is a void: a terrifying abyss of nothingness that, when encountered, transports the subject momentarily back into a pre-social, pre-symbolic realm. Encounters with the real can be understood then as a temporary return to an infantile state and the concomitant terrifying helplessness and dependency of this period.

Such a conceptualisation is significant for helping to make sense of the experience of brutalising violence. Neurologically, when witnessing or experiencing violence, the brain is overwhelmed by the sudden on-rush of stimuli, sending it into 'overdrive' which induces primitive defensive dissociation in a drastic attempt to deny, de-realise and de-personalise the horrific event taking place (Stein, 2007). In essence, the subject suffers an annihilation of their self; a deeply profound sense of being separated from oneself as their psychic integrity is disintegrated while they are still alive (Bollas, 1995; Zizek, 2006). Despite our conscious awareness of various dangers that are present in society and that we actively take precautions to avoid, most of the time we manage to generate an illusion of sanctity that, although entirely a falsehood, is essential for day-to-day life. This is what psychoanalyst Christopher Bollas (1995) terms 'generative innocence'; the ability to imagine and believe in the innocence of others, even when we have been harmed in some way by the direct or indirect actions of others. This is something to which we can return throughout our lives to soothe and heal ourselves in difficult times. Violent traumas represent moments of overwhelming emotional intensity, when the benign, unthreatening, familiar and meaningful texture of day-to-day reality suddenly transforms into something unfamiliar, threatening, and unspeakably 'alien'; no longer providing a comprehensible, familiar, safe and nurturing constitutive space for the individual that can be comprehended meaningfully.

Bollas (1995) likens trauma to the moment in the fairy-tale 'Little Red Riding Hood' when the seemingly unthreatening 'granny', dressed in her bonnet and wrapped in a duvet, announces to the unsuspecting heroine after she comments on the large set of white teeth staring at her: 'all the better to eat you with'. Bollas describes an initial moment of sheer disbelief characteristic of traumatic experience, where the subject struggles to comprehend what is happening. His insightful discussion of trauma is interwoven with what he terms Western societies' 'structure of evil'. A constituent of which is the pretence of vulnerability disguising predatory intentions. He continues to illustrate this through the analogy of Red Riding Hood, describing the wolf's impersonation of the vulnerable, sickly granny to effectively disguise its predatory desire to eat the tale's heroine.

In Western societies, the violent serial killer is a popular manifestation of such evil. The key point here for Bollas is that serial killers often exploit and trade upon the trust they are able to establish with victims. Like the malevolent wolf in Red Riding Hood, some serial killers will often project a façade of benign vulnerability and helplessness; reaching out to the unsuspecting victim for assistance and help. When the victim obliges, trust is effectively established, allowing the killer to exploit this relationship. The cold, calculated, mechanistic manner in which trust is breached here constitutes, for Bollas, the destruction of the fundamental foundation upon which human relations are built: elemental trust (see also Hall, 2012a; Hall and Wilson, 2014). Trust is so often established between humans, often without any recourse to premeditated thought, in a manner symptomatic of generative innocence. It is an inevitable and unavoidable prerequisite for human survival, without which humanity simply could not survive. As Bollas points out, this is exemplified in the relationship between the infant and its parents/carers – the human subject's first encounter with elemental trust. The infant cannot choose its carers and *has* to trust them; it has no other choice. Of course this is not done consciously, but it nevertheless must trust that its carers will look after it; sacrificing their own needs, if necessary, to meet the child's. And this 'elemental trust' extends to human relations in general. Physical violence of all kinds, particularly that which occurs from parent to child, which some of these men have experienced, is potentially so damaging, so catastrophic, and thus traumatic, because it breaches the subject's fundamental need to be able to trust others. The experience of brutal violence time-warps the victim into an infantile state, throwing identity structures out of sync and leaving in their place an obsessive identification with the act(s) committed against them. Those who face traumatic violence directly, particularly those who encounter it habitually, are left with a nagging insecure feeling that the everyday, benign, and thus *unassuming* contexts of their lives will at any moment fail to support them. This can remain a consistent and haunting presence throughout the life course.

Spectres of shame

The evidential basis for early exposure to violence, as a witness or victim, leading to the possible use of violence in later life, is particularly strong. Research on the effects of domestic violence upon male children finds increased risks of them subsequently becoming involved in physical aggression (McPhedran, 2009), as does research on the effects of witnessing violence being perpetrated by others (Gibson *et al.*, 2009). A large number of criminological studies using qualitative methods that were reviewed in Chapter 2 have also found many persistently violent men to have biographical histories characterised by abusive treatment. As Winlow (2012) points out, the early lives of persistently violent men are very often characterised by climates of insecurity. Insecurity, in this sense, arising out of profound feelings that their physical safety is under threat and which is experienced as anxiety; the kind of nagging feeling that was identified in relation to the experience of violent trauma and its effects. For the men who appear in this book, access to a sanctified cocoon free from the possibility of threats, intimidation and violence, has not been entirely possible, as their lives documented throughout the previous four chapters attest. Violence for them is not the sexy, sanitised, clinically executed mediatised spectacle that appears on TV screens; nor a distant, alien threat that exists somewhere else, beyond the realm of their immediate social space.

Of course, most Western states during the past several centuries have achieved a degree of success in monopolising the use of physical violence and in reducing its presence, particularly in public spaces (Hall, 2014; Hall and Wilson, 2014; Spierenburg, 2008). Although this previous statement bears the important caveat that this monopolisation has not achieved blanket success, as violence rates are variable by time, context and place (see Ray, 2011) with some specific geographical locales and communities bucking this broader trend (Dorling, 2004; Hall, 2007, 2014; Reiner, 2012). Further to this, for many of those who occupy the Western world, their day-to-day reality is structured by the benignity of advanced capitalism. Postmodern culture has generated a surrogate social world: a simulated, commoditised, sanitised, 'safe' unreality of consumption (see Winlow and Hall, 2013; Zizek, 2002) that attempts to create calming, unthreatening environments. From within these cocoons 'real' violence can be glimpsed, viewed, consumed, without the accompanying trauma. Advancements in technology have brought televisions and computers into the vast majority of homes in the Western world. And of course, through these media, individuals are regularly bombarded with disturbing images of physical violence and human suffering: films, media reporting and computer games, all regularly depict acts of violence, both 'real' and fictional. However, there is something wholly unreal about these images, some of which represent forms of santitised 'designer' violence (Pearson, 1995) devoid of the brutal and unspeakably 'real' quality of witnessing violence enacted before one's very eyes or upon oneself. In short, the benignity of these 'unreal' spaces and images are far removed from the physical violence the men who featured in Chapters 3 to 6 have encountered.

For Winlow (2014), however, traumatic early encounters with the real violence that can be distinguished from consumer culture's fantasy violence stultify the young male, who possesses limited means to adequately express and articulate the truly horrific and unspeakable nature of these experiences. In the formative years these men occasionally found themselves utterly defenceless against physically superior foes. The acute and unbearable feelings of helplessness experienced during these moments of terrifyingly traumatic intensity are repeated at other points in the life course. The psychic disintegration that results from such brutalising experience creates unbearable feelings of displacement, in which the sense of self is disturbed by the impact of these events and alternative subjective forms can develop in their shadow (Bollas, 1995); subjective forms that despise humiliation, that ruminate on it, are fearful that it will abruptly return, and that view the 'other' as hostile, threatening and harbouring predatory intentions.

Importantly, within immediate cultures in which the presence and possibility of violence is expected and regarded as something that must be confronted with one's personal resources, the young male becomes overwhelmed by powerful cultural injunctions and narratives around what it means to be a 'man' and the role of violence within this. As we saw in Chapter 4 particularly, this cultural atmosphere is characterised by persecutory narratives and injunctions. These instruct, insist and demand that males from such communities 'toughen up' and do not 'take any shit' from anyone (see also Winlow and Hall, 2009), which for some of these men was embodied in the domineering figure of their fathers as well as other significant males, who display a deep attachment to aspects of this particular 'hardened' gendered habitus (Winlow, 2012).

What is also significant here is the ambiguity that surrounds this. Importantly, these injunctions are often delivered by significant others with benevolent intentions. Contrary to assumptions that teaching individuals to deal with violence arises from 'uncivilised', archaic, nihilistic cultures, the purpose is rather to ensure a measure of dignity can be retained in the face of it (see Winlow and Hall, 2009). The aim is not necessarily to cause harm, but to help the inexperienced young male to 'take care of himself' in order that he may recuperate some dignity from potential confrontations. Despite generating some quite unrealistic expectations of males, these are still perceived to be necessary parts of socialisation and are instilled within individuals to engender resilience, fortitude, stoicism, as well as the confidence and courage to defend and look after oneself in the face of threats. Unfortunately, brutal physical abuse meted out at the hands of parents, carers and significant others is often justified by them as necessary to instil toughness via recourse to these gendered narratives. Those subjected to such abuse, too weak to defend themselves or escape, often eventually internalise, accept and reiterate these justifications or assume a sense of personal responsibility and even guilt for their victimisation, as if they had done something wrong to warrant their 'deserved' abuse for not emulating the standards and expectations demanded of them (Stein, 2007; Winlow, 2014).

There is a sense of isolation and individualisation that seems to have characterised these men's early relationships with violence and their attempts to psychologically deal with its presence in their lives. Their narratives often indicated intense and prolonged musings over specific events (stretching into the present time in some cases) as their psyches attempted to address long-held resultant traumas. The language and symbolic systems of meaning available to these men and with which they could make sense of their experiences with the unspeakable *real* of violence were narrow, rigid, and framed in terms which invoke a sense of personal responsibility to defend oneself and to respond to threats *adequately*. Significantly these were experienced psychosocially as incredibly shameful and humiliating; experiences compounded when parents and significant others utter the cliché '*they'll only do it again if you don't stand up for yourself*', that warns of the persistence and return of humiliation if action is not taken.

Violent traumatic experience formulates part of the roots of the humiliation and shame that were both repressed and acknowledged in the data presented in previous chapters. Although there is debate over exact definitions, shame is generally taken to represent a horrifying feeling of lack and inadequacy in relation to others, experienced when one's identity is under threat and no longer felt to be one's own (Jones, 2008). Gilligan (2000) conceptualises shame as a sense of dread at the possible cessation of social bonds and resultant personal isolation. It has its roots in experiences of infancy, when the child becomes aware of its parents/carers' disapproval at behaviour that is socially unacceptable. Feelings of shame are primitive and experienced as a horrific fear of being abandoned, rejected and un-loved, which would inevitably result in one's death due to an inability to effectively care and fend for oneself (Gilligan, 2000). Katz (1988) conceptualises humiliation slightly differently to shame, as a profound and incomprehensible loss of control over one's identity, generating feelings of isolation that fill the entire body and seem, momentarily, to be unending. Humiliation is experienced psychosomatically as an intense burning sensation in the stomach, which rapidly spreads throughout the body, animating it and making it feel uncomfortably 'alive' (Katz, 1988). Rage and anger often accompany the experience of these social emotions, because the purpose of rage is to destroy: to destroy the source of one's internal pain and discomfort.

These perspectives imply a position of control over a fairly stable identity that becomes threatened and against which violence is used in an attempt to regain control (see also Wieviorka, 2009). However, in the midst of an assault from a physically superior body there is no escape, so there is no control in the first place to be established and then subsequently threatened (see Hall, 2014; Hall and Wilson, 2014). During these terrifying moments the abused is at the total mercy and whim of this sudden and horrifically inexplicable incarnation of the *real*. The experiences of humiliation described in previous pages are the resonances of being dominated, of having an 'other' evacuate your identity while you are still alive and too weak to put up a defence in broader contexts that valorise the ability to defend oneself. Humiliation then, in this context, is the response to primitive feelings of never having had control and the absolute terror that the unfolding interaction will transport the individual back to those moments.

Winlow (2012, 2014) has identified similar attempts by men to address what are highly traumatic and humiliating experiences, which are often psychically 'smoothed out' (see Fink, 1996) in narcissistic self-narratives that are suggestive of subjective change, transformation and 'becoming'. These conventions were very much present in the life narratives described in previous chapters. Many of the men fixated, during conversations and interviews, upon particularly horrific, yet highly memorable, experiences during their formative years, usually those that involved being dominated by a more powerful, physically superior individual(s). Tremendous significance was attached to these more conscious aspects of traumatic memories, which seemed to represent epiphanies within the life course (see discussion by Goodey, 2000). Importantly these narratives emphasised their stoicism, fortitude and courage in the face of danger, but also attempted to perform the function of glossing over memories of such experiences that were far too painful and humiliating to vocalise. Although some of the men attempted on occasions to use their past experiences of being victimised as reasons for their own use of violence, their understandings and discussions of previous victimisations and traumatic experiences were far more complex than a simple 'blaming exercise'.

There is a sense of diminished inhibition and transformation following victimisation and also perpetration. Once you have experienced violence and been dominated you know what to expect. Although this experience is without doubt a painful one, violence is no longer purely unknown, uncertain, or so alien anymore. Once you have been through it and come through it still alive and relatively intact, physically at least, the possibility of going through it again is no longer filled with the trepidation and fear that was felt before. This is suggestive of something more complex than violent victimisation equalling simply an emasculating experience (see Stanko and Hobdell, 1994).

We must acknowledge and give sufficient analytical attention to the significance these men attach to being able to react appropriately to what become understood symbolically as inevitable and unavoidable threats that constantly attempt to 'test' and expose within them that which is culturally designated as weakness. The valorised quality of 'hardness', the 'hard' body, implies resistance to external forces that attempt to act upon and breach it (Ahmed, 2004). It encapsulates the ability to withstand pain and the mental capacity to face and accept this stoically (Jefferson, 1998). What is significant then is how you take the beating, what you take from it, and what you then do afterwards. This appears to be of utmost importance to these men who attempt to retain those aspects of experience as a symbolic 'badge of honour'; horrific rites of passage that when undertaken stoically imbue a sense of dignity and narcissistic self-righteous entitlement. Experiencing violence, particularly from a young age as discussed in Chapter 4, was described in painful, yet nevertheless somewhat beneficial terms, as it helped to reinforce to them something akin to a 'hidden truth' (Winlow, 2012): that the everyday world is dangerous, competitive, populated by ruthless individuals that you must be ready and willing to deal with, violently if necessary. Being able to '*handle*' and '*look after*' yourself was then a vital constituent of the masculine identities they sought to project and a strategy to deal psychologically with traumatic memories. And of course, lying just under the surface of these stoic tales were those harder to acknowledge, or unacknowledgeable, memories and experiences, particularly those involving physical domination and capitulation at the hands of others.

The specific cultures I have described and from which the men in this book have emerged have developed in tandem with transformations in political economy throughout history. These 'visceral cultures' (Hall, 1997) that characterised industrial working-class life emerged as a necessary suite of rigid psychosomatic attributes and dispositions – a durable habitus – that enabled members of the working class to cope with and respond to brutalising labour conditions and circumstances. And although the industrial workplaces where much of this, particularly masculine, culture was generated, enacted and reproduced have now largely disappeared, elements of this culture remain in contemporary forms of socialisation. This specific culture had historically served an economic purpose to further industrial capitalism's military and heavy-productive ends, but was largely discarded towards the end of the twentieth century during de-industrialisation and the expansion of the financial, informational and consumer-service economies. As we have seen, within these micro cultures a certain degree of acceptability is afforded to exposing the young male to violence and to his use of it against others.

Such micro cultures are situated in broader hegemonic contexts in which the equation of masculinity with the use of physical force is ubiquitous. Within Western culture, violence is a behavioural response that is available and, to a degree, acceptable for men in ways that it is not for women (Ellis *et al.*, 2013; Jones, 2008). Some scholars have, correctly, identified the emasculating and shameful consequences that are present in male cultures of displaying weakness or being identified by others as weak (Kaufman, 1994; Kimmel, 1994). They have also identified the pure hatred and rejection of anything that approximates 'feminine' that define some particularly rigid masculine cultures (Carrington *et al.*, 2010; Connell, 2005a; Edwards, 2006; Jones, 2008). Suffering defeat and capitulating to another's superior strength is without doubt ignominious, partly because of the unrealistic and thus harmful demands of such cultures (Jefferson, 1994; Kimmel, 1994).

As I have already alluded to, this represents a form of gendered socialisation that in some marginalised communities manifests in an acutely pragmatic way of being that is deemed *necessary* and of genuine practical utility in order to prepare these males for what is a perceived life of extreme interpersonal competitiveness (see Winlow, 2012). The value placed on the ability to compete with others, which I have begun to outline and will discuss in more detail later, is not a form of subjectivity confined solely to marginalised spaces and locales, although in such spaces it appears in more physical and visceral forms. Interpersonal competition, which manifests in varying degrees of intensity by social context, lies at the fundamental core of capitalism's socio-economic system. Importantly though, violence as a resource for engaging in the system's disavowed dominant norm (Hall, 2012a) is dimorphic and split along class-based lines between forms of symbolic and physical violence (Hall, 2000). As Johnston and Malabou (2013) argue persuasively, the human brain and its neurological system are defined by plasticity. Although the body's neurological constitution is highly receptive to first experiences during early life, the connections formed during this period are potentially pliable and flexible in accordance with the kind of life we are leading and through continuing experience. Frequent exposure to immediate environments characteristic of the kinds of grinding insecurity, threat, persecution and potential humiliation discussed so far, are liable to produce subjectivities neurologically primed to detect and respond to perceived *threats* to the self. As emerged from the data in previous chapters, how such *threats* are identified is complex and bound up within an amalgam of subjective experience, situational context and social conditions.

What the fuck are you looking at?

For Lacan, the early process of subjectivisation is contingent upon the subject submitting to the symbolic, allowing themselves to harness language and be represented through language. What this entails is the surrendering of the proto-self, but being given something in return, something that becomes one's own (Fink, 1996). Winlow's (2012) description of violent subjectivity identifies such a process, in which the child exposed to violence finally overcomes their early fixation with it and grasps that which was possessed by the other and incorporates it into the 'self'. This was often expressed verbally in the early fascination with the awesome prowess of significant individuals who wield violence and aggression competently. Later this became a process of 'self-becoming' and 'transformation' during which what was initially an unfathomable, alien, awesomely terrifying force possessed and wielded by the other, eventually becomes something 'for one's own'; the point at which they tried violence for themselves (Winlow, 2012). And as these men's testimonies demonstrate, this experience was highly memorable; expressed as an epiphany and revelatory in nature.

The data gathered from participants suggests that actual past events themselves may not be remembered directly or in their full actuality during confrontational moments believed to be threatening to the self. Rather, fragments of emotions are experienced as *concrete universals* (see Zizek, 2008a) – Hegel's link between the individual's emotional experience in early life and the subsequent recognition of their identification with a broader universal culture in later life. Primary identification and experience during early lives that are characterised by occasional brutalisation, humiliation and intense competition, becomes recognised in the whole culture and is believed to be representative of it, and therefore a *concrete* truth. So in particular situational contexts that are construed as 'threatening', these past traumatic events are recalled and experienced as an overwhelming and incomprehensible sense of dread. As outlined in previous chapters, this was often expressed by the men during interviews in statements like '*I just lost it*' or '*I couldn't cope with it*', which is the typical language used to explain feelings at the point of executing violence. The ethnographic material reveals the spontaneity and rapidity with which some of these men will become aggressive and violent in particular situations and contexts. Such reactions do not require recourse to premeditative thought or conscious decision-making, but are immediate. This may appear reductive and somewhat deterministic, but the data indicates strongly that in quite specific circumstances some men's destructive violent behaviour is not the product of rational thought, choice or agency. Rather, it seems language, thought and reflection are bypassed in some circumstances in favour of immediate action, of *acting out* dissociated rage that cannot be effectively articulated (Hall, 2012a, 2014).

Socially, physical confrontation is experienced and often expressed as a 'buzz', a brief moment in which all meaning seems to disappear (Willis, 1990). Driven by fear and adrenaline as it courses through the subject's veins impelling them to act, reality appears suspended as the individuals lose themselves momentarily.

Data presented in previous chapters attests to this feeling of losing control of one's body and being directed for a brief moment by a pure reckless force, which enabled them to impose physical dominance and superiority over opponents. The young men encountered in Bourgois *et al.*'s (2012) research described similar experiences in terms of a 'black out' that overcame them during physical confrontations. Bourgois *et al.*, found that these men valued this loss of control as part of the 'rage habitus', which operates both consciously and pre-consciously as a hyper-vigilant defence mechanism.

This feeling of '*losing it*', of '*seeing red*', and their equivalent colloquial expressions to communicate the feeling of becoming lost in the force of one's rage, often arises quite rapidly and in relation to some external cue. The rapidity of such aggressive reactions, even during what may appear to be fairly innocuous social encounters, suggests that vague feelings associated with past traumatic, humiliating experiences lodged in the memory, resurface in moments of perceived threat, recurrently haunting everyday social experience (Winlow and Hall, 2009). Winlow's (2014) recent work is helpful here, as he suggests that guilt and shame arising from abusive experiences, particularly in childhood, operate unconsciously as 'misfelt' feelings. These feelings manifest psychosomatically in edginess, oversensitivity to threats and an unwavering desire to challenge those deemed threatening in order to avoid experiencing shame. The participants' over-identification with horrific personal experiences as concrete universals – representations of a universally cold, ultra-competitive, asocial culture – and the vague persecutory feelings these arouse, generate for them a sense of existing within a determinative subjective structure that is bound closely to these experiences (Bollas, 1995). For Bollas (1995), much of this operates unconsciously, but can become vaguely conscious to individuals through an uncanny sense of being driven and determined by such experience and the potential for this to shape their future. In previous chapters, the men discussed displayed a vague awareness of having a particular fate, which revolved around the genuine possibility that violence would be required at some point in the future.

They knew violence was 'bad', some even had a grasp of its utter futility in broader economic and political senses, as well as the dangers that they exposed themselves to in using it. Yet, this often conflicted with their intensely overwhelming desire to not be dominated, to avoid humiliating experiences and ensure their sense of dignity was retained; so violence could always be justified. And when faced with circumstances that threatened the latter, their responses were often to engage in aggression and never to 'walk away'. The intense wariness and oversensitivity identified by Winlow (2014) in relation to this can be detected in forms of non-verbal communication and interaction with others. The unconscious is highly receptive to the non-verbal communication issued by others through what Bollas (1995) calls a 'separate sense' that is attuned to engaging in sensitive contact with others. In the case of men willing to use violence, sustained eye contact, particular facial expressions, tone of voice, language choice, bodily comportment and demeanour, are all understood to harbour signs of potential threat and attempts to undermine. And some of the ethnographic material provided in previous chapters of physical confrontations highlights this. These cues are interrogated closely in order to 'retaliate first' (Winlow and Hall, 2009) before the other has a chance to strike a blow.

As we saw in Chapters 5 and 6 particularly, the injunction to use violence was considered to be an absolute *must* in some circumstances: you simply *have* to, and there was often no sense of agency, choice or alternative possibility detectable within these men's narratives or in the behaviour I observed. The possibility of negotiation or avoidance in some situations was uncompromisingly rejected as a possible or even viable strategy. There was a deeply felt cynicism among them about the amorality and dangerousness of the worlds they inhabited: it is dog-eat-dog and you had better have a good appetite. And this palpable sense of threat was faced with a distinct air of fatalistic resignation.

Abby Stein (2007) elaborates further on the presence of traumatic past experiences and their impact upon subsequent interactions with others:

> During subsequent traumas, powerful emotions may come to be registered as emanating from other people, who are then perceived as causative agents of one's internal distress.
>
> (Stein, 2007, p. 118–119)

Stein's analysis of this internalised process is accurate enough in accounting for traumatic experiences that can remain lodged in the neurological circuits as raw experiences. These past experiences evade effective symbolisation and reflection, which can result in feelings of rage, even during what might appear, to an outsider, to be quite benign and seemingly unthreatening interactions and circumstances. Certainly the memories, both clearly formulated and those that remain vague and unarticulated, of past failures and inactions in relation to confrontations, are present in such moments and serve as a background static that recurrently haunts experience (Winlow and Hall, 2009). However, the broader context that envelops this process and that shapes forms of marginalised masculine subjectivity that exist constantly in the shadow of a difficult past is somewhat under-developed by Stein.

This raises several pertinent questions: who are these 'other people' (as found in this research mostly other men of similar socio-economic background) that seemingly invoke 'tension' that results in aggression? And what is it about 'them', these 'others', which generates these kinds of unbearable feelings and emotions? Further to this, and related to these previous points, this internalised process within Stein's analysis remains rooted in the familial context: internal turmoil and damaged intimate relations from brutal upbringings. Of course, Stein's research as well as evidence from others (see Gadd, 2000; Gadd and Jefferson, 2007; Gadd *et al.*, 2013; Jones, 2008, 2012) is convincing enough of the potentially disastrous consequences of traumatic insecure childhoods and damaged intimate relationships. But analyses of male violence such as these remain rooted within that microcosmic realm of the family and are not analysed in dialectical relation to socio-spatial contexts nor the hegemonic context of macro socio-economic relations.

'When the going gets tough' ... toughen up

As Hall (2012a) explains, the characteristics of the familial context and the intimate relations forged within it are not divorced from broader socio-economic and hegemonic-cultural conditions. Familial life and relationships do not exist within a vacuum. Put simply, parents attempt to *prepare* their children based on their own experiences and with one eye cast on 'life out there' beyond the familial home. Eventually individual men venture out of the micro context of the family, equipped with the ideological and neurological preparation their parents/carers and significant others have bestowed upon them (Hall, 2012a). And as we saw in earlier chapters, with this group of men and those similar to them, it is a preparation based upon a *concrete* belief that they will have to negotiate relations of extreme competitiveness. Such sentiments are anchored in an almost paranoid obsession with being able and prepared to defend oneself. Immense significance is attached to these men's abilities to react appropriately to those who they perceive are attempting to unduly dominate, which is partially rooted in their childhood experiences and parents' (often fathers') own anxieties and paranoia concerning the *adequate* preparation of their sons for entrance into such environments. In working-class communities there remains a place for the tough, stoical, no-nonsense male, who is willing to wield violence when necessary, retaining some cultural clout and a degree of respect for this.

The men who discussed relationships they now share with their own sons and nephews in Chapter 6 also displayed an acute sense of fear and foreboding concerning such adequate preparation and socialisation. There was a great deal of anxiety and uncertainty upon recognising their inability as father figures to completely protect children, and this was accompanied by a somewhat muted and grudging acceptance that their sons must inevitably be prepared to 'look after themselves'. Yet, given these men's own violence against others, what constitutes 'looking after yourself' is fraught with ambiguity. There is a strong sense from these men that everyday social life is negotiated under the oppressive weight of competitive, potentially hostile relations, in which trust should be invested cautiously. Violent potential and its supposed utility for addressing social conditions that are perceived as threatening and deleterious, is often handed down through a durable and specifically masculine socio-cultural inheritance.

These men have grown up in a context where growth, expansion, economic gain, competitiveness, individualism and personal entrepreneurship, have been embraced wholeheartedly, becoming 'the dominant organising principle of social life' (Currie, 1997, pp. 151–152). The hegemony that has been achieved by neo-liberal ideology across the political, economic and cultural spheres of the West, benefited from its well-timed dovetailing with increasingly postmodern cultural currents. As well as becoming the driving force behind political and economic change, neo-liberalism fused with a nascent postmodern cultural movement that had at its core a desire for greater individual freedom and self-expression (Harvey, 2005). Hobbs (2012) describes the inherent aggression within this broad process of trans-formation and change:

the end of industrial society signalled the gloves coming off, and predatory entrepreneurship is now the norm in a society emptied out of the flawed certainties of industrial society.

(p. 265)

These were the certainties, however flawed, of a more inclusive socio-democratic political economy that engaged a politically organised working class in conflict and collectivised struggle with the state and the market. This helped to encase interpersonal violence and sublimate aggression within an institutional symbolic framework that enabled the industrial working class 'to have a positive self-image, exploited and dominated as they may have been' (Wieviorka, 2009, p. 13).

In a socio-economic context devoid of those former certainties, where the 'gloves are off', physicality makes sense to some men socialised to recognise the physical side of violence's dimorphic nature (Hall, 2000) as a means to compete and to recuperate respect and dignity. These men 'bulk up', quite literally, specific cultural and bodily capital that will assist in the inevitable competitive struggles that take place with 'others' in more atomised and divided circumstances. The men who feature in this book have all invested, albeit to varying degrees, in an image of potential volatility and dangerousness within what have rapidly become depoliticised, competitive and more atomised working-class communities. Cultivating such an image is a direct response to the sense of mistrust and fear that abounds in contexts of marginality and rampant individualism (see Hall *et al.*, 2008; Hall and Wilson, 2014). Fortified bodies of intimidating physicality, bodily scars and the stoic tales of how they were attained, exaggerated swaggers, aggressive gesticulating, as well as clothing associated with extreme sports, militarism and physicality (see Treadwell, 2008), combined with occasional uncompromising displays of raw physical power. These men have made best use of the resources available to them to fortify themselves: their bodies, resource networks and alliances with other men, and personal reputations for being prepared to fight and to go further than other men will.

Preparation for an increasingly competitive socio-economic life is not unique to this social group though, as I alluded to earlier. What is significant contemporarily is the increased emphasis now being placed upon the ability of all humans in advanced Western societies to compete with others and ensure they are capable of looking after themselves. Importantly then, such a 'preparation' that involves psychosomatic 'toughening up' for an increasingly individualistic and competitive social life, is only different in degree, not in kind, to the 'toughening up' bestowed upon more privileged socio-economic groups; core preparation that is undertaken to equip individuals for the dominant cultural norm of liberal capitalist Western societies (Hall and Wilson, 2014). Their competition with others is conducted symbolically with a form of valued social capital that displays only physical pacification, and which occurs upon a gladiatorial battlefield where education, employment, personal connections and material success are the weapons of choice, rather than the physical violence described in previous chapters involving fists, knives and firearms. This dimorphic nature of violence (Hall, 2000) is split along class lines with the men described in this book and others like them, in receipt of the physical and mental qualities that constitute the tragically unreflexive visceral cultures that remain in the discarded zones of contemporary society; a form of being that historically buffered this group from the brutalising enforced conditions of heavy labour and that possessed some political bargaining power. Ultimately, what ties together all of these various manifestations of interpersonal competition is the institutionalised envy that is now ubiquitous throughout advanced consumer capitalism and the various consumer 'markets' it has generated (Briggs, 2013; Hall, 2012a, 2012b; Hall *et al.*, 2008; Hayward, 2004; Smith, 2013; Winlow and Hall, 2006).

The history and development of modern capitalism in the West must be understood then as an insistent force that perpetually generates conditions of interpersonal competitiveness and the threat of socio-economic insignificance and the concomitant shame of this, as the vital energy sources required to ensure its continuation (Hall, 2012a). Such conditions were historically enforced in economic pressures and law, but have become internalised and reproduced within and by individuals as they respond to the hegemonic positioning of this logic (Hall, 2014). And with the post-war dismantlement of the socio-democratic state to pave the way for minimalist intervention and regulation in economic affairs, we are now witnessing this logic emerging full blown in the ideological apparatus of neo-liberal capitalism and its diffusion into post-modern culture (Harvey, 2005). The shamed 'loser' in this increasingly competitive atmosphere is an invention of modernity (Sloterdijk, 2010). The losers are juxtaposed to neo-liberal capitalism's more visible 'winners': the various self-made entrepreneurs, plutocrats, oligarchs and 'celebrities' that constitute contemporary capitalism's elite and whose material success and 'special liberty' (Hall, 2012a; Winlow and Hall, 2013) is heralded as evidence of the system's supposedly fluid and ascendable meritocratic hierarchy.

Late modernity's 'losers' are those who have slipped into the terrifying abyss cultivated in parallel to neo-liberal consumer capitalism's manufactured reality of lifestyle imagery, symbols and fantasies (Zizek, 2002); those who find themselves being mocked and vilified for lacking the competence, personal finesse and self-respect required to distinguish themselves from the 'herd' (Briggs, 2013; Hall *et al.*, 2008; Hayward and Yar, 2006). It was made abundantly clear to me by the men I encountered, that their immediate spatial environments are awash with such losers, who became approximations of threatening and dangerous individual 'others' – 'bullies', 'nob heads', 'shit bags', 'scum bags', 'cunts', 'piss takers', 'divvies', 'wannabe gangsters'. This construction of the 'other' featured strongly in these men's accounts of their own identities and their violence, which is situated in a broader context of the gradual demise and fracturing of the working class, its traditional forms of employment, institutions, political affiliations and activism, resulting in a divided largely de-politicised collective.

The few scholars still willing to engage theoretically with the concept of 'the working class', and the even fewer scholars willing to conduct qualitative research among this fractured social group, have documented the suspicions and hatred that have begun to emanate from this growing divide (Anderson, 1999; Briggs, 2013;

Hall *et al.*, 2008; Hall, 2012a; Jones, 2011; Shildrick and MacDonald, 2013; Treadwell and Garland, 2011). Rather than recognising a mutual history, common identity, oppression, and a potential for political unity, members of the former industrial working class are more likely to increasingly regard each other as hostile, threatening and dangerous nomadic others to be out-competed and avoided; in particular, the 'undeserving', undesirable sections of the working class that are considered a drain on public resources (Jones, 2011; Shildrick and MacDonald, 2013) and whose consumption choices are mocked and vilified (Briggs, 2013; Hall *et al.*, 2008; Hayward and Yar, 2006).

Given all the talk of dangerous, threatening amoral 'others' though, certainly begs the question of who exactly these 'others' actually are. Should we assume they are simply paranoid delusions, merely products of these men's imaginations? Or are there genuinely a group of dangerous predatory 'others' who exist outside of the morally-rounded, respectful majority, intent on wreaking harm upon everyone else to their own benefit? Who therefore must be fought and dealt with without any hesitation or remorse? The reality I think it is fair to suspect, is actually much less 'Hollywood' than this, and is likely to be that the various 'others' to which these men refer are merely their own mirror opposites: equally fearful, insecure, victimised, marginalised men, attempting to negotiate the wreckage of the post-industrial landscape with the few resources at their disposal. And who, like them, have found violence to be a resource that still carries some potential cultural clout and currency.

The enemies within

It is entirely possible, and desirable, to formulate some analytical linkages between the micro and macro contexts that have been discussed so far in this chapter. Within micro moments of extreme pressure, when echoes of unadulterated anxiety rooted in primitive dissociative responses to trauma (Stein, 2007) awaken and begin to reverberate, the savage dissociated 'not me' comes forward in order to avoid the spectre of looming annihilation (Bollas, 1995) by doing what is 'necessary' (Hall, 2012a). In such moments the male subject is confronted with the terrifying *real* of previous violent experience, the shame and humiliation associated with this and that will engulf them if action is not taken quickly. In those brutal confrontations described in previous pages, these men imagined the potential suffering of themselves as 'losers' as far worse than witnessing the suffering of the 'other' confronting them.

Like Jekyll and Hyde, once the punches have been thrown, the brief upsurge of magmatic rage expelled, the 'not me' shrinks back into the shadows and it is as if the destruction wrought upon the 'other' was inflicted by someone else – 'not me'. As the narratives in Chapter 6 revealed, the victim is attributed with full blame and absolute agency during this dissociative manoeuvre, while the 'not me' who enforces this brutal morality is justified as a necessary evil. This brutal moral economy of male violence rests upon an asocial, narcissistic 'special liberty' (Hall, 2012a), which is informed via traumatic personal experiences that confirmed to these men that in some contexts violence is unavoidable, but nevertheless acceptable for them to use; a means to by-pass what were described in previous chapters as well-meaning, but in reality, hopelessly inadequate idealistic ethical prohibitions of the symbolic order. These are perceived as largely obsolete in a context of growing atomisation, where it is believed that only the stupidly naïve will heed them completely. Conspicuously absent here then is a firm unwavering commitment to a rigid and embodied sense of ethical values that might govern the subject's engagement with the social world (see Winlow and Hall, 2013) – instead, a vague, context-bound interpretation of morality, judged by the individual, that is no one else's concern, and that has flourished in the void left following post-political abandonment.

In a discussion of the linkages between experience and the potential flexibility of neural connections, Johnston and Malabou (2013, p. 56) suggest:

> every kind of event is integrated into the general form or pattern of the con-nections, and the series of events of our lives constitute the autobiographical self.

When one looks across some of these men's life courses, seemingly isolated events must be understood in connection to one another as a constellation of humiliations that coalesce and for these men are understood as cumulative. Some of the violence described in this book is totally excessive, unjustified and unjustifiable. One must acknowledge however, the various personal and socio-cultural conditions discussed here that form the roots of these men's feelings of paranoia, cynicism and fatalism, as well as hyper vigilance and an anxious obsession with self-defence and preservation. Such repeated humiliating experiences across already margin-alised life courses reinforce and connect with earlier traumas and their humiliating consequences, in such a way that reinforces and exacerbates subjective feelings of being repeatedly down-trodden, dominated, and to quote one of the participants 'walked all over' by others. This fuels the subjective sense of being constantly victimised, under threat, and the accompanying absolutist and narcissistic self-righteous 'not me' when violence is then inflicted upon others, what Hall (2012a) describes as a 'shadow-world of perception and motivation . . . etched into the brain and the neurological system' (p. 197) is this subjective realm that is brutally carved open by violent traumatic experience. Here, anxious insecurities, memories, images of threat, and fantasies of a powerful, respected, narcissistic idealised self, abound. And so it goes for these men:

> these injustices are not forgotten. They are accumulated, the wrongs are registered, the tension grows more and more unbearable, till divine violence explodes in a retaliatory destructive rage.
>
> (Zizek, 2008b, p. 152)

Men regularly involved in violence represent the marginalised and criminalised 'othered' men, who fight, maim and kill men of similar socio-economic lineage, who they see as the true 'enemy'. As discussed, this 'enemy' must be out-fought in what are seemingly 'all or nothing' battles, during which the sense of self-dignity and respect that they cling to so desperately, seemingly stands on the brink of evaporation into utter insignificance; lost forever, never to be regained unless fought for immediately and ruthlessly. These 'epic' confrontations in the West's marginalised and politically abandoned communities are minute struggles to retain self-dignity, respect, recognition, reputation, and avoid humiliation; but hugely momentous for those involved.

Such violence is of little actual concern for the elite, who regard it as merely the work of a minority of pathological, amoral individuals who do not share or abide by the values of liberal culture that have emerged from the hallowed economic and political arrangements of late modernity. The men I have worked with and whose stories appear in this book, are simply examples of yet more 'little evils' to be policed, controlled and punished – a small price to pay for our new found 'freedoms' (Hall *et al.*, 2008; Hall, 2012a). These threats to law and order are swiftly mopped up by the state, which contemporarily has little actual incentive or desire to expunge the required resources needed to rehabilitate the competitive, unequal socio-economic and post-political context in which violent criminality has been able to fester and burgeon in marginalised spaces and communities (see Currie, 1997; Dorling, 2004; Hall, 2012a, 2014; Ray, 2011; Reiner, 2012; Wilkinson and Pickett, 2010).

Of course, as was discussed in Chapter 1, violent crime has gradually declined over centuries and we have witnessed in recent years an apparent fall in overall rates of recorded criminality. However, this book and other research has documented the persistence of hyper-violent sub-cultures among specific groups of men, which are consistently found in and around the interstices of less dangerous spaces and groups that embody more 'passive' ways of being. Suggestions that such trends should be taken to infer a move towards more harmonious and peaceful social relations should be regarded with extreme caution and scepticism, particularly given the West's current politico–economic situation. As Zizek (2008b) explains to us, the material comforts, affluence and security that many citizens of Western liberal democracies continue to pursue day-to-day in the post-crash context is enabled by 'violence': military force, economic power, and the systematic exploitation and expulsion of relatively weak and powerless groups (see also Winlow and Hall, 2013). This is 'violence' that ensures the efficient operation of the West's political and economic systems, creating the sense of *order* and *calm* that is perturbed by outbursts of individualised physical aggression described in previous pages. The inherent aggression in the social transformations witnessed over the past several decades suggests that in the late modern post-political context, rage is always liable to *return* (Sloterdijk, 2010), and is not something that is being gradually extinguished and removed from everyday social and political life.

At the very moment when the Western world was approaching a situation of potentially greater inclusivity and equality, this was quite swiftly and uncompromisingly obliterated (Young, 1999). The solidarity project that emerged during the middle decades of the twentieth century, ultimately served an instrumental economic purpose. When it became powerful enough to threaten economic growth and productivity, it was branded expensive, and an unnecessary set of apparatus that was strategically severed to pave the way for lightly regulated free market capitalism. Rather than a gradual civilising process (Elias, 2000) in the post-crash context there exists, more accurately, a form of *pseudo-pacification* (Hall, 2007, 2012a).

> in the age of globalized flexible accumulation and competition between permanently uprooted individuals, this complex and expensive infrastructure is no longer a vitally necessary element of economic development, and therefore no longer a prudent investment beyond the retention of a minimal requirement of public order.
>
> (Hall, 2007, p. 98)

Why *some* men are physically violent is the central question that this book has sought to address. The pseudo pacification of Western populations since the middle ages has involved the gradual reduction of serious, physically injurious forms of personal violence, but not the elimination of aggression from socio-economic life. Aggressive competition remains in symbolic forms, harnessed to service the system's need to 'get things done' and do what is 'necessary' (Hall, 2012a). The minorities of men who continue to appreciate the personal ability to use physical violence, and its utility for 'getting things done', are those who have yet to embark on the journey to the other side of the dimorphic violence at the heart of this process (Hall, 2000) in a society that is, fundamentally, competitive.

Throughout, but particularly in this chapter, I have striven to emphasise the significance of a broader confluence of forces in these men's lives. To use violence then, is not just about trying to be a 'man', nor is it simply a product of growing up and living in marginalised circumstances. It is the product of a broader confluence of psychosocial experiences and forces in men's lives. Early, and ongoing, profound physical insecurity and emotional disturbance, relationships with significant others who are prepared to use violence, a palpable sense of marginality, masculine cultures and identities, and the ideological circumstances of current political economy, collectively 'congeal' in neurological and emotional constitution (Hall, 2012a, 2012b; Johnston and Malabou, 2013; Winlow and Hall, 2013) producing marginalised masculine subjectivities that display a firm commitment to psychosomatic 'toughness', 'preparation', and hyper-vigilant sensitivity as a means to compete, whether that is by keeping a pickaxe by the front door, a 'shooter' stuffed down the back of the trousers, or positioning yourself to deliver the knockout blow in an eyeballing and chest puffing contest while waiting for a taxi at 2am on a Sunday morning.

8 Rolling with the punches

It is a balmy summer afternoon; too pleasant to be inside. I am sitting outside one of the city centre bars that Vince 'looks after', making friendly conversation with him and several of his acquaintances. The conversation oscillates between everyone's holiday plans and football. Vince is sat across the table from me, stuffing a bacon sandwich into his mouth. The few patches of his pale skin not covered in tattoo ink are tinged pink with sunburn, while beads of sweat trickle down his forehead from the afternoon heat.

A man who I have never met before, a friend of Vince's, comes over to our table and shakes hands with us. He is eating a pasty that protrudes from a Gregg's bag, while taking regular swigs from a can of Coca Cola. Vince jokes with him that he cannot eat the pasty on the bar's premises. The man laughs, says his goodbyes, and then takes a seat just off the terrace with some other lads dressed in vests and shorts. Vince later tells me that the man with the pasty is a criminal from a nearby city, who now lives in the area. I overhear Vince telling one of the men present, as is often the subject-matter of his conversations, that he knocked a big lad out the other night for being cheeky. Gradually, Vince's various acquaintances leave to return to work and other pressing errands. Lewis, who has been sitting with us for around half an hour, works the doors with Vince on occasions. He is a painter and decorator by trade, but the recession has hit him hard and business is poor. He has temporarily returned to security work while the economic forecast remains bleak, and is working at a nearby law firm. We shake hands before he leaves the group to continue his shift.

The serenity of the afternoon is interrupted when Vince's phone starts ringing. He pulls the phone from his pocket, glances at the screen, and moves away from the table out of earshot to answer it. I watch him curiously. He remains on the phone for about a minute, hangs up, and immediately walks into the bar. He emerges several minutes later, walking towards me at a brisk pace and with a sense of purpose that is in stark contrast to the relaxed, laid back demeanour he had presented prior to the phone call. His body language has changed subtly and I sense that something is wrong. When he reaches the table I notice a slight grin on his face – a nervous one. He appears slightly on edge, adrenalized. He twitches slightly, as if there is something that he wants to reveal and is struggling to contain it.

'You busy now mate?' he asks.

'No, why?' I reply.

'I've got some bollocks I need to sort out, if you fancy coming?'

His vagueness and sudden change in demeanour leave me feeling uncertain and I want to ask him what he means by 'bollocks'. Before I even have a chance to articulate these thoughts, I blurt out:

'Yeah I'll come with you.'

'Sound,' Vince replies.

We walk down the street towards where his car is parked and get in. Vince starts the engine and Reggae music blasts from the speakers at high volume. He winds his window down, quickly lights a cigarette, and pulls away from the pavement at speed. The car's engine roars as Vince hurtles through the city streets, paying little attention to the speed limit and the pedestrians crossing the road, some of whom are forced to leap back onto the pavement. We pull up at some traffic lights that are on red. I take the opportunity to probe Vince for more information and to try and find out what I might have let myself in for. Vince remains vague with the details:

'It was my mate Gav on the phone, his sister Kelly is having some bollocks with this bloke and he asked me to go up to where she works.'

Vince drives for several more minutes and we pull up outside a large pub on a small high street. Vince parks the car outside the pub. We get out of the car and walk across the road into a hairdresser's. A young woman is stood in the doorway and greets us:

'Hiya Vince, thanks for coming up.'

'No worries Kelly love,' he replies.

She greets me and asks who I am.

'I'm Tony love, one of Vince's mates,' I reply.

Kelly asks us if we would like a drink. Vince asks for a coffee. I ask for a tea. A young woman, who also works at the hairdresser's, heads into the kitchen at the back to make our drinks. Vince takes a seat in one of the chairs, folds one leg across the other, and listens carefully; all the while fumbling with his phone as if he desperately needs to occupy his hands. I stand slightly away from Vince, making sure I keep quiet and listen to what is being said.

Kelly: I think you know who this guy is . . . he phoned me up earlier and started threatening me. My friend has been seeing him, but he's married. And basically he's been rumbled and thinks it's me that's told his wife. So he rang me earlier and started threatening me, telling me he was going to come and fuck me up, he said he was a gangster and that I shouldn't fuck around with him. So I phoned our Gav and he said to phone you. Gav rang him and said to him he's going to put him in a box if he comes near me.

Vince: Is he from [inner city estate notorious for gang-related violence]?

Kelly: I don't know.

The young woman returns with our drinks while Kelly gives a physical description of the man in question. She reiterates to Vince that he will know him because he sometimes drinks in the bars that Vince looks after. Vince thinks for a moment:

Vince: I still don't know who you mean.

Another young woman pulls up in a car and we all go outside. Vince walks over to her car to speak to her and the young male sitting in the passenger seat. Vince obviously knows them and I can hear him laughing and joking with them. Kelly rings Gav to tell him Vince is here and that his friend [me] is with him. I stand outside the hairdresser's sipping my cup of tea while trying desperately to look the part of the hardman that Kelly must be assuming I am. Despite the jovialities between Vince, Kelly and the two individuals that have just arrived in the car, the atmosphere is quite tense. I begin to feel adrenaline slowly secreting into my bloodstream. I can feel my heart beating in my chest; I hear it in my ears. I try to use this brief moment to consider what I will do if the man in question makes good on his threat. I can run, or I can stay; it is safe to say that I do not like my options. After a few minutes Gav arrives in a very nice and expensive looking 4x4 vehicle. He jumps out and swaggers in an exaggerated fashion over to Vince. They shake hands and start talking:

Gav: I'll put that cunt in a fucking box if he comes up here; who the fuck does he think he is abusing my sister?

Vince: Have you spoke to him then?

Gav: I did yeah, he started threatening me over the phone and I told him to get up here and I would put him in a coffin. He hung up when I said that.

The group begin talking again about the identity of the man who has threatened Kelly. Kelly reiterates his physical description and both Vince and Gav debate who the culprit is. They reach a consensus on the identity of the man and the young woman who arrived slightly later in a car says she thinks she knows where this individual lives. Gav and Vince discuss the possibility of going looking for him there. Gav begins pacing up and down the pavement, clenching and then unclenching his fists. We continue to wait for several minutes, but the individual does not turn up, much to my relief. As the individual is someone who regularly drinks in one of the bars Vince looks after, Vince decides to head back there and wait for him. As we drive back into the city I ask Vince how he plans to deal with this.

> **Vince**: I'll just talk to him, ask him if he has been having bollocks with anyone and I'll see what he says.

Vince's continued vagueness leaves me feeling it is better not to ask any more questions about it; and I do not. I know that I do not need to. If the conversation ever takes place, what is considered 'necessary' will be done.

In many ways this event, which happened towards the end of the fieldwork, communicates in quite succinct terms the general experience of doing this research. This period of fieldwork began in mundane normality, which was the prelude to this event: sitting in the sun with food and drinks, engaging in simple conversation. The focus of this book has of course been upon the more extreme aspects of these men's lives and experiences. As I pointed out during Chapter 1, physical violence is not something that they engage in all of the time. And the suggestion that by simply being in the presence of these men places you in imminent physical danger is not wholly accurate. For the majority of the fieldwork there was no 'action' to watch (see Pearson, 1993) and significant proportions of my time were spent 'hanging around' engaging in conversations that were both relevant and irrelevant to my research goals.

However, one phone call as in this example, and we can extend this to one 'wrong' word, one 'wrong' facial expression, 'wrong' place, 'wrong' time, and things can change very rapidly. It was the constant, underlying possibility of threat and violence that was both a source of data and personal emotional distress. Taken together, these provided a means of unique analytical insight (see Wakeman, 2014). As has been indicated at times when presenting data throughout previous chapters, the whole process of conducting this research has not been devoid of stresses and strains upon me psychologically and emotionally. As I stated in Chapter 1, I do not possess a history of using violence against others. At times in my life though, I have witnessed violence and spent time around some dangerous and potentially volatile individuals. Apart from a few brief inconsequential physical confrontations with other males, I have always been a relatively calm and pacified individual; keen to 'keep my head down' and stay out of trouble.

Ethical debates within the social sciences have traditionally been dominated by concerns for the researcher's personal safety and managing dangers that threaten this. What has been less acknowledged are the emotional dangers faced by qualitative researchers (Blagden and Pemberton, 2010), which can, as a consequence, be largely overlooked during the course of a research project (Lee-Treweek and Linkogle, 2000); emotional dangers that can be all the more acute when the topic being studied has some relation to the researcher's own biography and personal identity (Wakeman, 2014). Through completing this research, I too was forced to confront events and aspects of my own life and identity as a male from a working-class family; something that, perhaps rather naïvely, I did not envisage or foresee at the beginning of it.

As I discussed briefly in Chapter 1, I could often relate to and empathise with some of the things these men described to me, as I had encountered them myself. Certain issues the participants talked about awoke feelings and emotions within myself that emanate from particularly difficult personal experiences – some around confrontation and violence – that I had forgotten; and in some cases tried very hard to forget. Significant family members and peers had attempted to instil in me, although not so brutally, the same injunctions that some of these men had received to 'stand up for myself' and that if someone was to hit me, I should hit them back, and harder. And the same feelings of self-loathing and humiliation that these men described in relation to past events in their own lives resonated with some of my own. I found myself at times becoming angry and resentful about those instances when I had not followed these injunctions or failed to live up to expectations. The process of returning to some of these memories brought back quite powerfully the pain that I experienced at the time of the event(s), when I too felt I had been 'walked over', dominated, and stripped of my dignity.

At times like that described earlier, I had to, as I discussed in Chapter 1, play up aspects of my own masculinity. I had to appear to be 'tough', blasé, and unphased by what was going on; while inside I was often frightened and disturbed. What happened on that glorious summer afternoon was another close call. Perhaps too close. It was in the wake of this event that I decided that I had to begin to negotiate my way out of the field. The thought of becoming embroiled in the kinds of feuds and complexities, as described, was something that I was keen to avoid.

For periods during the fieldwork, and afterwards, I had quite disturbed and poor sleep. I found it often difficult to relax and focus my thoughts upon other things unrelated to the research and participants. At times I suffered from mild paranoia, anxious that I would be subjected to police investigation or harassment, or, that during the instances of covert research I would be discovered and that there would be potentially dire consequences. Those occasions when I was placed in con-siderable danger exacerbated these difficulties. I also found myself worrying obsessively over the psychological impact my research might have upon the participants, particularly when they had revisited aspects of their lives that were obviously difficult and traumatic for them. I also regularly felt intense feelings of guilt that I was somehow taking advantage of the participants and their kind-ness towards me. Some gave up extraordinary amounts of their time in order to participate. They welcomed me into their homes and introduced me to their friends and families. Given such kindness and helpfulness it was difficult not to feel a genuine sense of affection towards some of the participants, who have benefited my academic career in ways they will probably never realise, with minimal personal gain for themselves. Their occasional kindness and openness imbued me with a tremendous feeling of personal responsibility to ensure I produced an account which accurately reflects their lives and experiences and the pressures that come with trying to achieve this. Yet simultaneously, I was on occasions appalled, angered, and continue to be, by their behaviour and their flagrant disregard for those they have harmed. On those occasions when critical reflection and empathy towards victims was in short supply, and there was a clear and demonstrable lack of regret, I did feel both disturbed and disgusted.

The closeness to participants that I achieved during the research meant that I was also exposed to the harshness and difficulties that some of them had faced and continued to face: chaotic lifestyles, strained relationships with significant others, and economic hardship. At times I could not help feeling sympathy towards some of the participants and continue to do so at times when my thoughts return to them. Since completing the research and achieving the Ph.D. that I conducted the research for, I have managed to secure stable and prestigious full-time employment for myself. I have appeared on national radio to talk about men and their relationships with violence. I have enjoyed some of the various plaudits that come with academic success. And importantly, I have been able to return to a relatively safe and secure life, while some of those men who appear in the previous pages of this book remain in precarious situations, both economically and physically. An ability to escape the drudgeries, various difficulties and potential threats that some of the inhabitants of northern England's deprived ex-industrial communities face, was absent for many of these men. It was very much a case of having to face this stoically. For an ethnographer of such individuals and places there are no easy choices either, while in the field and long after vacating it. As I discovered was the case for both them and me, it is a matter of *rolling with the punches*.

References

Ahmed, S. (2004) *The Cultural Politics of Emotion*. Edinburgh: Edinburgh University Press

Ancrum, C. (2013) Stalking the Margins of Legality: Ethnography, Participant Observation and the Post-Modern 'Underworld'. In Winlow, S. and Atkinson, R. (eds), *New Directions in Crime and Deviancy*. London: Routledge 113–126

Anderson, E. (1999) *Code of the Street: Decency, Violence and the Moral Life of the Inner City*. New York: Norton

Archer, J. (1994) Violence Between Men. In Archer, J. (ed.), *Male Violence*. London: Routledge 121–140

Arendt, H. (1970) *On Violence*. London: Harcourt

Arendt, H. (2006) *Eichmann in Jerusalem: A Report on the Banality of Evil*. London: Penguin

Armstrong, G. (1993) Like that Desmond Morris? In Hobbs, D. and May, T. (eds), *Interpreting the Field: Accounts of Ethnography*. Oxford: Clarendon Press 3–43

Armstrong, G. (1998) *Football Hooligans: Knowing the Score*. Oxford: Berg

Athens, L. (1992) *The Creation of Dangerous Violent Criminals*. Urbana: University of Illinois Press

Ayres, T. and Treadwell, J. (2012) Bars, Drugs and Football Thugs: Alcohol, Cocaine Use and Violence in the Night Time Economy Among English Football Firms. *Criminology and Criminal Justice*. 12 (1) 83–100

Bairner, A. (1999) Soccer, Masculinity and Violence in Northern Ireland: Between Hooliganism and Terrorism. *Men and Masculinities*, Vol. 1, (3), 284–301

BBC (2013) UK Peace Index highlights rate of fall in violent crime. Available at: www.bbc.co.uk/news/uk-22275280, accessed 9 September 2013

BBC (2014) Sexual offences recorded by police 'up 20%'. Available at: www.bbc.co.uk/news/uk-28340196, accessed 27 March 2015

Becker, H. (1967) Whose Side Are We On? *Social Problems*, Vol. 14, (3), 239–247

Beynon, J. (2002) *Masculinities and Culture*. Buckingham: Open University Press

Blagden, N. and Pemberton, S. (2010) The Challenge in Conducting Qualitative Research with Convicted Sex Offenders. *The Howard Journal*, Vol. 49, (3), 269–281

Bly, R. (2001) *Iron John: Men and Masculinity*. London: Rider

Bollas, C. (1995) *Cracking Up: The Work of Unconscious Experience*. London: Routledge

Bourdieu, P. (1984) *Distinction: A Social Critique of the Judgement of Taste*. London: Routledge

Bourgois, P. (1996) In Search of Masculinity: Violence, Respect and Sexuality Among Puerto Rican Crack Dealers in East Harlem. *British Journal of Criminology*, Vol. 36, (3), 412–427

Bourgois, P. (2003) *In Search of Respect: Selling Crack in El Barrio* (Second Edition). Cambridge: Cambridge University Press

Bourgois, P. Karandinos, G., Hart, L. and Montero Castrillo, F. (2012) *Cultivating Rage in the US Inner City. Paper presented at 'Taking Bourdieu to Town' seminar organised by YECCE and CURB.* York: University of York.

Briggs, D. (2013) *Deviance and Risk on Holiday: An Ethnography of British Tourists in Ibiza.* Basingstoke: Palgrave Macmillan

Brittan, A. (1989) *Masculinity and Power.* Oxford: Basil Blackwell

Brittan, A. (2001) Masculinities and Masculinism. In Whitehead, S. M. and Barrett, F. J. (eds), *The Masculinities Reader.* Cambridge: Polity 51–55

Brownmiller, S. (1975) *Against Our Will: Men, Women and Rape.* London: Secker and Warburg

Burdis, K. and Tombs, S. (2012) After the Crisis: New Directions in Theorising Corporate and White-Collar Crime. In Hall, S. and Winlow, S. (eds), *New Directions in Criminological Theory.* London: Routledge 276–291

Butler, J. (1990) *Gender Trouble: Feminism and the Subversion of Identity.* London: Routledge

Calvey, D. (2008) The Art and Politics of Covert Research: Doing 'Situated Ethics' in the Field. *Sociology* 42 (5) 905-918

Campbell, B. (1993) *Goliath: Britain's Dangerous Places.* London: Methuen

Canaan, J. (1996) 'One Thing Leads to Another': Drinking, Fighting and Working-Class Masculinities. In Mac An Ghaill, M. (ed.), *Understanding Masculinities.* Buckingham: Open University Press 114–125

Carrington, K. and Scott, J. (2008) Masculinity, Rurality and Violence. *British Journal of Criminology* Vol. 48, 641–666

Carrington, K., McIntosh, A. and Scott, J. (2010) Globalization, Frontier Masculinities and Violence: Booze, Blokes and Brawls. *British Journal of Criminology* Vol. 50, 393–413

Casciani, D. (2014) Crime Stats: The Truth is Out There. Available at: www.bbc.co.uk/news/uk-politics-25831906, accessed 27 March 2015

Castells, M. (2000) *End of Millennium.* Oxford: Blackwell

Charlesworth, S. J. (2000) *A Phenomenology of Working Class Experience.* Cambridge: Cambridge University Press

Cohen, A. (1955) *Delinquent Boys: The Culture of the Gang.* London: Collier-Macmillan

Collier, R. (1998) *Masculinities, Crime and Criminology.* Sage: London

Collier, R. (2004) Masculinities and Crime: Rethinking the 'Man Question'? In Sumner, C. (ed.), *The Blackwell Companion to Criminology.* Oxford: Blackwell 285–308

Collins, R. (2008) *Violence: A Micro-sociological Theory.* Oxford: Princeton University Press

Collison, M. (1996) In Search of the High Life: Drugs, Crime, Masculinities and Consumption. *British Journal of Criminology,* Vol. 36, (3), 428–444

Connell, R. W. (1987) *Gender and Power: Society, the Person and Sexual Politics.* Cambridge: Polity

Connell, R. W. (2005a) *Masculinities.* Cambridge: Polity

Connell, R. W. (2005b) Globalization, Imperialism and Masculinities. In Kimmel, M. S. Hearn, J. and Connell, R. W. (eds), *Handbook of Studies on Men and Masculinities.* London: Sage 71–89

Currie, E. (1997) Market, Crime and Community: Toward a Mid-Range Theory of Post-Industrial Violence. *Theoretical Criminology* Vol. 1, (2), 147–172

Daly, M. and Wilson, M. (1988) *Homicide.* New York: Aldine De Gruyter

Davies, A. (1998) Youth Gangs, Masculinity and Violence in Late Victorian Manchester and Salford. *Journal of Social History* Vol. 32, (2), 349–346

DeKeseredy, W. S. and Schwartz, M. D. (2005) Masculinities and Interpersonal Violence. In Kimmel, M. S., Hearn, J. and Connell, R. W. (eds), *Handbook of Studies on Men and Masculinities*. London: Sage 353–366

Dobash, R. E. and Dobash, R. P. (1992) *Women, Violence and Social Change*. London: Routledge

Dorling, D. (2004) Prime Suspect: Murder in Britain. In Hillyard, P., Pantazis, C., Tombs, S. and Gordon, D. (eds), *Beyond Criminology: Taking Harm Seriously*. London: Pluto 178–191

Edwards, T. (2006) *Cultures of Masculinity*. London: Routledge

Eisner, M. (2011) Human Evolution, History and Violence: An Introduction. *British Journal of Criminology*, Vol. 51, (3), 473–478

Elias, N. (2000) *The Civilising Process* (Revised Edition). Oxford: Blackwell

Ellis, A. Sloan, J. and Wykes, M. (2013) 'Moatifs' of Masculinity: The Stories Told About 'Men' in British Newspaper Coverage of the Raoul Moat case. *Crime Media Culture*, Vol. 9, (1), 3–21

Emsley, C. (2005a) *Crime and Society in England 1750–1900*. Harlow: Pearson

Emsley, C. (2005b) *Hard Men: The English and Violence since 1750*. London: Hambledon

Engels, F. (1953) The Condition of the Working-Class. In Chambliss, W. J. (ed.), (1973) *Problems of Industrial Society*. London: Addison-Wesley 43–46

Ferrell, J. (1998) Criminological Verstehen: Inside the Immediacy of Crime. In Ferrell, J. and Hamm, M. S. (eds), *Ethnography at the Edge: Crime, Deviance and Field Research*. Northeastern University Press 20–42

Fink, B. (1996) *The Lacanian Subject: Between Language and Jouissance*. Princeton: Princeton University Press

Fisher, M. (2009) *Capitalist Realism: Is There No Alternative?* London: Zero

Fletcher, J. (1997) *Violence and Civilisation: An Introduction to the Work of Norbert Elias*. Cambridge: Polity

Freud, S. (1961) *Beyond the Pleasure Principle*. London: Hogarth Press

Fukuyama, F. (1993) *The End of History and the Last Man*. London: Penguin

Gadd, D. (2000) Masculinities, Violence and Defended Psychosocial Subjects. *Theoretical Criminology* Vol. 4, (4), 429–449

Gadd, D. (2004) Making Sense of Interviewee–Interviewer Dynamics in Narratives About Violence in Intimate Relationships. *International Journal of Social Research Methodology* Vol. 7, (5), 383–401

Gadd, D. and Jefferson, T. (2007) *Psychosocial Criminology: An Introduction*. London: Sage

Gadd, D., Corr, M. L., Fox, C. and Butler, I. (2013) *From Boys to Men: Phase Three Key Findings*. Manchester: University of Manchester

Garland, D. (2002) Of Crimes and Criminals: The Development of Criminology in Britain. In Maguire, M., Morgan, R. and Reiner, R. (eds), *The Oxford Handbook of Criminology*. Oxford: Oxford University Press 7–50

Gelsthorpe, L. (2002) Feminism and Criminology. In Maguire, M., Morgan, R. and Reiner, R. (eds), *The Oxford Handbook of Criminology*. Oxford: Oxford University Press 112–143

Gibson, C. L. Morris, S. Z. and Beaver, K. M. (2009) Secondary Exposure to Violence During Childhood and Adolescence: Does Neighbourhood Context Matter? *Justice Quarterly*, Vol. 26, (1), 30–57

Gilligan, J. (2000) *Violence: Reflections on our Deadliest Epidemic.* London: Jessica Kingsley

Goodey, J. (1997) Boys Don't Cry. *British Journal of Criminology*, Vol. 37, (3), 401–418

Goodey, J. (2000) Biographical Lessons for Criminology. *Theoretical Criminology*, Vol. 4, (4), 473–498

Gregory, M. (2012) Masculinity and Homicide–Suicide. *International Journal of Law Crime and Justice*, Vol. 40, (3), 133–151

Hall, M. (2010) *Victims and Policy Making: A Comparative Perspective.* Oxon: Willan

Hall, P. and Innes, J. (2010) Violent and Sexual Crime. In Flatley, J., Kershaw, C., Smith, K., Chaplin, R. and Moon, D. (eds), *Crime in England and Wales 2009/10: Findings from the British Crime Survey and Police Recorded Crime.* London: Home Office http://rds.homeoffice.gov.uk/rds/pdfs10/hosb1210.pdf last accessed 11th March 2011

Hall, S. (1997) Visceral Cultures and Criminal Practices. *Theoretical Criminology* Vol. 1, (4), 453–478

Hall, S. (2000) Paths to Anelpis 1: Dimorphic Violence and the Pseudo-Pacification Process. *Parallax: A Journal of Metadiscursive Theory and Cultural Practices*, Vol. 6, (2), 36–53

Hall, S. (2002) Daubing the Drudges of Fury: Men, Violence and the Piety of the 'Hegemonic Masculinity' Thesis. *Theoretical Criminology* Vol. 6, (1), 35–61

Hall, S. (2007) The Emergence and Breakdown of the Pseudo-Pacification Process. In Watson, K. (ed.), *Assaulting the Past: Violence and Civilisation in Historical Context.* Newcastle: Cambridge Scholars Publishing 77–101

Hall, S. (2012a) *Theorizing Crime and Deviance: A New Perspective.* London: Sage

Hall, S. (2012b) The Solicitation of the Trap: On Transcendence and Transcendental Materialism in Advanced Consumer Capitalism. *Human Studies: Special Issue on Transcendence and Transgression*, Vol. 35, (3), 365–381

Hall, S. (2014) The Socioeconomic Function of Evil. *The Sociological Review*, Vol. 62, (S2), 13–31

Hall, S. and Wilson, D. (2014) New Foundations: Pseudo-Pacification and Special Liberty as Potential Cornerstones for a Multi-Level Theory of Homicide and Serial Murder. *European Journal of Criminology*, Vol. 11, (5), 635–655

Hall, S. and Winlow, S. (2004) Barbarians at the Gate: Crime and Violence in the Breakdown of the Pseudo-Pacification Process. In Ferrell, J., Hayward, K., Morrison, W. and Presdee, M. (eds), *Cultural Criminology Unleashed.* London: Glasshouse Press 275–286

Hall, S. and Winlow, S. (2012) Introduction: The Need for New Directions in Criminological Theory. In Hall, S. and Winlow, S. (eds), *New Directions in Criminological Theory.* London: Routledge 1–13

Hall, S. Winlow, S. and Ancrum, C. (2008) *Criminal Identities and Consumer Culture: Crime, Exclusion and the New Culture of Narcissism.* Cullompton: Willan

Harvey, D. (1989) *The Condition of Postmodernity: An Enquiry into the Origins of Cultural Change.* Oxford: Basil Blackwell

Harvey, D. (2005) *A Brief History of Neo-Liberalism.* Oxford: Oxford University Press

Hatty, S. E. (2000) *Masculinities, Violence, and Culture.* London: Sage

Hautzinger, S. (2003) Researching Men's Violence: Personal Reflections on Ethnographic Data. *Men and Masculinities* Vol. 6, 93–106

Hayward, K. (2004) *City Limits: Crime, Consumer Culture and the Urban Experience.* Glass House Press: London

Hayward, K. and Yar, M. (2006) The 'Chav' Phenomenon: Consumption, Media and the Construction of a New Underclass. *Crime, Media, Culture*, Vol. 2, (1), 9–28

Hearn, J. (1998) *The Violences of Men: How Men Talk About and How Agencies Respond to Men's Violence to Women*. London: Sage

Hearn, J. (2003) Searching for the Body: Making Connections Between Health, Bodies and Men's Violence. In Ervø, S. and Johansson, T. (eds), *Bending Bodies: Moulding Masculinities* (Volume Two). Aldershot: Ashgate 170–192

Hearn, J. and Morgan, D. (1990) Men, Masculinities and Social Theory. In Hearn, J. and Morgan, D. (eds), *Men, Masculinities and Social Theory*. London: Unwin Hyman 1–18

Heidensohn, F. (1985) *Women and Crime*. Hampshire: Macmillan

Hobbs, D. (1988) *Doing the Business: Entrepreneurship, Detectives and the Working Class in the East End of London*. Oxford: Oxford University Press

Hobbs, D. (1994) Mannish Boys: Danny, Chris, Crime, Masculinity and Business. In Newburn, T. and Stanko, E. (eds), *Just Boys Doing Business: Men, Masculinities and Crime*. London: Routledge 118–134

Hobbs, D. (1995) *Bad Business: Professional Crime in Modern Britain*. Oxford: Oxford University Press

Hobbs, D. (2012) 'It Was Never About The Money': Market Society, Organised Crime and UK Criminology. In Hall, S. and Winlow, S. (eds), *New Directions in Criminological Theory*. London: Routledge 257–275

Hobbs, D., Hadfield, P., Lister, S. and Winlow, S. (2003) *Bouncers: Violence and Governance in the Night-time Economy*. Oxford: Oxford University Press

Hollway, W. and Jefferson, T. (2000) *Doing Qualitative Research Differently: Free Association, Narrative and the Interview Method*. London: Sage

Hood-Willams, J. (2001) Gender, Masculinities and Crime: From Structures to Psyches. *Theoretical Criminology* Vol. 5, (1), 37–60

Howe, A. (2008) *Sex, Violence and Crime: Foucault and the 'Man' Question*. Oxon: Routledge-Cavendish

Jacobs, B. A. (2000) *Robbing Drug Dealers: Violence Beyond the Law*. New York: Aldine De Gruyter

Jefferson, T. (1994) Theorising Masculine Subjectivity. In Newburn, T. and Stanko, E. (eds), *Just Boys Doing Business: Men, Masculinities and Crime*. London: Routledge 10–31

Jefferson, T. (1996) From 'Little Fairy Boy' to 'The Compleat Destroyer': Subjectivity and Transformation in the Biography of Mike Tyson. In Mac An Ghaill, M. (ed.), *Understanding Masculinities*. Buckingham: Open University Press 153–167

Jefferson, T. (1998) Muscle, 'Hard Men' and 'Iron' Mike Tyson: Reflections on Desire, Anxiety and the Embodiment of Masculinity. *Body and Society* Vol. 4, (1), 77–98

Jefferson, T. (2002) Subordinating Hegemonic Masculinity. *Theoretical Criminology* Vol. 6, (1), 63–88

Johnston, A. and Malabou, C. (2013) *Self and Emotional Life: Philosophy, Psychoanalysis and Neuroscience*. New York: Columbia University Press

Jones, D. W. (2008) *Understanding Criminal Behaviour: Psychosocial Approaches to Criminality*. Cullompton: Willan

Jones, D. W. (2012) Psychosocial Perspectives: Men, Madness and Violence. In Hall, S. and Winlow, S. (eds), *New Directions in Criminological Theory*. London: Routledge 183–198

Jones, O. (2011) *Chavs: The Demonization of the Working Class*. London: Verso

Katz, J. (1988) *Seductions of Crime: Moral and Sensual Attractions in Doing Evil*. USA: Basic Books

Kaufman, M. (1994) Men, Feminism, and Men's Contradictory Experiences of Power. In Brod, H. and Kaufman, M. (eds), *Theorizing Masculinities*. London: Sage 142–163

Kelly, L. (1987) The Continuum of Sexual Violence. In Hanmer, J. and Mynard, M. (eds), *Women, Violence and Social Control*. Basingstoke: Macmillan 46–59

Kelly, L. (1988) *Surviving Sexual Violence*. Cambridge: Polity

Kimmel, M. S. (1994) Masculinity as Homophobia: Fear, Shame, and Silence in the Construction of Gender Identity. In Brod, H. and Kaufman, M. (eds), *Theorizing Masculinities*. London: Sage 119–141

Lash, S. and Urry, J. (1987) *The End of Organised Capitalism*. Cambridge: Polity Press

Lea, J. (1997) Post-Fordism and Criminality. In Jewson, N. and MacGregor, S. (eds), *Transforming Cities: Contested Governance and New Spatial Divisions*. London: Routledge 42–55

Lea, J. (2002) *Crime and Modernity*. London: Sage

Lee-Treweek, G. and Linkogle, S. (2000) Putting Danger in the Frame. In Lee-Treweek, G. and Linkogle, S. (eds), *Danger in the Field: Risk and Ethics in Social Research*. London: Routledge 8–25

Liebling, A. and Stanko, E. (2001) Allegiance and Ambivalence: Some Dilemmas in Researching Disorder and Violence. *British Journal of Criminology*. 41, 421–430

Lloyd, A. (2012) Working to Live, Not Living to Work: Work, Leisure and Youth Identity Among Call Centre Workers in North East England. *Current Sociology*, Vol. 60, (5), 619–635

MacInnes, J. (1998) *The End of Masculinity: The Confusion of Sexual Genesis and Sexual Difference in Modern Society*. Buckingham: Open University Press

Maguire, M. (2008) Researching 'Street Criminals' in the Field: A Neglected Art? In King, R. D. and Wincup, E. (eds), *Doing Research on Crime and Justice* (Second Edition). Oxford: Oxford University Press 263–289

McGarry, R. and Walklate, S. (2011) The Soldier as Victim: Peering Through the Looking Glass. *British Journal of Criminology*, Vol. 51, (6), 900–917

McPhedran, S. (2009) Animal Abuse, Family Violence and Child Wellbeing: A Review. *Journal of Family Violence*, Vol. 24, 41–52

Messerschmidt, J. (1993) *Masculinities and Crime: Critique and Reconceptualization of Theory*. Maryland: Roman and Littlefield

Messerschmidt, J. (1997) *Crime as Structured Action: Gender, Race, Class and Crime in the Making*. London: Sage

Messerschmidt, J. (1999) Making Bodies Matter: Adolescent Masculinities, the Body, and Varieties of Violence. *Theoretical Criminology,* Vol. 3, (2), 197–220

Messerschmidt, J. (2005) Men, Masculinities and Crime. In Kimmel, M. S., Hearn, J. and Connell, R. W. (eds), *Handbook of Studies on Men and Masculinities*. London: Sage 196–212

Morgan, D. (1992) *Discovering Men: Critical Studies on Men and Masculinities*. London: Routledge

Morgan, D. (2005) Class and Masculinity. In Kimmel, M. S., Hearn, J. and Connell, R. W. (eds), *Handbook of Studies on Men and Masculinities*. London: Sage 165–177

Nivette, A. E. (2011) Violence in Non-State Societies: A Review. *British Journal of Criminology*, Vol. 51, (3), 578–598

Oakley, A. (1981) Interviewing Women: A Contradiction in Terms. In Roberts, H. (ed.), *Doing Feminist Research*. London: Routledge and Kegan Paul 30–61

Office for National Statistics (2013) Focus On: Violent Crime and Sexual Offences, 2011/12. Available at: www.ons.gov.uk/ons/dcp171778_298904.pdf, accessed 18 September 2013

Okely, J. (1983) *The Traveller-Gypsies*. Cambridge: Cambridge University Press

Paoli, L. (2003) *Mafia Brotherhoods: Organised Crime, Italian Style*. Oxford: Oxford University Press

Pearson, G. (1993) Foreword: Talking a Good Fight: Authenticity and Distance in the Ethnographer's Craft. In Hobbs, D. and May, T. (eds), *Interpreting the Field: Accounts of Ethnography*. Oxford: Clarendon Press p. vii-xx

Pearson, G. and Hobbs, D. (2003) King Pin? A Case Study of a Middle Market Drug Broker. *The Howard Journal* Vol. 42, (4), 335–347

Pearson, J. (1995) *The Profession of Violence: The Rise and Fall of the Kray Twins*. London: Harper Collins

Polk, K. (1994) Masculinity, Honour and Confrontational Homicide. In Newburn, T. and Stanko, E. (eds), *Just Boys Doing Business: Men, Masculinities and Crime*. London: Routledge 166–188

Polsky, N. (1967) *Hustlers, Beats and Others*. Chicago: Aldine

Ray, L. (2011) *Violence and Society*. London: Sage

Ray, L., Smith, D. and Wastell, L. (2004) Shame, Rage and Racist Violence. *British Journal of Criminology*, Vol. 44, (3), 350–368

Reiner, R. (2012) Political Economy and Criminology: The Return of the Repressed. In Hall, S. and Winlow, S. (eds), *New Directions in Criminological Theory*. London: Routledge 30–51

Roe, S., Coleman, K. and Kaiza, P. (2009) Violent and Sexual Crime. In Walker, A., Flatley, J., Kershaw, C. and Moon, D. (eds), *Crime in England and Wales 2008/09 Findings from the British Crime Survey and Police Recorded Crime* (Volume 1). London: Home Office http://rds.homeoffice.gov.uk/rds/pdfs09/hosb1109vol1.pdf last accessed 11th March 2011

Sennett, R. (1998) *The Corrosion of Character: The Personal Consequences of Work in the New Capitalism*. London: Norton

Shildrick, T. and Macdonald, R. (2013) Poverty Talk: How People Experiencing Poverty Deny Their Poverty and Why They Blame 'The Poor'. *The Sociological Review*, Vol. 61, 285–303

Slaughter, P. (2003) Of Crowds, Crimes and Carnivals. In Matthews, R. and Young, J. (eds), *The New Politics of Crime and Punishment*. Cullompton: Willan 178–198

Sloterdijk, P. (2010) *Rage and Time: A Psychopolitical Investigation*. Chichester: Columbia

Smart, C. (1976) *Women, Crime and Criminology: A Feminist Critique*. London: Routledge

Smith, O. (2013) Easy Money: Cultural Narcissism and the Criminogenic Markets of the Night-Time Leisure Economy. In Winlow, S. and Atkinson, R. (eds), *New Directions in Crime and Deviancy*. London: Routledge 145–158

Spierenburg, P. (1998) Masculinity, Violence and Honor: An Introduction. In Spierenburg, P. (ed.), *Men and Violence: Gender, Honor and Rituals in Modern Europe and America*. Columbus: Ohio State University Press 1–29

Spierenburg, P. (2008) *A History of Murder: Personal Violence in Europe from the Middle Ages to the Present*. Cambridge: Polity

Stanko, E. (1990) *Everyday Violence: How Women and Men Experience Sexual and Physical Danger*. London: Pandora

Stanko, E. (1994) Challenging the Problem of Men's Individual Violence. In Newburn, T. and Stanko, E. (eds), *Just Boys Doing Business: Men, Masculinities and Crime*. London: Routledge p. 32–45

Stanko, E. and Hobdell, K. (1994) Assault on Men: Masculinity and Male Victimization. *British Journal of Criminology*, Vol. 33, (3), 400–415

Stein, A. (2007) *Prologue to Violence: Child Abuse, Dissociation and Crime*. London: Analytic Press

Sutherland, E. and Cressey, D. (1966) *Principles in Criminology* (Seventh Edition). Philadelphia: Lippincott

Taylor, I. (1999) *Crime in Context: A Critical Criminology of Market Societies*. Cambridge: Polity

Tolson, A. (1977) *The Limits of Masculinity*. London: Tavistock

Tomsen, S. (1997) A Top Night: Social Protest, Masculinity and the Culture of Drinking Violence. *British Journal of Criminology* Vo.l 37, (1), 90–102

Treadwell, J. (2008) Call the (Fashion) Police: How Fashion Becomes Criminalised. *Papers from the British Criminology Conference*, Vol. 8, 117–133

Treadwell, J. (2010) *Firm Men: An Ethnographic Study of an English Football Firm*. Unpublished Ph.D. Thesis: Birmingham City University

Treadwell, J. (2012) From the Car Boot to Booting It Up? Ebay, Online Counterfeit Crime and the Transformation of the Criminal Marketplace. *Criminology and Criminal Justice: An International Journal*, Vol. 12, (2), 175–192

Treadwell, J. and Ayres, T. (2014) Talking Prada and Powder: Cocaine Use and Supply Among the Football Hooligan Firm. In Hopkins, M. and Treadwell, J. (eds), *Football Hooliganism, Fan Behaviour and Crime*. London: Palgrave Macmillan

Treadwell, J. and Garland, J. (2011) Masculinity, Marginalization and Violence: A Case Study of the English Defence League. *British Journal of Criminology*, Vol. 51, 621–634

Treadwell, J., Briggs, D., Winlow, S., and Hall, S. (2013) Shopocalypse Now: Consumer Culture and the English Riots of 2011. *British Journal of Criminology*, Vol. 53, 1–17

Varese, F. (2001) *The Russian Mafia: Private Protection in a New Market Economy*. Oxford: Oxford University Press

Wakeman, S. (2014) Fieldwork, Biography and Emotion: Doing Criminological Autoethnography. *British Journal of Criminology*, Vol. 54, (5), 705–721

Walby, S. and Myhill, A. (2001) New Survey Methodologies in Researching Violence Against Women. *British Journal of Criminology*. 41, 502–522

Walklate, S. (2004) *Gender, Crime and Criminal Justice*. Cullompton: Willan

West, C. and Zimmerman, D. H. (1987) Doing Gender. *Gender & Society*, Vol. 1, (2), 125–151

Whitehead, A. (2005) Man to Man Violence: How Masculinity May Work as a Dynamic Risk Factor. *The Howard Journal*, Vol. 44, (4), 411–422

Whitehead, S. M. (2002) *Men and Masculinities: Key Themes and New Directions*. Cambridge: Polity

Wieviorka, M. (2009) *Violence: A New Approach*. London: Sage

Wilkinson, R. and Pickett, K. (2010) *The Spirit Level: Why Equality is Better for Everyone*. London: Penguin

Willis, P. (1977) *Learning to Labour: How Working Class Kids Get Working Class Jobs*. Hampshire: Gower

Willis, P. (1990) *Common Culture: Symbolic Work at Play in the Everyday Cultures of the Young*. Milton Keynes: Open University Press

Willott, S and Griffin, C (1996) Men, Masculinity and the Challenge of Long-Term Unemployment. In Mac An Ghaill, M. (ed.), *Understanding Masculinities*. Buckingham: Open University Press 77–95

Winlow, S. (2001) *Badfellas: Crime, Tradition and New Masculinities*. Oxford: Berg

Winlow, S. (2012) 'All That Is Sacred Is Profaned': Towards a Theory of Subjective Violence. In Hall, S. and Winlow, S. (eds), *New Directions in Criminological Theory*. London: Routledge 199–215

Winlow, S. (2014) Trauma, Guilt and the Unconscious: Some Theoretical Notes on Violent Subjectivity. *The Sociological Review*, Vol. 62, (S2), 32–49

Winlow, S. and Hall, S. (2006) *Violent Night: Urban Leisure and Contemporary Culture*. Oxford: Berg

Winlow, S. and Hall, S. (2009) Retaliate First: Memory, Humiliation and Male Violence. *Crime Media Culture* Vol. 5, (3), 285–304

Winlow, S. and Hall, S. (2013) *Rethinking Social Exclusion: The End of the Social?* London: Sage

Winlow, S., Hobbs, D., Lister, S. and Hadfield, P. (2001) Get Ready to Duck: Bouncers and the Realities of Ethnographic Research on Violent Groups. *British Journal of Criminology* Vol. 41, 536–548

Wykes, M. and Welsh, K. (2009) *Violence, Gender and Justice*. London: Sage

Young, J. (1999) *The Exclusive Society: Social Exclusion, Crime and Difference in Late Modernity*. London: Sage

Zedner, L. (2002) Victims. In Maguire, M., Morgan, R. and Reiner, R. (eds), *The Oxford Handbook of Criminology*. Oxford: Oxford University Press 419–456

Zizek, S. (2002) *Welcome to the Desert of the Real*. London: Verso

Zizek, S. (2006) *How to Read Lacan*. London: Norton

Zizek, S. (2008a) *The Ticklish Subject*. London: Verso

Zizek, S. (2008b) *Violence*. London: Profile

Index

Made in the USA
Las Vegas, NV
22 July 2022

52006114R00101